PELICAN BOOKS

The Pelican Economic History of Britain
Volume 2 · 1530–1780
Reformation to Industrial Revolution

═══

Christopher Hill was Master of Balliol College, Oxford, from 1965–78 and is a Fellow of the British Academy. From 1934–8 he was a Fellow of All Souls College, Oxford, and from 1936–8 Assistant Lecturer in Modern History, University College, Cardiff. He was Fellow and Tutor in Modern History at Balliol College, Oxford, from 1938–65, and Special Lecturer in sixteenth- and seventeenth-century English History at Oxford University from 1958–65.

He is the author of many books, including *The English Revolution 1640* (1940), *Lenin and the Russian Revolution* (1947), *Puritanism and Revolution* (1958), *The Century of Revolution 1603–1714* (1961), *Society and Puritanism in pre-Revolutionary England* (1964), *Intellectual Origins of the English Revolution* (1965), *God's Englishman* (1970), *Antichrist in 17th Century England* (1971), *The World Turned Upside Down* (1972), *Change and Continuity in 17th Century England* (1975), *Milton and the English Revolution* (1977) which won the Royal Society of Literature Award and *Some Intellectual Consequences of the English Revolution* (1980). He also contributed to *Rebels and their Causes*, a collection of essays to celebrate the seventy-fifth birthday of A. L. Morton.

The Pelican
Economic History of Britain

VOLUME 2
1530–1780

Reformation to Industrial Revolution

—

CHRISTOPHER HILL

PENGUIN BOOKS

Penguin Books Ltd, Harmondsworth, Middlesex, England
Viking Penguin Inc., 40 West 23rd Street, New York, New York 10010, U.S.A.
Penguin Books Australia Ltd, Ringwood, Victoria, Australia
Penguin Books Canada Limited, 2801 John Street, Markham, Ontario, Canada L3R 1B4
Penguin Books (N.Z.) Ltd, 182–190 Wairau Road, Auckland 10, New Zealand

—

First published by Weidenfeld & Nicolson 1967
Published with revisions in Pelican Books 1969
Reprinted 1971, 1974, 1975, 1976, 1978, 1980, 1983, 1986

—

—

Printed and bound in Great Britain by
Cox & Wyman Ltd, Reading
Set in Monotype Ehrhardt

For Vivian Galbraith

WITH THE ACCUMULATED GRATITUDE

OF THIRTY-SEVEN YEARS

CONTENTS

Contents

PREFACE

SOME of the subjects discussed in this book have already been treated in my *Century of Revolution, 1603–1714* (Vol. 5 of the Nelson History of England, 1961). Where possible I have used different illustrative material. Spelling and punctuation have been modernized in all quotations. The Index may help readers to identify persons referred to briefly in the text. Where a footnote refers to a book by the author's name only, or author's name and a date, the full title will be found in the Bibliography on pp. 289–91. It was not possible to document this book fully, but I have tried to acknowledge specific debts. I have drawn a great deal on the writings of others, particularly for Part Four. I am especially indebted to the work of Professor T. S. Ashton, Sir G. N. Clark, Dr Dorothy Marshall, Professor J. H. Plumb, Professor C. Wilson. I have also benefited by discussions with Dr K. R. Andrews and Mr A. L. Merson, and from hearing Professor Plumb's Ford Lectures in Oxford in 1965.* Dr Eric Hobsbawm very kindly read part of the typescript, and Mr Edward Thompson the whole of it; both made many useful suggestions. Mr Paul Slack undertook the dreary task of reading the proofs and saved me from many mistakes. None of these, however, is to blame for the errors which remain. Nor is my wife, who read it all and helped at every stage in every way.

CHRISTOPHER HILL

* Now published as *The Growth of Political Stability in England* (Peregrine, 1969).

NOTE TO THE SECOND IMPRESSION

I am very grateful to Miss Penelope Corfield, Professor G. R. Elton, Professor F. J. Fisher, Mr S. Inwood and Mr W. E. Makin for pointing out misprints, errors and misleading statements, most of which have been corrected.   C.H.

NOTE TO THE PELICAN EDITION

I have made some revisions for this edition, arising especially from two important books published during 1967 – Dr Patrick Collinson's *The Elizabethan Puritan Movement*, and Volume IV of *The Agrarian History of England and Wales, 1500–1640*, edited by Dr Joan Thirsk. I am grateful to Dr Thirsk and Dr Alan Macfarlane for help in revising, though the responsibility for what has emerged is my own.   C.H.

Part One

INTRODUCTION

I

ARGUMENT

This is the reward I look for, that my labours may but receive
an allowance suspended until such time as this description of
mine be reproved by a better. – SIR WALTER RALEGH,
History of the World (*1614*)

I HAVE tried in this book to isolate and explain some of those
features which differentiate English history from that of the rest
of Europe in the years between 1530 and 1780. Movements of
population and prices were roughly similar all over Europe
during this period; but the Netherlands and England were
unique in having successful political revolutions which led to
greater commercial influence over governments; England was
unique in her Industrial Revolution at the end of our quarter of a
millennium. The sixteenth-century price revolution was
accompanied by industrial decline in Spain, industrial advance
in England. Some historians have explained the lowered living
standards of the sixteenth-century English peasantry solely by
rising population; but in fifteenth-century Czechoslovakia a fall
in peasant standards of living accompanied a *declining* population. Rising population contributed to industrial revolution in
eighteenth-century England; it probably increased poverty in
Ireland, China and elsewhere.* Since a great deal of arable land
in Britain was still uncultivated in the eighteenth century, we
might well ask, Why did the increasing population not lead to an
extension of peasant farming?

Nor can we attribute political crisis to demographic or monetary changes. The years 1530–1620 in England saw an inflation
and what some historians refer to as a population explosion:
they were years of relative social and political stability. The
ensuing half century of political crisis was one in which inflation
tailed off and the population increase is believed to have slowed
down. In the eighteenth century, when institutions and social

*See pp. 83–4, 247, below.

relations were again relatively stable, prices were stable too but population is believed to have increased faster again. Neither demography nor monetary factors furnish a single key to the understanding of historical change. The seventeenth-century economic crisis which affected the whole of western Europe led to a strengthening of absolutism in most continental countries, and in the Netherlands to the consolidation of a trading oligarchy; in England alone it created a political system within which commercial and industrial capital had freedom to develop.* The connexion between economics and politics is not simple.

Social history is therefore, in my view, not what G. M. Trevelyan called it, 'the history of a people with the politics left out'. Politics affected the social structure and so the economic and social life of the people. In this book I have stressed the significance of the seventeenth-century political revolution in transforming English social and economic life, in making possible what historians are beginning to recognize as the agricultural and commercial revolutions of the seventeenth century,† and preparing for the eighteenth-century industrial revolution: though of course the political revolution itself had economic causes too. My aim has been all through to emphasize *interaction* between politics and economics, seeing neither as a sufficient cause in itself. Some historians, for instance, are prepared to attribute far-reaching effects to the freedom to buy and sell land which prevailed in England between 1530 and 1660. This is harmless enough provided we recognize that the open land market was no act of God; its beginning and end were the result of legal changes made by men – the statutes of the Reformation Parliament and the strict settlement evolved by interregnum lawyers. Pressure from potential purchasers lay behind these changes, and this in its turn began and ended for reasons which can be analysed.‡ When we observe what Professor Wilson has called 'the drunken hopelessness' of the West Country weaver

*E. Hobsbawm, 'The General Crisis of the European Economy in the seventeenth century', *Past and Present*, Nos. 5 and 6.

† See below, Part 3, Chapters 3 and 4.

‡ See pp. 64, 146–8, 186–9, below.

in the eighteenth century, which was cause and effect of his economic decline, and contrast it with the sober independence of his prospering West Riding counterpart, we may well wonder whether the catastrophic defeat of Monmouth's rebellion in the West in 1685, the last kick of the Good Old Cause, may not have had something to do with it.

One way of appreciating the impact of politics on economic development is to ask whether the course of English history could have been different. Such a question is worth asking now that we can see western imperialism as a brief interlude in human history. Suppose the little England of the early years of Elizabeth had continued; suppose the outcome of the English Revolution had been a victory for the radicals who so nearly captured control of the army in 1647–49; that in consequence the pro-letarianization of small masters in industry, the disappearance of the yeomanry, had been very much slowed down; that Leveller opposition to the conquest of Ireland had prevailed in 1649; suppose the author of *Tyranipocrit* (also published in 1649) had persuaded his fellow-countrymen that it was wrong for merchants to 'rob the poor Indians', to make slaves, or for governments of the rich to use the poor to fight their battles for them. Suppose there had been no Navigation Acts, no powerful navy, no colonial monopoly empire, no commercial revolution. Dutch merchants would have continued to carry our trade, capital accumulation would have been far slower, there would have been no industrial revolution in England in advance of the rest of the world. The worker who in 1530 could earn his yearly bread by fourteen–fifteen weeks labour might not have had to work fifty-two weeks to earn the same amount two centuries later.

But let us not sentimentally conclude that all would have been gain if England had pursued the relatively peaceful path of a Denmark, or Switzerland, and had not become a world power. Milton's poetry, Newton's astronomy, Locke's philosophy, Watt's steam engine, Adam Smith's economics – all these would no doubt disappear too if we wished out of existence the relationship of social forces which made the English revolution go the way it did. The long-term factors which in England fostered economic growth also brought about the seventeenth-century revolution. This by hindering hindrances to the expansion of capitalism created the conditions for that uniquely favourable balance between population and resources in England from which the Industrial Revolution was to result.* We cannot change one variable without affecting all the others. That, in fact, seems to me the ultimate lesson to be learnt from history: that fair is foul and foul is fair. 'Perhaps this is that doom which Adam fell into of knowing good and evil, that is to say of knowing good by evil.' History, as Engels once said, is 'about the most cruel of all goddesses, who drives her triumphal chariot over heaps of the slain'.

---

*See a perspicacious review of the first edition of this book by Mr D. W. Jones in *English Historical Review*, LXXXIV, pp. 119–20.

1530–1780

Before 1640 [mercantilism] had been a policy imposed by the government on business interests; after it, it became, to an increasing degree, a policy imposed by business interests on the government. – R. H. TAWNEY, *review in* Economic History Review, *v (1935)*

WHEN I was a boy at school my text-books of English history used to give the impression that one fine day in 1485 Englishmen woke up and said with surprise, 'The Middle Ages are over. Modern times have begun.' This view now seems naïve and silly. We know that the passing of the crown from one dynasty to another is not an epoch-making event. But we must be careful not simply to transfer the silliness from one date to another – to 1461, or 1529, or even to the fifteen-thirties as a whole. There was no sudden break in most people's lives at any of these dates: only the historian looking backward can see, or think he sees, decisive transformations.

But there is a better case than most for taking the fifteen-thirties as the beginning of modern English history.

> Hops, Reformation, bays and beer
> Came into England all in a year,

the old rhyme tells us. As we shall see, lighter cloths (bays) were to be very important in transforming the major English export industry. That near-contemporaries should associate new developments in the clothing industry with a new industrial crop and the beginnings of a brewing industry – and with the Reformation – is interesting. But the Reformation itself was not merely the legislation of the Parliament of 1529–36. If by the Reformation we mean a change in men's outlook upon themselves, society and the world, it had begun over a century earlier, with the Lollards, if not earlier still; and the Reformation was not complete until protestantism became the dominant religion among English men and women (some time in the seventeenth century, perhaps), or until the Toleration Act of 1689 gave freedom of worship to protestant dissenters, or until the final abolition of political disabilities on dissenters, well on in the nineteenth century – or indeed until that future date when the Church of England will be disestablished.

But the very conception of a dividing line between 'the Middle Ages' and 'Modern Times' is debatable. What do we mean by either phrase? Clearly, if we compare 1967 with 1367, the differences in economic activity, social and political structure, and in modes of thought, are immense. But what are the crucial points at which change has taken place? Medieval society was overwhelmingly agrarian: modern society is industrial. If we take this as our criterion the decisive change came with the Industrial Revolution of the late eighteenth and nineteenth centuries. If we look at social structure, medieval society was dominated by great landowners: so was England in 1780, when this book ends. If we look at political structure, England in 1530, in 1780 and in 1967 was governed by the crown in Parliament: between the first and last dates the franchise has been extended, but this change too took place long after our period ends.

Finally, in more elusive 'ways of thought', modern society is much less superstitious (or at least its superstitions are different: belief in magic, in direct divine intervention in everyday life, has virtually disappeared); the assumptions of modern science, however little understood by most of us, are rational and demonstrable in a sense in which the assumptions of medieval catholicism were not (and the more philosophic of them were equally little understood by the mass of the population). Modern society is tolerant (or indifferent) about things of which medieval society was intolerant. In these respects English society by 1780 was clearly modern: witches and heretics were no longer burnt, 'sin' was no longer punished. The most important book published around 1530 was William Tyndale's *The Obedience of a Christian Man*, which assumed that religion was the cement of society, and that the crucial questions of politics were internal subordination and external sovereignty. The comparable books around 1780 were Adam Smith's *The Wealth of Nations*, which assumed (almost for the first time) that the economic structure and politics of a society were what mattered most and should be the first concern of its citizens; and Thomas Paine's *Common Sense*, one of the foundation documents of modern democracy.

These two books may make us reflect again about the apparent continuity of English social structure and political institutions. For the landowners who ruled England in 1780 were very different from those who ruled in 1530. Their power was no longer measured principally by the number of their followers, the men who would fight for them: it was determined by their wealth. The transformation was beginning by 1530, when moralists were already denouncing depopulating enclosure, the eating up of men by sheep. By 1780 it had been virtually completed: smaller tenant farmers were giving place to agricultural labourers. Great landowners still rode off to county elections with 'their' freeholders; but in fact money dominated politics too. A West India trader could buy his way into Parliament if he was rich enough. 1549 saw the last large-scale peasant revolt in England;* by 1780 we are in the world of urban radical discontent.

Parliament too is only in a formal sense the same institution in 1780 as it had been in 1530. In our first decade Henry VIII seemed more powerful than any English king, before or since, and he used Parliament for his own governmental purposes. Two hundred and fifty years later the rule of the 'Whig oligarchy' was at its zenith, and Parliament gave the king pocket money. A motion in the House of Commons in 1780 suggesting that 'the influence of the crown has increased, is increasing' naturally went on to conclude 'and ought to be diminished'. At the beginning of our period the House of Lords was still the dominant chamber; at its end real power lay with the House of Commons. In the fifteen-thirties the church was subordinated to the crown; by 1780 it was subordinated to the Parliamentary politicians in office. Merchants were of little social significance in 1530; by 1780 the Bank of England and the East India Company were two of the most important institutions in the country.

This book then is concerned with the making of modern

* The agricultural labourers who rose in 1830 were not peasants.

English society. We shall be looking for those elements of the new which are emerging. This is sometimes criticized as a 'Whig' approach – as though the historian of successful change necessarily approves of all aspects of all the changes which he records. It seems to me on the contrary the only possible historical attitude: anything else involves the dangers of sentimental antiquarianism. It is interesting to discover survivals of villeinage in early seventeenth-century England, but leasehold and wage labour were of greater importance, just as in the eighteenth century the City of London was more important than Tory backwoods squires. Catholicism continued to exist in England after the reign of Bloody Mary, and must not be ignored: but protestantism is the general historian's main concern, and catholicism for its effect on the fortunes and outlook of protestants. Any historian has to select, especially a historian trying to cover 250 years in as many pages. But it is desirable that he should declare the assumptions which lie behind his selection.

These two and a half centuries are a period of social transition. In 1530 the majority of English men and women lived in rural households which were almost economically self-sufficient: they wore skins, sackcloth, canvas or leather clothes, and ate black bread from wooden trenchers: they used no forks or pocket handkerchiefs. By 1780 England was being transformed by the factory system: brick houses, cotton clothes, white bread, plates and cutlery were becoming accessible even to the lower classes. But throughout there are some permanent features of what today we should call a 'backward economy'. It is a good reason for treating these 250 years as a unity. Men's lives were dominated by harvests and the weather to an extent inconceivable in modern England. (This had consequences for aesthetic theory: in a predominantly agricultural society, where most of the working population was exposed to sun and wind, to be interestingly pale was the fashionable thing for girls: the craze for sunburn develops only in a highly industrialized society, well after our period ends.) In the sixteenth century up to one-third of the corn harvested was required as seed. In a year of crop failure starving men and women would eat some of the seed corn. So one bad harvest tended to produce another until the run was broken by unusually good weather. Good harvests similarly tended to follow one another.

Down to the eighteenth century, it has been well said, manufacture may be seen more significantly as processing the harvest than as something divorced from it.* Bad harvests led to shortage of purchasing power, and so to a fall in demand for cloth; abundant harvests stimulated a boom in the clothing industry and in wool production. Much of the population was in the technical sense of the term 'underemployed'. That is to say, it was not rationally disposed in the most economic way. There were long periods of unemployment, in industry as well as in agriculture. Bad communications made for an intense regionalism. Bishop John Bale in 1544 thought that northern Englishmen would not be able to understand his language. He planned to rewrite one of his books so that northerners and Scots could read it without difficulty. Inadequate communications slowed down the development of a national market, and protected small household production; the Industrial Revolution was ushered in by the canal age and led to the railway age. In our period a national market was created, and the economic and cultural dominance of London over England was established.

It is instructive to compare Leland's *Itinerary* (written within fifteen years of the beginning of our period) with Defoe's *Tour* (published in 1724, fifty-six years from its end). For Leland the important features of the human landscape are castles – mostly ruinous by now, except in the North and Wales – religious houses, gentlemen's seats, forests, market towns: landlords dominate, trade is local. For Defoe gentlemen's seats still matter, but castles, monasteries and forests have mostly disappeared, market towns are far less important: almost all trade that matters is with London. Both writers are concerned with transport and communications. Leland records the charitable bridge-building of the fifteenth century, as for instance at Burford and Culham, which diverted the trade route from London to the West away from Wallingford. Responsibility for building bridges was taken over by J.P.s from 1531, and came to

*P. Mathias, *The Brewing Industry in England, 1700–1830* (1959), p. xxi.

be financed by parish rates rather than by private charity. Leland's interest in forests and rivers was also part of a concern for the opening up of the nation's trade routes: he observed that food was cheap in Wakefield because the town was well served with water communications. The cutting down of forests in Cardiganshire decreased the danger from robber bands lurking there, but contributed to the shortage of timber which beset certain areas in the late sixteenth and seventeenth centuries. Iron furnaces near Bury, Lancashire, were decaying for lack of fuel, Leland noted, and the men of Droitwich had to go far afield to get timber for their salt pans. The fuel famine was ultimately to be met by the sensational expansion of Newcastle coal-mining after the dissolution of the monasteries. But one of the prime arguments for colonizing Virginia at the end of the sixteenth century was its rich forests; by the end of the seventeenth century American timber was being used for shipbuilding.

The period 1530–1780 was thus one of slow economic change. But if we look at political history we see this gradual advance interrupted by a sharp break after 1640; and the seventeenth-century political revolution gave rise to revolutions in trade and agriculture which had far-reaching effects on the whole of society. They prepared for that take-off into the modern industrial world which England was the first country to achieve.*

---

*Since one reviewer has accused me of inconsistency and unclarity in my usage, it is apparently necessary to state that in this book the phrases 'the revolutionary decades' or 'the revolution' refer always and only to the years between 1640 and 1660.

Part Two

FROM REFORMATION TO REVOLUTION

I

NATIONAL UNIFICATION

We will not be bound of necessity to be served with lords, but
. . . with such men what degree soever as we shall appoint. –
HENRY VIII *to the Duke of Norfolk, 1537*

I

THE century after 1530 saw the establishment of England's
insular independence. From 1066 to the fifteenth century England had, intermittently, great possessions in France. These had
all but vanished by 1530, the last outpost, Calais, falling in 1558.
The next twenty-five years are the only period in English history
since 1066 when the country had no overseas possessions (except
Ireland). And the American colonies whose foundation dates
from the end of Elizabeth's reign were of little significance to any
but merchants and Puritans until they became the hub of an
imperial policy after the Proclamation of the Republic.*

This Tudor reorientation of national policy was not made by
choice. English armies had been driven out of France in the
fifteenth century, and Henry VIII squandered two fortunes in
the vain attempt to get them back. Our period begins with
England just recovering from a great national defeat. The
attempt of Cardinal Wolsey from 1512 to 1529 to put England on
a diplomatic equality with great powers like France, Spain and
the Holy Roman Empire had ended in humiliation and isolation.
The English Reformation must be seen against this background:
as an assertion of English nationalism, a refusal to submit to
dictation from outside.

The sixteenth century saw the integration of English towns
into a single national unit, to an extent which was not paralleled
on the Continent. During the fifteenth-century Wars of the
Roses the towns had invariably supported the winning side.
Their interests were in law and order, and thus in a strong

*See pp. 155–61, below.

central government, against the feudal anarchy which was made only the more dangerous by gunpowder and the bands of fighting men ejected from France. Unlike Germany and Italy, England had no big free towns dominating their surrounding rural areas: English towns could not rely on their own strength to preserve their independence. London was unique in its economic and political importance as well as in its size: at the beginning of the sixteenth century the capital contributed as much to a Parliamentary subsidy as all other towns together; by the end of the century far more.

Furthermore, in the sixteenth century the 800 or so market towns in England and Wales came more and more under the control of oligarchies of their richer burghers, as the latter grew in strength and ambition. They were now a class aspiring to rule in their own right, no longer merely the spokesmen of their communities against the feudal ruling class. Yet their growing estrangement from their communities left them still dependent on the patronage of local gentry: indeed, in the two generations before the civil war the expansion of urban trade led to many conflicts between market towns and manorial lords, as the latter tried to revive the collection of virtually obsolete tolls. Urban oligarchies also depended on the political support of the central government. In 1549 Norwich was powerless against Kett's rebellion until the government sent mercenaries down from London; and Exeter was very hard pressed to ward off the Cornish rebels in the same year. It has been suggested that the absence of major revolution in England (except in the seventeenth century) is due to this lack of secondary centres of civilization outside London, and to the domination of the capital itself by the government.* There had to be a revolution in the City in December 1641 before the English revolution could take off.

The significant expansion of London, and its growing power as a unifying force, may be dated to the post-Reformation era. It furnished a market for food which could be supplied only by improved means of cultivation. This called for enclosure and the investment of capital in farming for the market, at first in the South Midlands, Kent and East Anglia, then gradually over the

* S. T. Bindoff, *Tudor England* (Pelican History of England), p. 172.

whole kingdom. The standards and morality of the market-place radiated slowly out from London. In the mid-sixteenth century the idea that men could 'use their possessions as they list' seemed to Crowley tantamount to atheism; but individualism – 'City doctrine', Dekker called it in 1612 – soon became respectable, as London merchants brought more and more of the country into a single market. Taking advantage of the establishment of law, order and internal police, the ending of private war even in Wales and the North, the elimination of franchises and the slow improvement of communications, merchants from the City gradually broke down the privileges of local corporations. The process was helped by the Statute of Apprentices (1563), which insisted that apprenticeship in all towns should be regulated 'after the custom and order of the City of London'. In the same period protestant preachers, financed from London, worked to bring the dark corners of the kingdom to a real understanding of the religion accepted by the capital.

The growing economic and political dominance of London was not unwelcome to the gentry; it was viewed with more mixed feelings by the local oligarchies of merchants. Their members were apt in the sixteenth and early seventeenth centuries to maintain a solid front against the outside world, whether it was the king's government, the authorities of the church or London merchants. Yet in the last resort, just because they were oligarchies, the privileged position of local ruling groups depended on the support of royal power, and there was a point beyond which authority could never be resisted.

Historians are just beginning to appreciate also the cultural significance of this imposition of London standards and London speech on the rest of the country. Professor Dickens speaks of the first two decades of Elizabeth's reign as a period which saw 'not only a waning of regional survivals, but a sweeping process of assimilation to the dominant national patterns'.

> For they of the country ever take heed
> How they of the City do wear their weed,

sang John Hall in 1565. By Elizabeth's reign any young man with literary ambitions had to move to the capital. Meanwhile London merchants, by means of great charitable endowments, were extending education, protestant preaching and an ethic of self-betterment from the capital into the provinces.

2

Throughout the Middle Ages there had been a tug-of-war over control of royal administration. Government originated in the king's household: the chancellor was the king's secretary, the treasury was a chest belonging to the king. As business became more complex, formal departments began to be differentiated. They ceased to accompany the king on his wanderings round the country, and settled at Westminster. Once an office had thus 'gone out of court', it was easier for a baronial opposition to capture control over it, to put in its nominee as, say, Lord Chancellor or Lord Treasurer. A weak king would have to accept baronial domination: a strong king would try to recover independence by bringing business back into the Household. The Chamber or the Wardrobe would then acquire new importance in national finance. A new seal – the Privy Seal, the Griffin, the Signet – would stamp the directly personal correspondence of the king, as opposed to the formal business left to the Lord Chancellor's office. Throughout the Middle Ages this see-saw continued: more 'bureaucratic' government under baronial control when the king was weak or a minor: 'Household' government under the king's personal control when he was strong. But in the sixteenth century this cycle was broken. Departments 'went out of court' without the king losing control over them: he could delegate a great deal of authority to a Wolsey or a Thomas Cromwell and still disgrace either of them with a word. Even when Cromwell met the vast influx of financial business which the Reformation brought by setting up a series of new courts outside the Household, no threat to royal control was implied: nor did the crown lose authority when they were mostly absorbed into the Exchequer under Mary. *All* government was now national government, the king's government.

We should be wary of attributing this development to the administrative genius of a Wolsey or a Cromwell, though they both helped. Deeper reasons for the change lay in the structure of society (and not only of English society: similar changes took place in many west European countries at about the same time). England had been moving towards some such system in the early fifteenth century, until the Wars of the Roses, the last faction fight between organized gangs of barons for control of the government, interrupted the process. With the return of peace and order under the Tudors it was resumed; and by now with a difference. The numbers, wealth and political influence of the greater aristocracy had been diminished: by death on the battle-field or the scaffold, by lack of male heirs, by habits of ostentatious living and a traditional reluctance to take part in trade, by the growing expenses of war and its diminishing profitability as the English were expelled from France, by losses of lands in France, by fines and attainders in England, by the secularization of the abbeys and consequent loss of patronage and perquisites. Fuller in the seventeenth century observed that 'although many modern families have been great gainers by the destruction of monasteries, yet the ancient nobility . . . found themselves much impoverished thereby, both in power and profit'.

In one sense the crown was the sole heir of the feudal baronage: the reforms of Thomas Cromwell can be said to have 'nationalized feudalism'. In another sense the residuary legatees of the lords were the wider sections of the gentry whom the House of Commons represented. Their power and social significance were based not on troops of retainers who would maintain their lord's cause on the field of battle or by intimidation in the law courts, but on sheep farming and agricultural production for the market. They were prepared to support the national centralization for which the Tudors stood – not in order to control the central government, as the feudal barons had wanted; they hoped to make money out of the tenure of many minor offices rather than to monopolize the few great offices. 'I serve only the King' was the motto of Sir Ralph Sadler, not the least successful of the new men who prospered by such service.

So the 'Tudor Revolution in Government', as Dr Elton called it, was a consequence of social changes which were increasing the importance of the House of Commons *vis-à-vis* the House of Lords, which secularized the monasteries, which led to enclosure for sheep-farming and to a society in which wealth came to be measured in £ *s. d.* rather than in military followings. Indeed, by the end of the Wars of the Roses, with the growing importance of gunpowder, money was needed even to raise private armies. The dependence of the Tudors on the gentry and greatest merchants (and on the peerage once they accepted a position of great social prestige *under* the king and no longer aspired to rival him) explains why Henry VIII said that he never stood so highly in his estate royal as in the time of Parliament. The realities of social power meant that the king could not rule without the support of the landed class. The gentry, said Sir Walter Ralegh, 'spread over all, are the garrisons of good order throughout the realm'. Parliament was to Henry VIII what his army was to the King of France. The private armies of the barons were disbanded, and the King of England, unlike his brother of France, had neither standing army nor bureaucracy. So effective power lay with 'the county' – the alliance of ruling landowners which had replaced the great lordships –, with the armigerous. The gentry officered the militia, and no one below the rank of gentleman carried a sword or a gun without permission. Consequently the order which was maintained had to be their sort of order.

England being cut off from the Continent, once the French adventures were abandoned, national defence was the affair of the navy – which could not be used for internal repression. Henry VIII strengthened the navy, and its mere existence protected trade; the expansion of the mercantile marine created a reserve of ships and seamen for the navy in time of war, and so was supported by governments. Thanks to the early development of sheep-farming in England, wool had become a useful source of taxes. Medieval kings therefore did nothing to discourage its production, and gradually became more and more dependent, in the absence of an army, on Parliament which voted taxes, and on the gentry whom the Commons represented and who assessed and collected the taxes. The fact that the Lord Chancellor sits on the woolsack symbolizes the close connexion between wool-growing and the survival of Parliament in England. Wool also helps to explain the Whiggish predilection of the English landed classes, very early shown, for sending their younger sons into trade, the co-operation of burgesses with knights of the shire in the House of Commons, and the representation of boroughs in that House by gentlemen.

Thus England, in the words of Professor MacCaffrey, became a hybrid political society, in which centralized monarchy existed side by side with a kind of confederation of local political interests. Parliament represented these interests to the central government. The latter depended on the gentry as M.P.s for taxes, on the gentry as J.P.s and deputy lieutenants for the maintenance of order, and used gentlemen increasingly as civil servants. Since it needed their support for the break with Rome, it allowed them to purchase monastic lands (or allowed members of other classes to make themselves gentlemen through the purchase of monastic lands) – in order that, as one gentleman purchaser put it, 'his heirs may be of the same mind for their own profit'. Tudor governments thus inevitably favoured the process which Professor Tawney called 'the rise of the gentry'. By the time that the gentry became collectively as strong as the feudal baronage had been in the fifteenth century, able to claim privileges and powers for the House of Commons such as had previously been claimed for the House of Lords, it was too late for Stuart governments to reverse the process.

The task of government in this period was not to make but to declare and interpret law. Parliament was still only an occasional part of the constitution, but its share in the Reformation settlement enormously enhanced its status, and the idea of its legislative function was slowly developing. In 1542 the Lord Chancellor recommended that Parliament should establish new laws if it found new evils. By the middle of the sixteenth century most boroughs as well as all counties were represented by gentlemen. This homogeneity of the Commons' representation probably contributed to the separation of the two Houses, which dates from the beginning of our period. The Commons had their own *Journal* from 1547.

Before our period began an alliance had been formed between common lawyers and the Commons against the fusion of church and government under Wolsey, against the latter's use of prerogative courts and flirtation with Roman law. The House of Commons, as many remarked between Francis Bacon and Blackstone, represented property. On property issues it showed its independence. Henry VIII's Statute of Uses, designed to enforce prerogative fiscal rights against tenants-in-chief, was doggedly opposed and ultimately modified; under Edward VI the government was forced to abandon its enclosure policy; under Mary the restoration of monastic lands was prevented. Under Elizabeth the church settlement and the Statute of Artificers were drastically modified; and by 1601 (as in 1621, with greater economic self-confidence) the Commons were able to take advantage of an economic crisis to challenge the crown's financial policy. It was therefore natural for the House to resolve in 1628 that 'every free subject of this realm hath a fundamental property in his goods and a fundamental liberty of his person'. The many who were not free were less fortunate.

3

The fifteen-thirties marked a step forward in national unification. The defeat of the Pilgrimage of Grace (1536–37), a mixture of feudal and peasant revolt, was utilized to replace the great ruling families in the North by 'mean persons' from the gentry, dependent on London support. When the Duke of Norfolk protested against this policy of arming small thieves to hunt down the big, the Council rebuked him, saying, 'If it shall please his Majesty to appoint the meanest man to rule and govern in that place, is not his Grace's authority sufficient to cause all men to serve his Grace under him without respect of the very estate of the personage?' Mary's attempt to reverse this process and set the Percies up again in the North collapsed with the failure of the last northern feudal revolt in 1569, and so the unification of England was completed. A pamphlet of 1569 asked rhetorically, 'Is Percy and Nevil more ancient, more beloved and dear unto you, than your natural sovereign lady, the Queen of England, or England itself? Doth one small tenancy move you more than the holding of the whole realm?' Thereafter the Puritan Earl of

Huntingdon as Lord President of the Council in the North, helped by a succession of near-Puritan Archbishops of York, consolidated the influence of the central government in the North, in continuing alliance with some of the gentry and urban ruling groups. The extension of London's authority into the out-lying regions is witnessed by Parliamentary representation. In 1547 three Yorkshire boroughs and six Cornish sent M.P.s to Parliament; in 1640 the figures were fourteen and twenty-one.

The year 1536 also saw the union of Wales with England, the division of Wales and Ireland into counties and the introduction of the English system of shire administration in order to over-ride local liberties – rather as the introduction of departments by the French revolutionary government after 1789 aimed to obliterate the traditional feudal independence of the provinces. Councils in the North and in the Marches of Wales were set up in the same year 1536–37, to control these outlying and turbulent regions. Tudor sovereigns often made bishops presidents of these two courts. Both in church and state the authority of the central power over all subjects was being made effective – e.g. by another act of 1536 resuming franchises to the crown. Destruction of 'liberties', it has been well said, was the great service of the Tudors to liberty.

The Justices of the Peace were the agents of this royal national-ism. From the Reformation the ecclesiastical machinery of the parish was at their disposal, supplying what they had hitherto lacked, subordinate officers to carry out their commands. J.P.s were appointed by the crown, and the dependants of great magnates were deliberately excluded from the commission of the peace. It instructed justices to act 'as well within liberties as without', thus encouraging them to break down the immunities of feudal lords. Society ceased to be, in Aubrey's vivid phrase, 'like a nest of boxes', with villeins holding of lords of manors who held of a superior lord who held of the king. Wars against Scotland and Ireland deflected the energies of potential rebels in the border areas of the North and Wales.

'The greatest triumph of the Tudors,' said Professor Stone, 'was the ultimately successful assertion of a royal monopoly of violence.' Gunpowder made feudal anarchy more dangerous, but monopoly control easier. The last great private castle to be built was the massive fortification of Thornbury, constructed by the Duke of Buckingham shortly before his execution in 1521. When the German Thomas Platter visited England in 1599 he commented on the absence of castles, which had been destroyed 'so that the inhabitants should not rise up against their king'. Nevertheless the Tudors still needed the arms of the nobility and gentry to keep the peasantry in place, and the process of disarmament was not complete until the beginning of the next century. Proclamations against retainers were being issued as late as 1583, and James I in 1603 was amazed by the equipage of the northern lords who joined him on his march southwards to claim his crown. Yet even in the North the unsuccessful risings of 1536 and 1569 were the last of their kind; the Earl of Essex's attempted revolt in 1601 was a fiasco even in Wales. By James's reign private war was unusual though not yet extinct; liveried servants had replaced armed retainers.

4

The church had long been a source of power, patronage and wealth to rulers of major powers like France and Spain. Those governments which broke with Rome in the early sixteenth century were on the fringes of catholic civilization, secondary powers whose rulers had not been strong enough to drive so hard a bargain with the papacy – like England, Sweden, Denmark, Switzerland, Scotland. An American historian has called the Act of Supremacy of 1534 'Henry VIII's Declaration of Independence'. Before the Reformation English kings had had to ally with the Pope in order to control their greater clergy, who were privileged landowners and franchise-holders. Henceforth they were royal servants, and played a much less independent role in political life. Cardinal Wolsey was succeeded by Sir Thomas More, the first lay Chancellor for seventy-five years. In 1540 Henry VIII proclaimed himself King of Ireland, to extinguish any idea that Ireland was a papal patrimony. The patriotic aspects of the Reformation must have struck contemporaries far more forcibly than any doctrinal change. The king became in theory as well as in practice head of church and state: the concept of national sovereignty arose as an incident of foreign policy.

The English Reformation was enacted by statute. The authority of the king over the church became the authority of the king in Parliament. Tax-payers benefited by the diversion to the king of revenues which had previously gone to Rome. First-fruits, tenths and monastic lands added over £200,000 a year to royal revenue previously more like £100,000 – and might have added considerably more, but monastic lands were soon sold, and chantry lands followed under Edward VI, when lands worth £1½ million were handed over by the government to its friends. So a vast vested interest in protestantism was created to guarantee the Reformation settlement.

It has been said that the Tudors treated the realm as though it was their manor, and the church as if it were their parish. But in both spheres their power was shared. The Reformation not only subordinated the national church to the king, it also subordinated parishes to squires. Gentlemen succeeded monasteries not only as landowners but also as recipients of tithes and as patrons of livings. After the Reformation nearly 4,000 of the 9,000 English parishes were impropriated – i.e. tithes were paid to a lay rector, and only a small stipend was reserved for the vicar or curate, whom the local squire very often appointed. Here was a vast accession of wealth and patronage. In Germany the Reformation led to a system described by the formula *cuius regio, eius religio*: each petty princeling determined the worship of his own dominions. Something of the same sort grew up in England, as the result of lay patronage combined with a growing divergence of political outlook among patrons. Lacking the support of an international church, or even of a bishop who was not a royal civil servant, the parson could not look the squire in the face as an equal. On his voyage round the world Sir Francis Drake not only subjected his chaplain to civil penalties, he also excommunicated him 'out of the church of God and from all the benefits and graces thereof', just as Elizabeth and James I suspended Archbishops of Canterbury.

The Reformation thus nationalized the church of which all Englishmen were members. It prohibited any appeal outside

England, and forbade any foreigner to intervene in English affairs on pretext of religion. It reduced the franchises and privileges of the church. In 1526 the Bishop of London had spoken of 'our subjects'. Post-Reformation bishops, even more than pre-Reformation bishops, were royal civil servants, rather like the Intendants of seventeenth-century France. In sixteenth-century Spain the Inquisition served as a royal instrument for national unification. So did the protestant church in Tudor England. Under Elizabeth the High Commission exercised a supervisory control over church courts, overriding the boundaries of dioceses, just as Star Chamber overrode local franchises. Episcopal visitations from time to time invigorated the lethargic activities of church courts. But the church after the Reformation had coercive powers only through its alliance with and dependence on the crown: as its courts came increasingly into rivalry with the common-law courts, so its dependence on the crown increased too.

A natural concomitant of the suppression of local liberties is an ideology of nationalism. For most ordinary Englishmen the changes decided on in London between 1530 and 1560 must have seemed bewildering, but not quite so fundamental as they do to historians. Looking back, we stick on labels like 'protestant' and 'catholic'; at the time men must have thought of themselves simply as members of the English church, which was undergoing some modifications. It is only in retrospect that reform becomes 'the Reformation'. The majority of clergymen retained their livings throughout the changes of these three decades, and we should be wrong to think of them as merely time-serving. Most of the laity must altogether have missed what seems to us the point.

Nevertheless, in the long run the consequences which followed from the break with Rome were momentous. 'Religion,' as Sir Lewis Namier used to say, 'is a sixteenth-century word for nationalism.' The early protestant reformers were staunch supporters of the English monarchy. Becon, for example, in 1550 stressed the popular nature of English patriotism, and rejoiced 'to see how glad my countrymen are to serve the commands of their own country, England'. By the early sixteenth century a right of revolt was likely to be claimed by feudal magnates like those who led the risings of 1536 and 1569, or by catholics in response to papal excommunication of the monarch, or by the ungodly and heretical multitude. Protestants could hope to spread their teaching only with the backing of the secular power: they thus advocated absolute submission to the king and denied that feudal lords or the Pope had any comparable claims on the loyalty of subjects. The protestant martyr William Tyndale said, 'The king is, in this world, without law; and may at his lust do right and wrong, and shall give account but to God only.' A tyrant is better than a weak king.

For Archbishop Cranmer royal headship of the Church of England was so much an article of faith that he found himself in the utmost philosophical confusion when Queen Mary told him she was not head of the church. Hence the recantations and re-recantations which he finally purged by the unforgettable gesture of holding out into the flames the hand which had signed them. When Bishop Ridley was preparing for the public trial which preceded his martyrdom he was confident of his theological position; but he was far less happy about the charge which he knew would be brought against him, that he disobeyed the Queen's orders in refusing to conform to catholicism. He finally found arguments which seemed to him satisfactory; but it is significant that it was at this non-theological point that sincere protestants (the martyr Bishop Hooper is another example) felt least sure of their position, so strong was the emotive power of loyalty to the secular sovereign.

Ridley did indeed, as Latimer urged him at the stake, 'play the man', and lighted a candle which has not yet gone out. But he gave an example not only of loyalty to his faith but also of disobedience to his sovereign, however reluctantly: both examples were to be followed by radical protestants in the next century. The dilemma lies very deep in protestant attitudes, which elevate both the monarch and the conscience of the individual. Tyndale, whom I quoted on the duty of absolute subordination to monarchical power, also said, 'The most despised person in his realm is the King's brother and fellow-member with him, and equal with him in the kingdom of God and of Christ.' Here was the 'two kingdoms' theory which Andrew Melville was to preach to 'God's silly vassal', James VI of Scotland, later James I of England. Henry VIII had already observed, presciently, that Luther 'robs princes and prelates of all power and authority'.

It was a long time before the emphasis on individual conscience was elevated to a theoretical right of resistance to constituted authority. Radical protestants continued to look to the king or to some great royal favourite – the Duke of Northumberland, the Earl of Leicester, the Earl of Essex, the Duke of Buckingham – to act as the ungodly agent of a godly policy. They did not advocate resistance, because they were far too conscious of its explosive possibilities. Monarchy, said Sir Robert Filmer in 1648, was crucified between two thieves, the Pope and the people; but the monarchy had first crucified these thieves. Throughout the sixteenth century church and state were identical. Sir Thomas More, the catholic martyr, thought that religious heresy should be punishable as sedition no less than did Queen Elizabeth, under whom Jesuits were executed as traitors, not heretics.

The Reformation contributed to a long-term social change by which the crown replaced the church as the chief patron of scholars and administrators as well as of artists. Thomas Cromwell in the thirties employed a number of humanist-educated lay scholars like Richard Morison and Thomas Starkey. The former wrote a propagandist pamphlet in 1536, pointing out to the northern rebels that the monarchy served the interests of the common man by opening up a career to the talents. So long as England's national independence was in danger, the loyalty of the educated gentry and merchants to the monarchy was unwavering. The crude anti-foreign feeling and violent jingoism of many middle-class Englishmen in the sixteenth century were often associated with a deeply-felt protestantism.

5

Protestantism depended on the new craft of printing. The widespread dissemination of vernacular translations of the Bible, some in pocket editions, made possible *individual* study of the

Scriptures: the scruples of the nonconformist conscience were trained in Bible-reading. In the sixteenth century advances in middle-class wealth were reflected in more domestic comforts, more privacy: the economic achievements made possible more widespread study and discussion of the Bible. Now that celibacy was no longer compulsory for intellectuals, and printing had put books within the reach of the middle class, the home could become a cultural and discussion centre as well as a family circle. Closed parish churches and family worship were both characteristic of protestantism. Artisans, spinsters and apprentices, a catholic complained, sang the 'variable and delightful tunes' of Sternhold and Hopkins's metrical psalms, and lapped up heresy with them. We can mark the rise of a new confidence in the Marian martyrs, mainly small merchants and craftsmen. Their Lollard predecessors had almost invariably recanted when caught. The Marian martyrs differed not in doctrine so much as in determination. They no longer felt themselves to be an isolated remnant, but an army on the march. This gave them the courage to die, and their deaths helped to bring victory to their cause.

The protestant emphasis on Bible-reading, vernacular preaching and congregational participation in worship (as against ceremonial and parrot-like repetitions) called for higher educational standards, in clergy and laity alike. The myth that the Reformation destroyed a national educational system has been completely discredited:* it is now known that very few chantry priests taught, and most of those only Latin responses for choir-boys. The whole trend of educational advance during the century before the Reformation had been towards a more secular, lay-controlled education in the vernacular. The dissolution of monasteries and chantries gave an opportunity for creating a national educational system. The land-grabbers prevented the wealth of the church being used for this purpose as completely as the radical reformers would have wished, or as was done in Presbyterian Scotland. But, thanks to pressure of municipalities and to endowment of grammar schools by merchants and gentle-

*What follows draws heavily upon Mrs Joan Simon's admirable *Education and Society in Tudor England* (Cambridge University Press, 1966).

men, by the end of the sixteenth century England had a far better educational system, in quantity and in quality, than before the Reformation. It was also a more socially mixed educational system. Gentlemen's sons, who would previously have been taught in monasteries, now sat side by side with plebeians in village and grammar schools, and flocked into the universities, which by the early seventeenth century were fuller than ever before, or than they were to be again until the later nineteenth century. In the long run the gentry used its power to monopolize the better schools and Oxford and Cambridge colleges, to the great detriment of those lower in the social scale.* But this tendency was not fully developed in the first century after the Reformation.

In all sorts of ways protestant theology appealed to the individualism of the middle class. The abolition of mediating saints and a mediating priesthood set individual consciences face to face with God. Tyndale rejected the argument for mediation of saints with words which must have boomeranged against social hierarchies: '"If a man have a matter with a great man or a King, he must first go unto one of his mean servants, and then higher and higher till he come at last to the King." This enticing argument is but a blind reason of man's wit. . . . With God, if we have belief, . . . there is [no] porter to keep any man out.' Monks and nuns no longer prayed for the community: the individual household had its own family prayers. 'The putting down of monasteries argues purgatory not to be.' The medieval doctrine of purgatory conceived of society (the church) as a single community. The merits of individual Christians (including those of dead saints as well as those of living monks performing their highly specialized social tasks) were paid into an ecclesiastical bank from which, through the mediating priesthood, they could be drawn upon by individual Christians if they did penance. Protestantism popularized the idea of the individual spiritual balance sheet, the profit-and-loss book-keeping of diaries. This presupposes an atomic society of individuals fighting for their own salvation, no longer a community working out its salvation, as it cultivated its fields, in common. The phrase 'the individual' in its modern sense dates from the late sixteenth or early seventeenth centuries. We can

See p. 207, below.

see the new spirit in a number of spheres – in the emphasis of Puritans and dramatists on the right to choose one's matrimonial partner, which proved so liberating for women, in more realistic portraiture and sculpture, resulting from post-Reformation secular patronage of the arts: Holbein, the first painter of genius to work in England, came over in 1527. The miniatures of Nicholas Hilliard and Samuel Cooper are paralleled by the poetry of introspection. Sir Walter Ralegh's long *Cynthia* has only one subject – the poet's own state of mind. Metaphysical poetry was meant to be *read* in private, not sung or declaimed in public: miniatures were private and personal keepsakes.

The Reformation stimulated not only individualism but also, in the long run, a scientific outlook. Protestants inherited a long-standing Lollard tradition of scepticism about the miracle of the mass. Tyndale denounced the Pope as a magician. As in so many other respects, the aura which the church lost fell first of all on the monarchy. Shrines and saints lost their magical powers and (more slowly) the adulation of the populace; at the same time the supposed ability of the sovereign to cure scrofula was increasing and was deliberately emphasized – for Elizabeth especially after she had been excommunicated by the Pope in 1570. James I accepted the belief despite his Calvinist scruples. The thaumaturgic powers of royalty were difficult to maintain in an increasingly industrial and scientific age, an age which was losing faith in witches. They finally disappeared only after the establishment of Parliamentary sovereignty: Queen Anne was the last to 'touch'.

In the early seventeenth century the king ceased to exhibit himself to his subjects as he ate his way round estates scattered all over England. He settled at Westminster: and royal propagandists began deliberately to use control of pulpit and printing press to project a new image of monarchy. The adulation of Elizabeth as Gloriana started it; court poets treated James and Charles with increasing reverence as they declined in the respect of the country. But an image is different from the real thing: it can be counterfeited or manipulated, as Charles found in 1642 when Parliament claimed to be fighting to defend him from a group of evil councillors who had somehow kidnapped him.

6

If we think again of our period as a whole, it extends not only from Reformation to Industrial Revolution but also from Reformation to the Gordon Riots.* For 250 years protestantism and patriotism were closely interwoven. Protestantism, as many of its partisans emphasized, put an end to the centuries-old border conflict with those who were now 'our brethren of Scotland'; catholicism lost Calais, and so less gloriously ended another centuries-old story. John Foxe's *Acts and Monuments* popularized a national historical myth which saw God's Englishmen from Wyclif's day (at least) fighting against Antichrist, who in the sixteenth century was represented by the Pope and Spain. The Spanish Armada in 1588, Guy Fawkes's Plot in 1605, the Irish Revolt of 1641, the Popish Plot of 1679, all fitted into this pattern, though by 1679 the spontaneous feelings of protestant patriots were worked upon by unscrupulous politicians, just as in 1780 no-popery was a cry which justified looting the rich. But for 250 years protestantism strengthened patriotism, and the existence of an internal (papist) enemy, as well as the neighbouring popish Irish, helped to bind Englishmen together in national unity. The struggle of pious protestants to extend English religion and English civilization, first to the 'dark corners' of England and Wales, then to Ireland and the Highlands of Scotland, was a struggle to extend the values of London, and so to reinforce England's national security. It was no accident that Leland, so interested in the development of internal communications, was also a keen protestant, a friend of Thomas Cromwell, and intended his *Itinerary* as a contribution to English patriotism.

A by-product of the protestant national myth was a hatred of cruelty, which was portrayed as something especially Spanish and popish. John Foxe the martyrologist was a genuine humanitarian, who hated cruelty to animals as well as to men and women, and who was almost unique in his time for disliking persecution even by his own side. One result was that, though English law remained harsh and brutal, especially to the lower classes, there was a strong protestant sentiment which opposed cruelty. The

*See pp. 277, 283, below.

great Puritan preacher William Perkins attacked cock-fighting on humanitarian grounds. The separatist Henry Barrowe was against the death penalty for theft, since such a punishment was unknown to the Mosaic law. A representative Englishman like John Taylor the Water-Poet, rather conservative in his general outlook, was very shocked by the judicial cruelty he found in Hamburg in 1616. Charles I was the last English king to have a court fool. Some of the 'Puritan' legislation of the interregnum gave effect to this new sensitivity. Macaulay's jibe that Puritans disliked bear-baiting not because of the pain it gave the bear but because of the pleasure it gave the spectators is wholly unfair.

The struggle against cruelty needed all the ideological help it could get. Judicial torture seemed perhaps less shocking to the men and women of the sixteenth and seventeenth centuries because of the frightful pain which all had to endure in everyday life. There were no pain-killing drugs, teeth were extracted and limbs sawn off without anaesthetic. Public floggings and hangings were common sights, and schoolboys and undergraduates even of the well-to-do classes were regularly beaten. The theologians had to emphasize the eternity and special intensity of the torments of hell if they were to have the desired deterrent effect. It may be, ironically, that popular protestant humanitarianism helped to sap belief in that eternal torture which protestant divines had unquestioningly taken over from their catholic predecessors.*

*See pp. 204–6, below.

2

THE PEOPLE

Old Barnacle: We that had
         Our breeding from a trade, cits as ye call us,
         Though we hate gentlemen ourselves, yet are
         Ambitious to make all our children gentlemen:
         In three generations they return again.
         We for our children purchase land: they brave it
         I' the country; beget children, and they sell,
         Grow poor and send their sons up to be prentices.
         There is a whirl in fate.
                         JAMES SHIRLEY, The Gamester (*1633*)

I

WE know very little about population in England before the
eighteenth century. The population of western Europe had perhaps been halved by economic stagnation and plague in the four-
teenth century. After a slow recovery in the fifteenth century,
the pace was quickening in the sixteenth, and population continued to increase throughout our period. But we cannot be sure
about the rate of growth, or whether it was steady or phased, local
or general. Economists make elaborate guesses, not always supported by firm historical evidence. It is wise to be very sceptical
of arguments for this period which are based on assumptions
about population movements: they can neither be disproved nor
proved.

In the sixteenth century many migrants came to England from
the Continent, Wales and Ireland: we do not know how many.
The halving (as we guess) of the Irish population in the sixteen-
forties and -fifties presumably slowed down migration to England. There was also migration within England. Population
growth was probably more rapid down to the sixteen-thirties,
when mass emigration began, followed by civil war. If we say
that England's population was about three millions in 1530, over
four millions in 1600, over five and a half millions in 1700, over

44

six millions in 1750, seven and a half millions in 1780, we shall be wrong; but not perhaps seriously enough to matter much. In the sixteenth century pressure of population on natural resources was beginning to be shown – by roving bands of beggars, by internal colonization, by draining of marshes, cultivation of forests, enclosure of the waste, and by schemes for emigration and colonization, whether of Ireland or of America.

Rising population meant expansion of the towns, most of all London, and of such rural industrial areas as Somerset, Wiltshire, Gloucestershire and the West Riding of Yorkshire. The population of London may have quadrupled in the sixteenth century, rising to 200,000 or more by 1600: and it probably doubled again in the next fifty years. This of course was due to migration as well as to natural increase. In the first two decades of our period migrants came to Bristol from no less than forty-five English and Welsh counties.

More important for our purposes than the absolute numbers is the structure of the population. In the sixteenth century, with the collapse of demesne farming, the dissolution of the monasteries and the breakup of many great feudal households, the number of those who had lost their land-holdings (or their source of maintenance from a feudal superior) and thus were becoming wholly dependent on wage labour or charity seems to have been on the increase. Wage labour and the Poor Law rise together and complement one another. The harsh penalties imposed on sturdy beggars from the fifteen-thirties were intended to force the idle to work; later provision for the impotent poor was a delayed recognition of the fact that landless families starve if they have no employed wage-earner.*

Men and women who became dependent for their subsistence on wages were far more at the mercy of famine, unemployment and similar catastrophes than those with agricultural holdings. The number of persons on the poverty line in London and other great cities was very great. In 1520, according to Professor Hoskins, one-third of the urban population was exempt from taxation because of poverty; the proportion probably rose during the next century. In 1602 a judge said that there were 30,000

*See pp. 55–9, below.

'idle persons and masterless men' in London. It was a guess, and probably not a very good one; but it helps to explain the anxiety of the ruling class in time of hardship, and its harsh repression (e.g. when a series of bad harvests coincided with a clothing slump, as in the fifteen-fifties and sixteen-twenties, or with war, as in the fifties, nineties and sixteen-twenties). At the same time the increase in the proportion of the population which had to buy food meant that prices fluctuated sharply according to the nature of the harvest, though the general trend of real wages was relentlessly downwards until the agricultural revolution of the seventeenth century began to take effect.* The first effect of industrialization, as we have seen in our own day, is to increase the risk of famine: the faster the industrialization, the greater the initial danger. It is only when the national market is fully integrated that it evens out regional fluctuations in grain prices.

There were, however, important checks to population growth in this period, when English territory was almost immune from the great continental regulator – war. The first was the killing power of the insanitary cities, with many endemic diseases and frequent outbreaks of plague. As population expanded, its surplus drifted to London and other great cities, there to be killed off, with the assistance of the medical profession. The plague of 1635 removed nearly half of Newcastle's inhabitants.† It has been estimated that in the sixteenth century only two children out of every five born to royalty and the aristocracy reached maturity. The fourth Duke of Norfolk lost three wives in succession in childbirth. Ten of the eleven children born to the Rev. John Owen (1616–83) died in early youth. If such were the figures for the upper classes, the lower orders must have fared far worse. In 1662 John Graunt calculated a London child's expectation of life at birth as seventeen-and-a-half years. One London child in ten survived to the age of five. Since the population nevertheless continued to expand very rapidly, the natural increase in the country as a whole must have been considerable.

Dirt and disease were the main killers. But the law did its bit. In 1598 seventy-four persons were sentenced to death in Devon-

*See Part III, Chapter 3, below.

†R. Howell, *Newcastle upon Tyne and the Puritan Revolution* (1967), p. 9.

46

shire. Over the nine years 1607–16 the yearly average of persons executed in Middlesex was seventy-eight. These figures may be exceptional, since 1598 was a famine year, and Middlesex had a larger and more rootless population than most counties. Nevertheless, if say 2,000 persons were executed every year, and we add to this the number (quite impossible to determine, but probably far greater), who died in the fever-ridden prisons, it is clear that the law eliminated a respectable proportion of those in the age-groups most likely to beget children. We can understand the unwillingness of juries to find men and women guilty of the trifling thefts for which they were liable to the death penalty.

2

Turning now to the social classes into which sixteenth-century England was divided, let us look first at the peers. Here we have to record a double phenomenon – loss of some power but survival of privilege and great influence. The Reformation transformed the balance of the House of Lords, converting a clerical majority into a lay majority. Thirty-one mitred abbots disappeared, and only five of the new bishoprics created survived. There thus remained twenty-six bishops: there were never less than thirty-six lay peers in Henry VIII's reign. But the lay peerage was transformed too. Twenty-five out of thirty-nine families ennobled under the first two Tudors owed their elevation to political and administrative services to the crown. By Elizabeth's accession, twenty-six of the sixty-one lay peerages had been created since the Reformation. There was never a majority of peers who had inherited their titles until the reign of James I. Since bishops were royal nominees, we can understand why the House of Lords usually found itself in agreement with royal policy. Simultaneously the royal attack on franchises meant that the old nobility was losing its independent territorial power. As Spelman put it about a century after the Reformation:

The whole body of the baronage is . . . fallen . . . from their ancient lustre, magnitude and estimation. I that about 50 years ago did behold with what great respect, observance and distance principal men of counties applied themselves to some of the meanest barons, and so with what familiarity inferior gentlemen often do accost many of these of our times, cannot but wonder either at the declination of the one or at the arrogance of the other. . . . God, to requite them [for their participation in the spoliation of the church] hath taken the ancient honours of nobility, and communicated them to the meanest of the people, to shopkeepers, taverners, tailors, tradesmen, burghers brewers and graziers.

The Lords then became only one of two Houses instead of being the essential component of Parliament. The sixty-one lay peers of 1558 had fallen to fifty-nine in 1603. Elizabeth's failure to ennoble the rising gentry meant that the peerage as a social group ceased to coincide with the biggest landowners: and when James and Charles renewed creations, merchants were rich enough to buy them. By 1626 there were about a hundred lay peers. But in compensation the sixteenth century also saw the working out of a law of peerage, of the theory that the crown could not summon whom it wished to the Upper House, but only those who had a hereditary right to attend. As Bacon observed, the 'rights and pre-eminence of the nobility' were in no way diminished by their loss of military power. A peer did not expect to receive the same treatment in the law courts as a commoner. He could not be put on oath. He was exempt from torture. He could not be arrested for debt – a most important privilege. He was assessed to taxation at a very low figure. 'When did you ever see a lord hang for anything?' asked Lord Fee-Simple in *Amends for Ladies* (1618); 'we may kill whom we list'. Their dependants could still overawe juries. A J.P. would not arrest a man who wore the livery of a powerful peer, as many of the gentry still did. In 1620 two serjeants of the Counter were punished for arresting 'a gentleman belonging to the Earl of Oxford'. 'Will any man think that a justice will contend with as great a man as himself?' asked an M.P. in 1621.

Especially in the seventeenth century, when the government no longer feared the political power of the aristocracy, it enforced the peers' social privileges with savage penalties. In Charles I's reign a man who called the Earl of Danby 'a base cheating lord' for enclosing, and said 'I am a better man then he', was imprisoned during His Majesty's pleasure, fined £1,000 plus

£1,000 damages. Even Laud at the height of his power dared not bring the wife of a peer to penance until he knew the king's pleasure. The king himself would intervene to protect a noble debtor or murderer. Peers could issue 'protections' which enabled bankrupt debtors to evade their creditors: some peers sold these at 5s. apiece.

Sumptuary laws helped to maintain class distinctions. Just as in the army today a disagreement can be ended by a glance at the shoulder-straps or sleeves of the contestants, so in the sixteenth century the validity of a man's argument was established by his garments. But the frequent reissue of proclamations on the subject of apparel is evidence of the breakdown of this symbol of a static hierarchical society. Significantly, a sumptuary bill was opposed in the House of Commons in 1621 on the ground that 'although the honour and difference betwixt the nobility and us was confessed, yet there was no reason there should be so much as is between silk and cloth, and so little left betwixt us and our servants as betwixt October and May'. There spoke men whose social aspirations were greater than the social position traditionally allotted to them. After 1640 sumptuary laws broke down.

The litigiousness for which sixteenth-century England was notorious should be seen against this social background. In any society at this stage of development, litigation tends to be private war carried on by other means: juries were rigged or terrorized, all sorts of pressures were brought to bear on judges. Nevertheless, by the seventeenth century a great change had taken place, at any rate in the South and East of England. The property rights of 'the meanest' in England could be defended at law (by those who could afford it); and Whitelocke contrasted this with 'those countries where the boors and peasants do wholly depend upon the will of their lords ... and dare not dispute any matter of right with him'. He pointed out that there were still fewer lawsuits in the North of England than in the South.

When it came to civil war in 1642, Charles I must sometimes have regretted that the Tudors had been so successful in disarming the great feudal families of the North and West on whose military support he now depended. 'One of the reasons why

King Charles lost the civil war', Professor Stone observes, 'is that the English aristocracy no longer knew how to fight.' Yet in 1642 even the Parliamentarians felt compelled to give military commands to peers wherever they could persuade one to accept – and nearly lost the war in consequence. Both Baillie and Clarendon thought the prestige of the Earl of Essex was necessary to hold the Parliamentary army together. Essex himself demonstrated his feudal power at the beginning of the war when he warned his tenants to 'expect no friendship after if they did not help to furnish him'.

The numbers of those who called themselves gentlemen seems to have expanded very rapidly in this period. At the beginning there were many parishes with no resident gentlemen. (Leland noted it as remarkable that there was a gentleman in nearly every village of Northamptonshire.) It would be interesting to know more about these villages which were not squire-ridden: they seem to have become fewer by the later seventeenth century, when three villages out of four had a resident squire. But – as with so many statistics in this period – we have to admit that we are not sure how new this was. It may be that far more persons had been accepted as gentlemen than the surviving records tell us, and that it was only in the sixteenth century, with the increase in the number of rich plebeians, that it became important to be *legally* recognized as a gentleman. But it looks as though pressure upwards into the gentry reinforced the domination of the country by an enlarged armigerous class. For as the great magnates lost their franchises, the gentry stepped into their places, controlling local government in the king's name.

At the beginning of our period there was still a personal element in the relation of J.P. to central government: Elizabeth, a 'gentleman's queen', went through the list of justices, marking those whom she wished to retain on the commission. She believed that she knew them all personally. But as the prestige and profit of the office grew, so pressure to be made J.P. for social reasons grew, inevitably; and their numbers increased. J.P.s at first were under the close control of the Privy Council and prerogative courts, just as they themselves looked to London for support against riots. But as the country was disarmed, so later the central government found it impossible to enforce unpopular policies on the justices. By 1621 the House of Commons was making itself the spokesman of the J.P.s against a royal project for removing the licensing of ale-houses from their control – an essential element in the maintenance of law and order and of the local patronage which justices expected to exercise. In the victorious session of 1624 an act practically removed J.P.s from supervision by higher courts.

There is a natural connexion between the growing importance of the gentry in local government and their desire for a seat in the House of Commons, which was both effect and cause of the growing importance of the lower House in our period. If Elizabeth created few peerages for the richer gentry, she compensated them by creating borough seats which remained under the patronage of a local gentleman. And although the line upwards out of the gentry was difficult to cross, the line from below into it was not: gentlemen 'be made good cheap in England', said Sir Thomas Smith in 1565. All who lived without working and yet were able to keep up the part of a gentleman, all who had degrees at Oxford or Cambridge, could be accepted as gentlemen. There was some difficulty in reconciling this *de facto* social mobility with the prejudices of the age: it was the job of the newly founded College of Heralds to perform this work of reconciliation. The earliest Heralds' Visitation was in 1529, the last in 1686. In 1530 the Heralds decided that any man of good reputation with free lands worth £10 a year or movable goods worth £300 could buy a coat of arms. So from the very beginning of our period blue blood was purchasable. At the dissolution monastic lands were normally sold in tenure by knight's service, for reasons which were fiscal rather than military. Thus landownership was still further separated from its traditional military liabilities, and more landed families were brought into dependence on the crown through wardship: though later in the century purchasers of monastic lands found ways of escaping feudal tenure.

3

'Even our cities and corporations here in England, such as need the protection of great men,' Sir Walter Ralegh observed, 'complain otherwhiles of their patrons' overmuch diligence, either in searching into their private estates, or behaving themselves master-like in point of government.' The relation was still one of feudal dependence, just as the Venetian Ambassador described trading companies under James I as 'burdened and protected' by the king.

Certainly boroughs had cause for complaint. They needed the protection of a local peer or gentleman for many reasons – to win favours from the government, to see that their interests were not disregarded by Parliament. But they often had to pay a heavy price. Leland tells us that though the salt industry of Droitwich was thriving in his day, 'yet the burgesses be poor for the most part, because gentlemen [have] for the most part the great gain of it, and the burgesses have all the labour'. The Earl of Cumberland had the profits of the weekly market and two annual fairs at Kirkby Stephen. When in 1618 the Earl of Suffolk fell from power, this ruined the Oswestry cloth market, which he, as lord of the manor, had been able to defend against the competition of Shrewsbury. In the fifteen-nineties Sir George Grey wrote to the city fathers of Leicester about a criminal they had arrested: 'Have him I will; . . . therefore send him me, for as I live I will try all the friends I have in England, but I will be righted. . . . If you be able to cross me in one thing I can requite your town with twenty.' Increasingly in the sixteenth century all but the greatest boroughs wished to be represented in the Commons by gentlemen, who would not ask for their wages to be paid, and who might be more influential at court than burgesses.

But we should not look only at the relationship of oppression–protection between gentlemen and towns. The relative weakness of English towns (outside London), which kept them dependent on the local landlord, also helped national unification under a single capital. It made possible the escape of newer, freer, expanding industries from the walls and regulations of corporations which were on the defensive for their privileges. Here there were links of greater equality and friendliness between the gentleman sheep-farmer and the clothier, who had so many interests in common – interests which the House of Commons represented.*

Above all we must emphasize the great London merchants. They were still relatively uninfluential in politics, but in the fifteen-seventies, after the sack of Antwerp, they were beginning to be more significant as a source of loans to the government. At the very beginning of Elizabeth's reign the great merchant financier, Sir Thomas Gresham, told the Queen that the English merchants 'must stand by you at all events in your necessity', and would thus save her from dependence upon foreigners. Within the City of London 'Her Majesty cannot lack in money matters, if it was for £40 or £50,000', said Gresham in 1570. In that year Elizabeth visited the newly opened Bourse which Gresham had built in imitation of Antwerp's: she symbolically christened it the Royal Exchange. England's independence automatically enhanced the importance of those who could finance it. Next year the taking of interest up to ten per cent was legalized.

By the seventeenth century some merchants were as rich as peers, though their fortunes were usually made in one lifetime. Such men were quite independent of all but the government. They were busy breaking down the privileges of local corporations where these impeded internal trade; and they were using their wealth to reconstruct the society in which they lived, its schools and colleges, its poor relief, its opportunities for able young people to better themselves. The relationship of such great merchants to the state evolved very differently from that of the aristocracy. At the beginning of our period traders needed strong centralized government for the maintenance of internal peace, law and order, as well as external support to oust foreign rivals and to protect the interests of English merchants in foreign countries. For all this it was worth paying a good deal. But by the early seventeenth century England's national independence and internal order had been secured, the foreigners had gone. Now the burdens of government seemed more obvious than its

*See pp. 68–9, 76, 120–21, below.

advantages. Merchants had to pay for their own defence against pirates in the English Channel, for maintenance of their own ambassadors overseas: Stuart governments were half-hearted in pressing the interests of English traders against foreign competitors, and tended to back up the privileges of local oligarchies against Londoners. They interfered in all sorts of ways with mercantile activities. Yet by this time the interests of merchants were shared by other classes in society: many gentlemen would agree with Thomas Mun that 'foreign trade is the only means to improve the price of our lands'. As the government slid back into alliance with an increasingly parasitic aristocracy, a growing number of gentlemen came to feel that their interests coincided with those of merchants, that jointly they formed 'the country' as against the narrow 'court' clique. On the other hand, the compact ruling oligarchy of London was drawn more and more into money-lending, first to peers, and then to the government. As Professor Robert Ashton puts it, 'the court and country alignment . . . extended into the City itself. . . . The distinction in terms of economic interest is not that of Court *versus* City, but of Court and a section of the City *versus* the rest.'

Below the landowners and greater merchants comes an important group of those whom I have called 'the middle class'. Attempts have been made recently to discredit the use of this term in the sixteenth and seventeenth centuries, but it seems to me indispensable provided it is carefully defined. In the middle class I include most merchants, richer artisans, the independent peasantry (yeomanry) and well-to-do tenant farmers. These were differentiated from the landed gentry and the ruling oligarchies of London and the bigger towns, on the one hand, by their lack of privilege; and from the mass of the rural and urban poor and vagabonds, on the other, by the possession of enough property to be economically independent. Their survival was precarious in an arbitrary world of natural catastrophes (plague, disease, inadequate medicine, no insurance), and of human violence and oppression; but with luck and industry many of them might survive and even prosper.

Such men were unprivileged but not rightless. The property of freeholders was protected by common law. The disappearance of villeinage in England by the end of the sixteenth century left copyholders, the villeins' successors, in an ambiguous legal position; but increasingly those who could afford to take legal action – i.e. the more prosperous – were likely to be able to get their tenure protected by the law courts. Alternatively they could buy their freedom – often at very high rates. These groups, increasing steadily in numbers, wealth and education, formed the Bible-reading class, the class for which the literature discussed in L. B. Wright's admirable *Middle-Class Culture in Elizabethan England* was written. Such men supported the Tudor monarchy – even the accession of the papist Mary in 1553. For in the sixteenth century the threat to the unprivileged came not so much from the central government as from the local feudal lord, against whom the monarchy might be conceived as a protector. This was often found to be an illusion, from Wat Tyler to Kett and later: the king's interests were inseparably bound up with those of the landed ruling class. Yet he *had* an interest in preventing the grosser forms of injustice, and in the maintenance of law and order.

'A much greater gulf,' Mr Barley says, 'by Charles I's time divided the successful and ambitious farmer from the poor commoner.'* Among the rising yeomanry the tradition of sturdy English independence was to grow up: beef-eating, beer-drinking, God-fearing English common men. Such men were the backbone of Puritanism and of the New Model Army. Many events conspired to fortify this class in England, at a time when wooden shoes were regarded as the normal wear of the lower-class inhabitants of foreign popish countries. It was such independent men of small means who established the new ideology of the middle-class home, as against the great households (aristocratic, monastic) of the Middle Ages.

4

The common people 'are held in little more esteem than if they were slaves', a Venetian ambassador declared about 1500: he commented at the same time on the prosperity of merchants.

*Thirsk, 1967, p. 766.

Another foreign observer remarked about 1619 on the uppishness of the common people because they were too rich: he clearly referred to those whom I have called the middle class. Contradictory accounts of the wealth of the English common people spring from the angle of vision of the observer: for the very poor were beginning to be differentiated from the richer plebeians with a sharpness that was new.

England and Scotland were unique in Europe (except for Scandinavia) in having escaped from villeinage by the end of the sixteenth century, though some labour services survived – e.g. an act of 1555 imposed *corvée* duties on the roads on all ablebodied men for four days a year (the rich of course could buy themselves off). Rents in kind were still very important, at least on ecclesiastical lands. This situation was not an unmixed blessing for the poorer peasants: 'villeinage ends, the poor law begins', was Professor Tawney's terse comment. Landlords had no scruples about evicting tenants who no longer owed them compulsory labour service. The law was heavily weighted against the poor. Men violently evicted could bring an action for forcible entry only if they were able to lay down costs in advance. English justice was already 'the best that money could buy'; and Chancery too seems to have favoured manorial lords against their tenants.* Wage labourers with no land were in a much less secure position than those who still retained their holdings. Villeinage ends, leasehold and wage labour extend. A statute of 1550 protected small cottagers building on wastes and commons. 47 years later it was laid down that no new cottages should be built without four acres of land attached; but J.P.s – themselves employers of wage labour – were in a position to enforce this or not as they pleased. A judicial decision of 1605 laid it down that inhabitants as such had no common rights on the waste. And real wages were declining steadily all the time.

On one point all members of the ruling class were agreed: the lower orders had no political rights. Henry VIII told rebels that he had 'never heard or known that princes' counsellors or prelates should be appointed by the rude or ignorant common people'. Sir Thomas Smith in 1565 said that 'day labourers,

*W. J. Jones, *The Elizabethan Court of Chancery* (1967), pp. 264-5, 461-2.

poor husbandmen, yea merchants or retailers which have no free
land, copyholders and all artificers ... have no voice nor
authority in our commonwealth, and no account is made of
them, but only to be ruled'. The great Statute of Artificers of
1563, the product of the joint wisdom of government and House
of Commons, is the best evidence that, in Sir John Clapham's
words 'legislators still thought of all people who had no property
as semi-servile', with a duty to work for their betters. Entry into
skilled occupations was restricted to children of the well-to-do,
so that 'gentlemen and others of living might have some means
to ... place their younger sons ... in reasonable countenance
and calling'. Semi-skilled labourers could be compelled to work
in their crafts, others in agriculture, women as domestic servants.
A memorandum of 1573 which I have just quoted, commenting
on this statute, held that it was only right and proper that
children should not be allowed to depart from the occupations of
their parents. The statute not merely attempted to freeze a static
hierarchical society: it also insisted that the gentry should benefit
in the first place from such mobility as was unavoidable. Henry
VIII's debasement of the coinage had caused especial impoverishment among the poorest classes; the abolition of chantries had deprived the poor of one form of social assurance. Now
the Act of 1563 imposed a stringent control over the working
population, a control exercised by J.P.s from the employing
class.

One object of the 1563 Act was to keep a pool of cheap labour
available in country districts, so that landowners should not go
short. As population increased, labour lost the scarcity value
which it had enjoyed in the fifteenth century. A servant had to
buy a ticket of release (at 1*d*. or 2*d*.) from his previous employer
before he could bargain with another. If he took wages higher
than the legal maximum (fixed by J.P.s: in most counties official
wage rates remained almost unchanged from about 1580 to 1640,
while prices continued to rise), he could be punished by a
crippling fine and imprisonment, his employer only by a relatively light fine. This clause was not always enforced. On
occasion, in areas where there was a shortage of labour, J.P.s
would wink at its infraction. But always it could be enforced at

their discretion. By an act of 1610 any able-bodied man or woman who should *threaten* to run away from his or her parish was liable to be sent to the house of correction and treated as a vagabond. Think what power this gave to the employing class!

Under all these circumstances – racking of rents, eviction and vagabondage, cutting down of great households, a wage freeze during a price rise, the poor flocking into the towns, where the majority lived at or below subsistence level; a legally enforced retention of a pool of labour in the villages – poor relief was necessary to subsidize wages, if the lower orders were not to be forced into revolt by mass starvation. An act of 1531 first distinguished between sturdy rogues (who are to be punished) and the impotent poor (who may beg). After 1563 a poor rate might be levied, though in many parishes this was not done. It was very unpopular with the propertied class, and down to 1660 (at least) the poor received far more assistance from private charity than from the state. On the other hand, in Charles I's London there were whipping posts for sturdy beggars every few hundred yards. Vagabonds preferred gaol to houses of correction. The Poor Law, said Thorold Rogers, was 'in origin purely a matter of police regulation, and the desire to succour those in distress merely an unavoidable corollary imposed by necessity, not dictated by philanthropy'. On average every fourth year before the sixteen-twenties was a year of shortage. By ensuring a minimum subsistence for the aged and sick, poor relief prevented starvation and revolt in time of dearth; it also helped to keep wages down. Protestant theology contributed to this grim determination to hold the poor in their poverty, by its heavy emphasis on the wickedness of idleness and the importance of self-help. Divines recommended restricting charity to the 'deserving'. So did a playwright like Dekker, popular with London citizens. When indiscriminate charity was defended in one of his plays, the speaker was a devil.

In the fifteen-thirties J.P.s were made responsible for the enforcement of this legislation, and the parish became its administrative unit. J.P.s took over control of the formerly ecclesiastical area of the parish, just as crown and Parliament had taken over central control of the church. J.P.s' power was immense. As a sympathetic parson put it in 1550, 'if the poor oppressed complain to the justices of peace or suchlike in the county where he dwelleth that hath the injury done unto him, little redress, as I hear, can be had, one so serveth another's turn, even as the mules scratch one another's back'. It was said of Sir Walter Waller twenty years later that 'by the means that he is a J.P. he overbeareth the poor men with ... disordinate dealings both against law and conscience'. Not all J.P.s were like this, of course: but there was no remedy against tyrants. An editor of quarter-sessions records before 1612 comments that 'many instances of illegal procedure, of high-handed injustice, ... are recorded as mere matters of fact, publicly and unhesitatingly done'. We may imagine some of the things that happened unrecorded.

During this period a proletariat began to be differentiated from the rest of society organized in gilds and manors. Industrial specialization, especially in mining, produced workmen who were dirtier than their fellows; being less well fed their teeth tended to decay early, their children to be deformed by rickets. Newcomers often formed a separate industrial community. In 1606 the tenants of a Shropshire village protested that a new colliery was introducing 'a number of lewd persons, the scum and dregs of many [counties] from whence they have been driven'. But the most marked physical differences in pre-industrial England were probably those between the ruling class and the mass of the population. The former, in the words of Mr Laslett, 'must have been taller, heavier, better developed and earlier to mature than the rest'. This no doubt confirmed the ruling class's belief in its own innate superiority. In seventeenth-century plays, and in the fairy stories, any beautiful peasant girl who shows sensitivity turns out to be a princess in disguise. Even that medieval folk-hero, Robin Hood, was in the sixteenth century transformed into a dispossessed earl. This inheritance of physical class distinctions, still dinned into most of us in the fairy tales on which we are brought up, seemed to be justified in our period by the physical differentiation which the under-nourishment of the lower classes produced: similar circumstances produce similar results in South Africa today.

The unprecedented profits of the rich were, and were known to be, made at the expense of the poor: and during this century some at least of the rich felt some conscience about it. Professor Jordan has traced the charitable foundations by which thirteen out of every fourteen paupers who received any relief at all were maintained – overwhelmingly at the expense of those merchants who were the greatest employers of the poor. England acquired a system of organized charity in the century when merchants had become rich and socially influential enough to afford it, and before they shared in control of the state sufficiently securely to feel that the problem could be left to official action: in the century when men ceased to endow masses for the dead and began to think it virtuous to help the living to help themselves.

The poor were rightless in another sense. They were liable to conscription: those who paid taxes very rarely were. In the early sixteen-twenties impressment of craftsmen for Mansfeld's ill-fated expedition to Germany helped to relieve the unemployment of those crisis years. 'The meaner sort of people and servants,' on the other hand, were not to be employed in the militia, the home guard of property, partly because, as Charles I put it, 'their residence cannot be expected to be constant'; partly because 'the government feared to arm and train the lower orders.'* As the Russian historian A. N. Savine showed fifty years ago, half of the surnames of a Norfolk village totally disappeared between 1607 and 1650: in Clayworth, Nottinghamshire, over sixty per cent of the population disappeared between 1676 and 1688.† These villages may not have been typical, but it was a pretty foot-loose society so far as the unpropertied were concerned. No wonder Francis Quarles tells us that the poor feared to have children.

*Lindsay Boynton, *The Elizabethan Militia* (1967), pp. 62, 109 and *passim*.
†P. Laslett and J. Harrison, 'Clayworth and Cogenhoe', in *Historical Essays, 1600–1750, presented to David Ogg* (ed. H. E. Bell and R. L. Ollard, 1963), p. 174.

3

AGRICULTURE AND AGRARIAN RELATIONS

> Hospitality, which was once a relic of gentry and a known cognizance to all ancient houses, hath lost her title merely through discontinuance; and great houses, which were at first founded to relieve the poor and such needful passengers as travelled by them, are now of no use but only as way-marks to direct them. But whither are these Great Ones gone? To the court, there to spend in boundless and immoderate riot what their provident ancestors had so long preserved. – RICHARD BRAITHWAITE, The English Gentleman (*1633*)

I

IN Gregory King's tables of 1688, eighty-eight per cent of the population was given as engaged in agriculture. Though many no doubt had subsidiary employment in industry, this should prevent us from attaching too great importance to trade and industry before that date. Historians are coming more and more to agree that capital accumulated in agriculture, often in the form of small savings, may in the long run have been more important than the contribution of trade and industry.

The sixteenth-century price revolution created new problems and new opportunities for landowners and subsistence farmers. The estate of gentlemen and nobles, Edward VI observed in 1551, 'has alone not increased the gain of living, ... yet their housekeeping is dearer, their liveries dearer, their wages greater. ... The gentleman, constrained by necessity and poverty, becomes a farmer, a grazier or a sheepmaster; the grazier, the farmer, the merchant, become landed men and call themselves gentlemen, though they be churls.'* Agricultural prices rose faster than industrial prices, so prudent men producing food for the market throve. Those with fixed incomes were in difficulties

---

*Ed. W. K. Jordan, *The Chronicle and Political Papers of King Edward VI* (Cornell University Press, 1966), pp. 163–4.

– e.g. landlords who had let their lands on long leases, though when the leases fell in they would get a windfall fine, a loan in advance. Tenants with long leases had every chance of prospering.

There were many stimuli to the commercialization of agriculture. There was a marked rise in yields per acre, thanks largely to enclosure. But population, especially urban population, increased more quickly than the farm surplus. That is why prices for agricultural products rose faster than industrial prices. Consumption of corn in London is estimated to have grown by 230 per cent between 1605 and 1661, and the London market stimulated large-scale market-gardening. By 1640 milk was being peddled in the streets of London. The years 1570–1640, Professor Bowden tells us, showed 'a sudden leap forward in the volume, organization and impact of agricultural trading in the English economy'.* The growing demand for food affected first the home counties and then all parts of England with access to water communications. Grain imports to London from three north-eastern counties rose fourteen times in the sixty years before the civil war. That great triumph for English export merchants, the closing of the Steelyard in 1598, also had consequences for agriculture, since the Hansa merchants had paid for cloth with corn, and their withdrawal – after a series of bad harvests too – increased the pressure for home production. A character-writer in the reign of James I remarked of 'An Ingrosser of Corn': 'He wishes that Dantzig were at the Moluccas, and had rather be certain of some foreign invasion than of the setting up of the Steelyard.'

Increasing demand for food led to internal colonization; the line of settlement advanced in Cumberland, Westmorland and south-western England. There was also pressure to cultivate common and waste lands, and royal forests. There was a large movement of surplus labourers from the open villages to forest settlements in many parts of England – Gloucestershire, Worcestershire, Northamptonshire, Kent cottages were built on heaths, corners of waste land, and woodlands, were squatted on by cottagers. Dr Thirsk and Professor Everitt have recently suggested that a sharp distinction should be drawn between woodland and

*Thirsk, 1967, p. 587.

pasture areas on the one hand and arable on the other. The former were much more extensive in our period than now, and included, for example, North Essex, the Weald, the 'cheese' area of Wiltshire, as well as forests like Sherwood and the New Forest, and the Highland zone generally. Since cottagers could squat in woodland areas, these were able to supply plentiful labour (whole- or part-time) for expanding industries, old or new. These areas were consequently more susceptible to change than the open-field districts, where the stable routine of arable farming still predominated. Professor Everitt sees 'a relatively free and mobile society in heath and wood parishes, and a relatively static and subservient one in the parishes of the field and plains'. John Norden in 1607 said that 'the people bred amongst the woods are naturally more stubborn and uncivil than in the champion [open-field] countries'. John Aubrey described woodlanders as 'mean people', who 'live lawless, nobody to govern them, they care for nobody, having no dependence on anybody'. In such areas, the feudal ties of subordination could be most easily broken by the intrusion of rural industry. Dr Thirsk and Professor Everitt go on to suggest that pastoral regions like the Weald of Kent were 'the most fertile seed-beds for Puritanism and dissent', and have speculated whether the heath and forest lands may not have supplied most of the troops of the Parliamentarian armies in the civil war.*

The rapid expansion of wool-growing and developments in the coal industry also contributed to eviction and proletarianization. 'Wherever coal-mining became important,' Professor Nef tells us, 'it stimulated the movement towards curtailing the rights of customary tenants and even of small freeholders.' 'Not only must the tenants be prevented from digging themselves, they must be stripped of their power to refuse access to minerals under their holdings, or to demand excessive compensation.' 'The trend of legal opinion throughout Lancashire and Yorkshire was against permitting a copyholder to break the soil without special licence from the lord.' Economics made law. 'Copyholders lived in constant fear of the discovery of coal under their land.'

*Thirsk, ibid., pp. 111–12, 435; cf. Chapter I *passim*, and pp. 411–12, 462–5, 562–3, 573.

2

In the century and a quarter after 1530 land was more freely bought and sold in England than ever before. The Reformation threw monastic and chantry lands on the market. The combined effect of the statutes of uses and wills (1536 and 1540) was to facilitate the mobility of land. The sales of a century culminated in the orgy of confiscations and sales of the revolutionary decades. But by then the market was saturated, and in any case more attractive investment possibilities were opening up – government contracts, state loans, public offices, overseas trade and ship-building, joint-stock companies. (The extreme generosity which merchants and Puritan gentry had shown before 1640 in endowing education, preaching and poor relief may, among other things, have been influenced by the lack of outlets for investment.) From the sixteen-forties the strict settlement* developed to close the land market – because the pressure which had kept it open for the preceding century had lessened.

Meanwhile monastic lands had been sold, and crown lands to the value of £2¼ million between 1558 and 1640. In addition there were landowners great and small who were unable to adjust their management processes or who sold to reorganize. There was relatively cheap land to be bought by anyone who had capital to invest and social aspirations to satisfy. The mobility of land naturally upset conservatives. The existence of a 'land-buyers' society' in the sixteen-thirties seemed to one observer 'tending to the destruction of gentry' and to 'the making of a parity between gentlemen and yeomen and those which before were labouring men; the begetting of pride and stubbornness in them, and by this means to become more refractory to the government of the country'. Those who acquired land in significant quantity became gentlemen, if they were not such already – a process sometimes misleadingly referred to as the rise of the gentry. By 1600 gentlemen, new and old, occupied a far greater proportion of the land of England than in 1530 – to the disadvantage of crown, church, aristocracy and peasantry alike. Gentlemen leased land – from the king, from bishops, from deans

*See pp. 146–8, below.

and chapters, from Oxford and Cambridge colleges – often in order to sub-let at a profit. Leases and reversions sometimes lay two deep. It was a form of investment, there being no banks; like the purchase of office in France. The smaller gentry gained where big landlords lost, gained as tenants what others lost as lords. Savine called this the gentry 'stooping to conquer': it led to their final triumph as a class, though individual families failed to survive.

3

The sixteenth century offered great opportunities to landowners and farmers, though not all took advantage of them. One of the myths that has been finally dispelled of recent years is that the 'mere' country gentlemen could not prosper during this period from farming alone, without investment in trade, industry, privateering or the even greater hazards of a career at court. On the contrary: whilst the general price level rose some five times between 1530 and 1640, rents in some areas that have been investigated rose on an average at least eight times. Income from sheep-farming rose from four and a half to seven times in East Anglia. The biggest profits seem to have been made by capitalist farmers, men who leased land in order to produce for the market, including the rapidly expanding export market, but landlords who shortened leases could share in these profits. Smaller husbandmen probably soon found their surplus swallowed up by rising rents and taxes. The years 1580–1620, Professor Bowden tells us, saw 'a massive redistribution of income in favour of the landed class, a redistribution which, in the final analysis, was as much at the expense of the agricultural wage-earner and consumer as of the tenant farmer'.* The shift from oxen to horses as draft animals during this period is evidence of the growing prosperity of some farmers. Horses cost more to feed, but they do three to four times as much work as oxen.

In the inflationary century it seems to have been farmers, yeomen, lesser landlords, who first developed the bourgeois

*Thirsk, 1967, p. 695.

qualities necessary to success – thrift, industry, readiness to rack rents and watch markets, moderate consumption and reinvestment of profits. Peers and greater gentlemen with traditional standards of expenditure to maintain were slower to adapt themselves, and continued to spend sums for which their rent-roll gave no justification. Such men became increasingly dependent on court favour for economic survival. The timber shortage may have been accentuated by indebted landlords living on capital. Land put to pasture was worth three times as much as land on which timber was grown: so men decided, in the words of a pamphleteer of 1611, 'there is sea-coals enow to supply many wants thereof', and cut down their woods without replanting.

'Live not in the country,' the prudent Lord Burghley advised his son, 'without corn and cattle about thee; for he that puts his hand to purse for every expense of household is like him that thinks to keep water in a sieve.' The profits to be made by agricultural improvement derived from careful management, land drainage and reclamation, the use of fertilizers, hedging and ditching enclosed land: for all these capital was needed. As fixed rents and dues were dwindling, it was necessary to get rid of freeholders and copyholders, and to convert long to short leases. Increasing entry fines and racking rents seemed a revolutionary breach with custom: but it was the only means by which landowners could keep pace with rising prices. In the short run it was farmers and smaller landowners who benefited most. But greater landowners soon followed their example. 'The gentlemen,' Sir Thomas Wilson wrote about 1600, 'which were wont to addict themselves to the wars, are now for the most part grown to become good husbands, and know as well how to improve their lands to the uttermost as the farmer or countryman, so that they take their farms into their hands as the leases expire, and either till themselves or else let them out to those who will give most . . . whereby the yeomanry of England is decayed' – except those who enjoy long leases.

4

The combined effects of inflation and of the royal policy of drawing the aristocracy to court were to force the latter to depend on the king for favours and perquisites, and to diminish the feudal dependence of their tenants on them. By the seventeenth century the aristocracy was no longer primarily a military class. Even the Earls of Northumberland had ceased to be northern feudal potentates and had become Sussex landowners. Peers could share in the profits arising from the concentration of wealth and power in the monarchy, but only through submission and good behaviour. They lost their financial and political independence. This function of the court as redistributor of wealth helps to account for 'the country's' hostility to it, and for the Puritan sense that the idle aristocracy was parasitic. Such feelings were intensified when James I began to distribute largesse to Scots and non-noble favourites.

Archbishop Mathew and Professor Trevor-Roper have pointed out the importance of court favour as a path to windfall wealth, and so to the capital with which estate reorganization or commercial investment could be undertaken. But of the many who were called to court, few were chosen. And in the meantime, in pursuing a will o' the wisp, the real basis of wealth, the land, suffered from lack of that unremitting vigilance which the stay-at-home Puritan squire devoted to it. 'The court,' said Arthur Wilson, is 'a kind of lottery, where men that venture much may draw a blank, and such as have little may get a prize.' Sir John Oglander, who bound his fortunes up closely with the court, had expenses which were some £1,000 a year in excess of his income. Sir John Reresby later in the century complained of his father's losses by following the court for thirty years before his death in 1619.

As great landowners lost their military power, they had to adapt themselves to the new society in which money was king. So gradually they came to take a more direct interest in estate management, to cut down hospitality, to rack rents, to lease mining rights, etc. Many families who tried to keep up traditional standards of ostentatious expenditure in an inflationary age had to sell lands before they could balance their budgets; but most of the great families had managed it by the seventeenth century. In the first two decades of the century the Earls of Northumberland completed a drastic financial reorganization of estate management, a switch to leasehold, which considerably increased their revenues. The Herberts of Wiltshire undertook a similar reorganization at about the same time with equally beneficial results. Those who could not make the transition were replaced by others more capable of taking advantage of the intellectual and technical revolution in estate management. (The professional surveyor dates from Elizabeth's reign; the new mathematics soon made him adept at precisely calculating the value of lands and possible improvements, especially at the expense of copyholders, who hated surveyors.)

'The improvement of the ground,' observed Francis Bacon, 'is the most natural obtaining of riches; ... but it is slow; and yet, where men of great wealth do stoop to husbandry, it multiplieth riches exceedingly.' Bigger landlords, with limitless credit, were better placed to take advantage of such techniques, and to undertake mammoth operations like, for instance, fen drainage. With the end of the inflation in the twenties, the adoption by the landowning class of enhanced rents and entry fines, 'the hardening of the lines of social cleavage [within the landed classes] itself reflected and was supported by a shift in the balance of economic advantage from the yeoman leaseholder to the nobility and gentry landlords'. As tough absentee landowners most of the peers, at least in the South and East of England, had by 1640 forfeited the feudal allegiance of their tenants, without regaining the preponderant position in the state which their former military power had given them.*

The House of Commons, almost by definition, represented the prospering section of the gentry: a landed family would not long maintain a position of leadership in the county if its revenues declined significantly; conversely, a new family would be accepted into county society within a generation or two if it was rich enough. So the House of Commons tended to express the wishes

*L. Stone, p. 31. The preceding paragraphs owe much to Professor Stone's book.

of the well-to-do gentry. We can trace the triumph of capitalism in agriculture by following the Commons' attitude towards enclosure. Governments opposed depopulating enclosure, primarily for military reasons. But enclosure also led to loss of taxable income, and to smaller tithe payments: the opposition of parsons to enclosure may not always have sprung from purely altruistic sentiments. The famine year 1597 saw the last acts against depopulation; 1608 the first (limited) pro-enclosure act. (In 1607 there had been revolts against enclosure in the Midlands, and a state paper suggested that enclosure was necessary if the growing population was to be fed.) In 1621, in the depths of the depression, came the first general enclosure bill – opposed by some M.P.s who feared agrarian disturbances. In 1624 the statutes against enclosure were repealed. At the end of the decade there were anti-enclosure riots and risings in Dorset, Gloucestershire, Worcestershire, Shropshire and Wiltshire. This was followed, in the absence of Parliament, by Laud's Enclosure Commissions, which made a good deal of money by fining enclosers – though the crown itself was an enclosing landlord. But they did little to restore the evicted to their holdings, and indeed 'Charles I's commissions were not aimed at the prevention of enclosure, any more than his scheme for retail tobacco licensing aimed to prevent the smoking of pipes'.* Enclosure fines became an irregular tax levied on one section of the landed class, and gave no adequate protection to the poor. Again the Long Parliament was a turning point. No government after 1640 seriously tried either to prevent enclosures, or even to make money by fining enclosers.

5

Sir Thomas More's bitter joke about sheep eating men turned out to be truer than he knew. For in the sixteenth century, whilst the living standards of men and women of the lower classes fell catastrophically, the living standards of sheep improved equally remarkably. Enclosure and the floating of water meadows led to better grass; this produced sheep with coarser and longer wool,

*M. W. Beresford, 'Glebe Terriers and Open-Field Buckinghamshire' *Records of Bucks.*, XVI, p. 8.

though more of it. This in its turn contributed to the decline of English broadcloth, made from short-staple wool of under-nourished sheep, and to the rise of worsted and the New Draperies, utilizing coarser, longer wool.*

The main opposition to enclosure came from rank-and-file peasants, mostly copyholders. Legal changes of the sixteenth century began to assimilate copyhold to freehold, but the security of copyholders' tenure would vary with the length of their purses and their courage in standing up to their lords. Similarly the rights of peasants to compensation at enclosure are apt to look more impressive on paper than they were in fact. Much enclosure was by 'agreement' between the freeholders of a village. It is difficult to avoid the suspicion that on occasion 'agreement' was extorted from the weak by the strong. Near Wakefield an en-closure made 'by consent' was thrown open again as soon as civil war conditions made this possible. We must recall too the loss of the right to pick up timber, hunt animals etc. on the common lands – the total loss of which must have been very serious for families near the margin. Enclosure moreover increased the dependence of villagers on their landlord, who now often became their employer as well.

The danger of peasant revolt was far more effective than government action in restraining the advance of the new methods in agriculture. There were minor revolts in 1596, 1607, 1628–31, and in one part or another of England agrarian revolt was endemic throughout the sixteen-thirties. But there was no suc-cessful national agrarian revolt in seventeenth-century England – not successful even in the sense that 1381, 1450 and 1549 were successful, still less in the sense that agrarian revolt succeeded in the French and Russian Revolutions. One reason was that the English peasantry had already ceased to be a homogeneous class. Many yeomen and better-off husbandmen were producing food or wool for the market, themselves employing wage-labour, and shared the outlook and interests of gentlemen and merchants rather than of landless labourers and subsistence husbandmen. Even an open-field farmer like Robert Loader of North Berkshire was continually concerned in the years 1610–20 with the profits

*Bowden, *passim*.

of marketing wheat and barley. Men with a marketable surplus might *profit* by a bad harvest which would ruin a subsistence farmer. Less successful husbandmen were selling their livestock and lands, and sinking into the ranks of wage-labourers. Hence the failure in the revolutionary decades of the radical movements for winning security of tenure for copyholders, and preventing enclosure. We can understand why men and women of the poorer classes were prepared to face the risks of drowning in the Atlantic or starving in a New England winter, in the hope of ultimately winning free land and a regular source of livelihood. Nearly 80,000 men, women and children left England between 1620 and 1642.

4

TRADE, COLONIES AND
FOREIGN POLICY

Men are gaining possessions without your knowledge. . . .
Merchants ignore the interests of their sovereign, and are con-
cerned only with their own commercial profit. – TSAR IVAN
THE TERRIBLE *to Queen Elizabeth, 1571*

I

WORLD trade was increasing in the sixteenth century, thanks to
the discovery of America and of the sea route to the Far East.
Use of the mariner's compass, improved astronomy and navigational mathematics contributed to the expansion of long-distance
trade. But even more important, in the short run, was increasing
demand in Europe itself from the prospering upper and middle
classes. English cloth exports expanded rapidly in the earlier
part of the century to meet this demand. Although the boom
was checked by a collapse of the export market around 1550, and
the ensuing crisis was aggravated by debasement of the coinage,
ultimately new markets were found (e.g. in Russia) for cloth
exports. Tsar Ivan was right: the capital of the Russia Company
multiplied over thirteen times in the first thirty years of its
existence after 1553. And – more significant in the long run – by
the end of the century a new line of lighter cloths – the New
Draperies – was being produced which opened up new markets
in the Mediterranean area and in Africa. John Hawkins in 1584
believed that 'the substance of this realm is trebled in value'
since Elizabeth's accession.

Especially after peace with Spain in 1604 there was great
commercial prosperity. But from 1615 economic disasters followed one another rapidly. The Cokayne Project of 1614 led to a
crisis of over-production and widespread unemployment in the
clothing industry. Recovery had barely begun when an even
graver crisis started with a collapse of cloth markets in eastern

Europe, and was intensified by the outbreak of the Thirty Years War in 1618. Throughout the twenties and thirties the economy stagnated. But even during this period the reorientation of England's trade continued. By 1640 half London's cloth exports were going to Spain and the Mediterranean. The value of the capital's exports had trebled since 1600.

Governments needed the richest merchants as lenders, and were also interested in trade to the extent that its increase brought enhanced customs revenue. As Bacon thought it necessary to remind the new royal favourite, Sir George Villiers, about 1616, 'the constant trade of merchandising will furnish us at a need ... with mariners and seamen' for the naval defence of the island of Britain. The ruling class as a whole, moreover, welcomed the luxury imports which overseas trade provided. But otherwise governments were little concerned to further the interests of trade. Between 1613 and 1619, when English merchants appealed to James in their disputes with the Dutch, he regarded his role as that of neutral mediator between two brawling groups: this at a time when the Dutch East India Company was practically a department of state, and the furtherance of its trade a main object of government. Charles I in 1629 surrendered Canada to France, and so gave a hold on American soil to the power which was to be our chief colonial rival for the next century and a half.

The traditional medieval way of pillaging trade was by the imposition of tolls, tribute levied by the lords of any area through which the goods passed. Customs were royal tolls, pillage on a national scale. Thus the government both wanted and did not want a strong commercial class. It wanted customs and taxes and a navy; it did not want any unbalancing of the hierarchy of degree by excessive commercial wealth. Similarly merchants wanted a unified state and legal system, uniform coinage, weights and measures, with a government strong enough to give protection against foreign enemies and pirates, and to break down internal privileges and barriers to trade. Yet there was no guarantee that a strong state would rule in their interest, and every chance that it would not. The ambivalence of Tudor economic policy turned into incompetent predatoriness under

Charles I; and the merchant class polarized between the small group of government-privileged monopolists and the mass of rank-and-file traders.

Nevertheless, even without significant government support English merchants emerged in the sixteenth century from their semi-colonial status of dependence on foreign merchants. The Venetians, who once almost monopolized England's woollen exports, ceased regular visits to London after 1533; they were last seen at Southampton in 1587. The North German Hanseatic merchants lost their privileged position under the radical rule of Northumberland in 1552, regained it under the papist Mary, lost it again under protestant Elizabeth. They were finally ousted in 1598. Thirteen years later English merchants were invited to Hamburg and given 'magnificent' privileges there, similar to those which the Hansards had once enjoyed in England. The relative power positions had been reversed within two generations.

Edward VI himself discussed establishing in England a market which would replace Antwerp as the entrepôt for European trade, and diversifying the industrial structure of England 'so that all may not stand by clothing'.* But after the interlude of his reign, governments seemed to pursue a policy of deliberate restriction of trade, concentrating it in the hands of a few rich London merchants. The great trading companies were needed to control monopoly areas, to force down the buying price and force up the selling price. Theirs was a predatory form of foreign trade, involving a relatively small turnover with very high profits; it would have been impossible without government support for their monopolies, and for this support they had to pay dear.

Sir William Cecil in 1564, after observing that 'the people that depend upon making of cloth are of worse condition to be quietly governed than the husbandmen', went on to argue the advantages of a *reduction* in exports, cutting out smaller clothiers and concentrating production in the hands of richer manufacturers. (Duties on exports had been raised in 1558.) In James I's reign we find ten per cent of the exporters exporting fifty per

*Ed. W. K. Jordan, *The Chronicle and Political Papers of King Edward VI*, pp. 168–73, 180.

cent of the cloth from London. This deliberate policy of restriction succeeded in binding a group of Londoners closely to the
government, and made them willing lenders; but it led to resentment and interloping from lesser merchants and merchants of
the outports. It also led to royal interference in the internal
affairs of the companies. Although the connexion of the City's
ruling oligarchy with the court brought perquisites and baronet-
cies for some merchants, in the long run the growing
bankruptcy of the crown made the financial connexion lose its
attractions even for those in the inner ring: for those outside,
hostility to government policy grew steadily during the reigns of
the first two Stuarts.

We should therefore not be deceived by the apparent activity
of aristocrats and courtiers in the trading and colonial companies
under James and Charles (with exceptions, like the Earls of
Middlesex and Warwick, who became peers because they had
been successful businessmen rather than vice versa). Merchants
in effect ran the companies, or at any rate those which were
successful; aristocrats worked the court and took a rake-off.
Where merchants were not in control, they held back from
court-sponsored enterprises. As a royal official told the Duke of
Buckingham in 1622, 'Men of ability will not join in partnership
with your lordships, for merchants are jealous to hazard their
goods with their betters.' This was true even of the proprietary
colonies, where a great aristocrat was given ostensible control,
but was normally interested only in the money which he could
make out of his dignified position. Thus the Earl of Carlisle left
management of his Leeward Islands and Barbados to a group of
London merchants.

The government also failed to perform the duty of protecting
the seas to the satisfaction of English merchants. In 1609 there
were said to be a thousand pirates at work off the Irish coast. In
the next seven years 416 ships were captured, and their crews
enslaved. One of the English pirates – Henry Mainwaring –
became rich enough to retire and buy a knighthood from James I,
who appointed him Lieutenant of Dover Castle. In 1631 Turkish
pirates were making slave raids on the Irish and English coasts.
'If the Turks be suffered long to continue,' wrote the Governor

of Pendennis Castle to Secretary Coke, 'they will disable the English from any trade hereafter.' South coast towns had to build fortifications against the raiders. Meanwhile the presence of English merchants in the Mediterranean in increasing numbers created new demands for naval protection, demands which were not met until the fifties. Charles I, on the contrary, in 1633 forbade English merchants to enter the Mediterranean.

The foundation of joint-stock companies from Edward VI's reign was a great advance in the capitalist organization of English society. First a group of merchants would club together for a single voyage, then for several voyages, ultimately for an indefinite period. By this means the circle of investors could be widened, and the savings of persons not immediately engaged in trade or industry could be mobilized. By the early seventeenth century many gentlemen were investing in overseas trading ventures, including a large number of M.P.s. What is interesting is that most of them invested *after* sitting in the Commons. Parliament helped to spread London's influence into the counties: through Parliament merchants and a section of the gentry were bound into a single capitalist interest.* This development looks forward to a society in which the *rentier* could safely invest in branches of the economy with which he had no direct connexion. But in the short run companies trading as a body were more liable to interference and control from above. Full freedom for capitalist joint-stock companies was ensured only when governments accepted the principle of non-intervention with private property, after 1688.

Trade, it was agreed in the sixteenth and seventeenth centuries, should amass treasure, wealth which could be converted into capital. But 'increasing the national wealth' begs a number of questions. Wealth for whom? For the business community? For the state? Do merchants exist for the state, as James I thought they should? Or does the state exist to help merchants? Against royal bullionism and restrictionism, attempts to control the direction and amount of investment, Thomas Mun and

*T. K. Rabb, *Enterprise and Empire: Merchant and Gentry Investment in the Expansion of England, 1575–1630* (Harvard University Press, 1967), Chapter 1.

76

others put forward a new version of mercantilism, the '-ism' of merchants. Their thought shifted more and more from the sphere of circulation to that of production. Royal theorists wanted to cut imports to balance exports; merchants wanted to expand exports in order to win for England a favourable trade balance. This could be done best by breaking away from the company form of organization; but the companies could be dispensed with only if the state took over protection of trade.*

2

Throughout this century the decisive considerations underlying the formation of English foreign policy were financial. Henry VIII used the plunder of the church to build up a powerful navy. But the vast cost of wars between 1542 and 1562 led to financial chaos, devaluation and sales of crown land – a lesson which was not lost on Elizabeth and her successors. An expensive foreign policy would lead to dependence on Parliament, and Parliament would be likely to use this dependence to demand, for example, a more radical religious settlement. Elizabeth's 'parsimony' sprang from a complex of constitutional, political, religious and social causes, as well as from her own personal inclinations. The Spanish and Irish wars at the end of her reign forced further land sales, and concessions to Parliament over monopolies; the foreign adventures typical of Buckingham's rule in the sixteen-twenties finally wrecked relations between crown and Parliament, and led to Charles I virtually abdicating from foreign affairs during his eleven years' personal rule.

Yet though war was disastrous for governments, it brought advantages to other sections of the community. Bullion worth some £4½ million was coined in Elizabeth's reign, most of it believed to be plunder seized from Spain. Prize goods brought in by privateers between 1585 and 1603 amounted to some ten to fifteen per cent of total imports. These were welcome windfalls to a commercial class whose most crying need was for capital. At the same time the exotic imports looted from Spanish vessels created new consumer demands. The national unity of these

*See pp. 155–61, below.

years is symbolized by the alliance in privateering of the sea-dog gentry of Devon and Cornwall with the City merchants who came more and more to finance them.*

There were in fact two alternative foreign policies open to governments during this century. The Howards normally led the pro-Spanish, catholic, conservative group, from the days when they successively overthrew Wolsey and Thomas Cromwell: they were overthrown themselves in 1547 to guarantee the protestant succession. In Elizabeth's reign the Duke of Norfolk – the most powerful subject in the land – first wanted Elizabeth to marry a Habsburg; in 1572 he was executed for conspiring with Mary Queen of Scots and Spain in what Froude called 'the last combined effort of the English aristocracy to undo the Reformation and strangle the new order of things'. Yet from Mary Tudor's reign onwards the conservative group faced insoluble contradictions. The economic and political basis of the church and of the old aristocracy had been so gravely weakened that it was impossible to re-establish their rule except with outside help. Hence Mary's marriage to Philip of Spain, and her close dependence on Rome and Madrid, which offended the patriotic sentiments of gentry and merchants no less than the religious sentiments of protestants and the cupidity of possessors of monastic lands. Wyatt's rebellion in 1554 was an expression of nationalism rather than of protestantism. The loss of Calais in 1558 and the burning of three hundred heretics were equally attributed to the baneful influence of Spain. Consequently Elizabeth could never carry her flirtation with Spain too far. Only after England's independence had been secured was there a reversion to a positively pro-Spanish policy under James I, coinciding with a return of the Howards to dominance. Support for this policy came from those conservatives who were least prepared to see the increase in Parliament's influence over policy which would inevitably result from an aggressive foreign policy. (Not that the pro-Spanish policy was necessarily cheap. The ridiculous trip of Prince Charles and Buckingham to Spain to woo the Infanta in 1623 cost well over £100,000.) If James reverted to the policy of appeasing Spain which Elizabeth had

*Andrews, pp. 128, 232–5.

pursued at the beginning of her reign, his son almost returned to the abject dependence on Spain and Rome of Mary Tudor. The mantle of patriotism was eagerly taken up by Puritans and the opposition in the House of Commons.

On the other side, from Thomas Cromwell through the Dudleys to Oliver Cromwell, there were proponents of a more positive protestant foreign policy. Ralegh and Hakluyt became the spokesmen of an expansionist anti-Spanish policy: it was endorsed by the House of Commons in 1624 and many times later. In the thirties it was represented by John Pym and the Providence Island Company, at a time when Wentworth was leader of the pro-Spanish conservatives, and Charles's government signed an alliance with Spain, even considering a partition of the protestant Dutch republic between England and Spain. The social issues underlying foreign policy were clear to contemporaries. It was 'the inbred malice in the vulgar against the nobility' which Burghley gave, among other reasons, for wanting peace with Spain. Pamphleteers in the sixteen-twenties described the pro-Spanish party as consisting of courtiers and great aristocrats, many of them in receipt of Spanish bribes; the common people, it was agreed, were pro-Dutch and fiercely anti-Spanish.

One section of the commercial interest supported an expansionist foreign policy, but there were others who preferred peace with Spain. For the East India Company, founded in 1600, the main enemy was the Netherlands. Some of the New Draperies were manufactured from Spanish wool, others were exported to Spain. Sir Thomas Wentworth and Cromwell's Major-General Lambert, representing the West Riding clothing interest, were both consistently pro-Spanish, though it is difficult to think of any other political matter on which they would have been in agreement. Wentworth had another reason for wanting peace with Spain, in his Lord Deputyship of Ireland. Ireland was always the wide-open backdoor to Spanish invasion. In the last decades of Elizabeth's reign this door was kept closed, but at vast expense. The monarchy's resources were insufficient for complete conquest and subjugation of the island. The joint-stock principle on which Elizabeth attempted to subdue Ireland as well as to fight Spain (privateers, private colonization of America no less than of Ireland) could not bring a final solution. Ireland was conquered and Spain brought to her knees only in the sixteen-fifties, when England's resources were fully mobilized.

3

A similar story of failure to support commercial interests and of disastrous intervention by the Stuart kings could be told of Far Eastern trade. In 1600 the East India Company bought a charter which gave its members a monopoly of this trade. Four years later Sir Edward Michelbourne, a courtier who had been expelled from the company for non-payment of dues, was licensed by James I to trade to the East Indies in violation of the royal charter. In 1617 James granted another charter to a Scottish East India Company, to which Englishmen were admitted. The London company had to buy them out. In 1622 the company captured Hormuz. Buckingham, the Lord High Admiral, so far from expressing pleasure at this accession to English naval power brought by private enterprise, at once demanded £10,000 as his share of the alleged profits, and detained the company's ships until they paid. Inspired by this example, the King demanded – and got – a similar cut. In 1635 Charles went one better than his father by licensing a second East India Company to trade in the waters of which the existing company had bought a monopoly. This 'association of squires' ignored agreements entered into by the legitimate company, and caused great trouble in the Far East, ultimately taking to piracy. Its patent was revoked in 1639, when it was becoming obvious that a Parliament would soon be meeting.

These are only examples from many that could be given. Increasingly in the early seventeenth century commercial interests (and the gentry associated with them) came to criticize the government's appeasement of Spain and its failure to protect English trading interests against the Dutch. There was rivalry over questions of organization. The government preferred regulated companies: interlopers appealed to Parliament. Within the companies themselves there were disagreements between royal nominees and others; again these quarrels were reflected in the House of Commons. There were rival colonial policies. Proprietary colonies were used to subsidize the aristocracy; real colonial advance was left to private enterprise, with little support and some positive hindrance from governments. There was the familiar unreliability of government favour even when paid for. Charles I made a regular practice of selling monopoly rights in the same colony to rival groups or individuals. Many forfeitures were made by Laud's Commission for the Plantations in the sixteen-thirties. So Dutch ability to out-trade English merchants was hardly surprising. Only the very biggest merchants in old-established regulated trades, often with court connexions, held their own; elsewhere all was frustration and lost opportunities. The Dutch came to monopolize not only the East India trade, but also that from Spanish America to Europe, and very nearly that from the Baltic. Yet England's eclipse was, and was recognized by contemporaries to be, the consequence of defective policies, not of lack of resources or opportunities. At the end of the sixteenth century Sir Walter Ralegh, the Venetian Contarini and a Spanish diplomat had all foreseen that England could become the most powerful nation in the world if she built up a great navy to win and maintain commercial supremacy. This happened; but only after the commercial interest and its gentry associates had won a say in the formation of policies such as it had never enjoyed before 1640.

'The trade, and more especially the navigation of this kingdom,' said a petition from London merchants in 1641, 'is of late years very much decayed and fallen into the hands of neighbour nations . . . by reason of the great burdens which are laid upon [merchants], and for want of such due encouragement and regulation by law as is necessary for the maintenance and support of them.' The petitioners hoped for a more sympathetic hearing from Parliament.

5

INDUSTRY AND GOVERNMENT
ECONOMIC POLICY

The Parliament, as well for the better service to be done in
husbandry (whereunto the children of husbandmen and
labourers are most apt) as for the avoiding of other inconveni-
ences that groweth by the evil education of artificers' children,
hath provided that each sort of such children should be applied
to the trade that their parents were of before them. – *Memorandum on the Statute of Artificers, ?1573*

I

ENGLAND'S insular position gave her tremendous advantages
once national unity and internal peace had been established.
There were no inland tolls. England was already the largest free-
trade area in Europe. The proximity of all parts of the country
to coast and river navigation further reduced transport costs. So
though England was a late starter in the race towards the modern
world, her geographical advantages enabled her to develop
rapidly in this period, taking advantage of modern industrial
techniques, often imported by Dutch or French protestant
refugees, or by German capitalists seeking profitable investment.

Geography provides conditions 'without which': it does not
offer a causal explanation of why England's advance came precisely when it did. To understand this we must link the internal
peace and national unity given by Tudor rule with the price
revolution. Historians today are more cautious than they were
thirty years ago of attributing too much to the sixteenth-century
inflation, and still more cautious of giving the influx of American
silver as its sole cause. Prices were already rising before any
American metals arrived in Europe. In England contemporaries
and some historians blame (at least in part) racking of rents by
landlords, debasement of the coinage and war expenditure for
the price rise. The fifteen-forties and -nineties, the decades in

which prices rose fastest, were decades of war. Expanding population, with increased demand for food, also contributed, as well as expanding credit facilities, de-hoarding, the melting down of plate, the liberation of funds tied up in decoration of churches and chantries or praying for masses.

The effects of the price revolution differed from country to country. In England it stimulated (or was accompanied by) a considerable industrial development. In Spain it first stimulated an industrial boom, then led to (or was accompanied by) industrial decline. In France it seems to have had no very marked effects on industry. We cannot use the price revolution as a *deus ex machina*: its effect was probably only to accelerate economic changes which were going to take place anyway.

In England the general price level rose five times between 1530 and 1640, wheat prices six times. This had a dual effect. First, since English prices lagged behind those on the Continent, there was a great stimulus to cloth exports in the years 1530 to 1550; and though the boom broke in the latter year, a considerable degree of prosperity continued until the sixteen-twenties, especially in the years of peace after 1604. This offset government attempts to restrict industrial production and exports. Second, there was a savage depression of the living standards of the lower half of the population, since food and fuel prices rose more sharply than those of other commodities. In the building industry real wages in the later sixteenth century were less than two-thirds of what they had been in 1510, and in the fifty years before the civil war they were less than half. The mass of the population was forced down to a diet of black bread. For those who possessed no land this was a catastrophe. For those with land but who produced little or nothing for the market, it meant that wives and children were forced to by-earning in the clothing industry. Some time between 1580 and 1617 the word 'spinster' acquired its modern sense of unmarried woman: for of course such a woman would have to spin. Competition was so great that female wages rose even less than male in the late sixteenth and early seventeenth centuries.

There was a large labour supply. Population had been increasing steadily since the later fifteenth century. The end of the

French wars closed one avenue of employment, the cutting down of great households during the sixteenth century led to un-employment. Enclosure and eviction too may have contributed to the army of vagabonds which starts to alarm publicists from the beginning of our period. The process is circular. Low wages stimulated industrial production, especially in the clothing industry. The clothing boom encouraged enclosure for pasture, and so eviction. Although ley husbandry increased output of meat and dairy products, food prices and profits rocketed. Land-less labourers were at the mercy of employers: the existence of a pool of unemployed no doubt kept wages low far more effectively even than the activities (or inactivity) of J.P.s. Mass pauper apprenticeship in the towns also contributed to drive wages down. In the last two decades of the sixteenth century, and again in the depressed sixteen-twenties, preachers and pamphleteers talk of men, women and children dying of starvation in the streets of London. Professor Bowden confirms that the decades from 1620 to 1650 'witnessed extreme hardship; ... and were probably among the most terrible years through which the country has ever passed'.*

The conception of rising population, monetary inflation and declining real wages may be difficult for those to grasp who think in terms of modern economic models. But in this pre-industrial society much of the labour force was employed only part-time, much labour was semi-forced. In 1625 the Society of the Mines Royal was given the right to conscript labour in Wales. Men did not work more but less when wages were high. The Poor Law, whether by accident or design, encouraged the payment of low wages, which had to be subsidized by the parish if the families of the labourers were to survive. 'Contemporary opinion always associated the coming of industry with a rise in the poor rates,' observed Professor Hoskins. Among Sheffield's 2,207 inhabitants in 1615, only 100 householders had a surplus; 160 were unable to relieve others. A third of the inhabitants were 'begging poor'.

*Thirsk, 1967, p. 621.

2

One effect of low wages was to retard the development of a mass home market for manufactures. But every evicted person had perforce to become a cash purchaser, where previously he had no doubt clothed and fed himself, and so at the very lowest level there was an increase in demand. We should not exaggerate the self-sufficiency of the medieval peasant household; nevertheless it is true that to a large extent it grew its own food, brewed its own drink, spun and wove its own clothes (or wore the skins of its own animals), built its own houses, collected its own fuel. Urban concentrations made demands on the rest of the population for food, clothing, housing, fuel, the London food market extending its tentacles all over England and Wales. The fishing industry expanded rapidly, as did a series of industries producing consumers' and processed goods – glass, cutlery, domestic pots and pans, salt, sugar, beer, soap. So too did the shipping, ship-building and wagon-making industries necessary for the transport of these goods, as well as naval ship-building. The historian of shopping regards this century as 'a critical point ... in the slow evolution of retail trade', with 'consumers feeling a new authority in their purses, a new confidence in the exercise of choice', beginning to be wooed by retailers.*

Equally important was the stimulus to the building industry caused by the rising prosperity of the upper half of the population. Few churches or castles were built now, but there was an orgy of conspicuous building by the aristocracy, and a great deal of new building in stone by gentry and yeomanry, housing themselves in greater comfort. As Professor Stone has shown, the half-century after 1575 was a great era of country-house building. London and some of the greater towns were expanding continually. All these activities must have led to increased purchasing power among labourers, mostly itinerant craftsmen without gild affiliations. But aristocratic builders often used the semi-forced labour not only of 'their own tenants, but all the country round about them', complained a preacher at Paul's Cross in 1615.

*D. Davis, p. 55.

85

Most mysterious of all is the clothing industry. We have no figures for the home market in cloth. Historians who attach weight only to export statistics believe that this, England's major industry, boomed in the first half of the sixteenth century and stagnated in the second half, with the collapse of the export market in cloth. But is it likely that an economy in which the demand for food, housing, furniture, fuel and so many other consumers' goods was expanding, was not also demanding an increased production of clothes? (Hat-making, we know, was a new industry in Elizabethan England.) The rising standard of living of so many English merchants, yeomen and artisans in the late sixteenth and early seventeenth centuries must inevitably have led to a greater domestic demand for cloth, even though the aristocracy was simultaneously switching to silk and velvet. A pamphlet of 1592 refers to a courtier as Velvet Breeches, a yeoman as Cloth Breeches and labourers (a rope-maker, a bricklayer) as Leather Breeches. It must have been fairly recently that yeomen had moved up from leather to cloth. (But the leather industry still remained very important for the home market, as the habit of wearing boots and shoes spread downwards in the population.)

By the middle of the seventeenth century a man like George Fox the Quaker, who rode about the countryside clothed all in leather, was beginning to be regarded as something of an oddity. Would he have been so regarded a century earlier? May not the century after 1530 be that in which a significant portion of the English population was reclothed as well as rehoused? The reclothing no doubt came by the rich handing down their cast-off clothing earlier to the poor; but this happened because more men were in a position to buy clothes more frequently. Respectable members of the middle class would normally buy their clothes second-hand. Blankets, feather beds, counterpanes were also coming into more common use.

The early sixteenth century was the great age of broadcloth exports, though they were beginning to decline by the end of the century. Their place was taken by the New Draperies, whose export started to expand from the later sixteenth century, in Yorkshire only in the seventeenth century. The crises of 1615–18 and of the twenties and thirties led to English broadcloths being priced out of the North European market by Silesian and Polish cloths. By 1640 London's broadcloth exports were barely one-third of what they had been in 1606. Recovery came only with a re-direction of England's export trade to the Mediterranean area. By 1640 exports of the New Draperies had caught up with broadcloths in value. England's export trade was being reorientated in a way which suggest the need for Oliver Cromwell's Mediterranaen policy. The advantages of diversification of exports led to an economic discussion which points forward to the Navigation Act of 1651.*

The switch from heavy and expensive broadcloths to the New Draperies is often explained in terms of a search for new markets after the collapse of old markets in Northern Europe in 1550, and again after 1614. But the switch may equally well be due in the first instance to the demand for cheaper cloth for the home market. The Flemings who introduced the New Draperies came after all from the most urbanized and most prosperous area of the Continent. They would be familiar with the sort of market which seems to have been opening up in England.

We must beware of optical illusions created by the accidental survival of evidence – in this case export figures. Here is another example. We know about the expansion of consumer demand in housing and household goods from wills of yeomen, craftsmen, merchants. These show a significant rise in living standards of a substantial section of the middle class. But the bottom fifty per cent or so of the population left no wills because they had no property worth leaving: and all the evidence suggests that this stratum of the population was getting poorer, not richer, in the century after 1530. The century of the great inflation saw a re-distribution of wealth as well as a rise in total national wealth. It was a great divide. Some of the rich and many of the middling sort grew richer; the poorer (and the improvident or unlucky among their betters) grew poorer. The great price rise was accompanied by a wage freeze enforced by the whole power of the state and the ruling class.

In medieval England wool export had been monopolized by

*See pp. 155–60, below.

big landlords, including monasteries, who made bulk sales to
foreign merchants. After the fifteen-thirties Italian merchants no
longer came to England, and the monasteries were dissolved.
The early sixteenth century completed the transition from export
of the raw material to export of the finished product, produced
by numerous small clothiers linked by merchant middlemen,
especially from London. After 1614 wool export was prohibited.
The completeness of this sixteenth-century transformation is
shown by a speech of William Hakewill's in the House of Commons in 1610. He quoted the concessions made by Magna
Carta to merchant strangers and added: 'It is improbable that
the makers of the law should be more careful to provide for the
indemnity of merchant strangers than of England'. He argued
that therefore English merchants must have shared the same
privileges – so completely had the colonial status of medieval
England been forgotten.

There were many other stimuli to industry. Much of the coal-
bearing land of England and Wales was at the beginning of our
period in monastic possession. The dissolution threw this land
on to the market just when the beginnings of a timber famine
were stimulating the search for other fuels. While the coalfields
of Belgium and the Ruhr were still battlefields, England became
far and away the biggest coal producer in Europe. Coal was the
basis of many new industries (paper, armaments, sugar refining)
and of new techniques in old industries (bricks, glass, salt,
brewing). Coal-mining itself called for heavy capital investment;
so did the building of furnaces for the use of coal in other
industries. So the switch to coal as an industrial fuel stimulated
the development of capitalism in industry. But here too the
whims of royal policy interfered. Charles I's attempt to collect
money by fines for encroachment on royal forests led to the
ironmaster Sir Basil Brooke being fined £98,000, of which he
actually paid £12,000. The dispersal of monastic lands may have
had similar beneficial effects on the salt and metallurgical
industries. Copper and lead mining were expanding in the sixteenth century, though held up in the early seventeenth century
by fuel shortage. English production of tin, largely from Cornwall, was still the largest in Europe. Cheaper iron and brass

helped to make England secure behind the heavily armed fleet which Henry VIII built up, setting new standards by the size of the naval guns with which he equipped the *Great Harry*.

3

The way in which capitalist relations came to pervade all sectors of society can be illustrated from an industry not often considered by economic historians – the entertainments industry. Before 1577 theatrical productions had been small-scale, once a week at most, either private performances by the dependants of a great lord or the amateur productions of a community, whether guild, Oxford or Cambridge college, or one of the Inns of Court. The financial genius of James Burbage brought playing from a small-scale private enterprise to a big business. The Theatre and the Curtain were both opened during 1577, with the object of producing plays to which the general public would be admitted on payment. The capital for the Globe was provided in part by the actors themselves, on a joint-stock basis. For prudential reasons the patronage of the royal family or of leading aristocrats was retained (under an Act of 1572 actors not so protected could be treated as vagabonds), but henceforth the profit motive prevailed. The drama was the first of the arts to be put on sale to the general public. Larger theatres brought bigger profits if the dramatist could draw his public. This created exciting new possibilities for writers, though capitalism had its drawbacks too. 'Should these fellows come out of my debt,' said the biggest theatre-financier of all, Philip Henslowe, under James I, 'I should have no rule with them.' It was this quite new commercialism in the theatre, plus the fact that the new theatrical buildings were outside the City and so immune from control by the City authorities, that led to the so-called 'Puritan' attack on the stage – which in origin was not Puritan at all and was restricted to an attack on the commercial stage.

4

In medieval theory the right to trade, under protection, was a privilege to be bought from a landowner or from the crown. It then became an exclusive property right, and the guild thus 'enfranchised' with its 'liberty' could demand that the coercive power of the state be turned against those who infringed its monopoly privileges. But coal was not urban, and other industries grew up around coal, away from towns – e.g. the metallurgical industries around Birmingham, free from guilds. Especially the clothing industry escaped from towns to the rural districts. The success of the Lancashire textile industry is attributed to the absence of a guild system. (The clothing areas, incidentally, were the one part of Lancashire, except Liverpool, to support Parliament during the civil war.) England beat Italy in competition for cloth markets because English cloth was cheaper. It was often inferior in quality, but it supplied the new middle class market, while Italian exports still held the luxury market. The hands of Italian industry were tied by guild regulations. The maintenance of these obsolete forms of economic organization led to high production and labour costs. Taxation, moreover, was heavier in Italy, and there were more internal tolls. In Italy too, industries ultimately shifted from the cities to escape from guilds and to find cheap labour; but this move came too late to emulate the English system of small-scale production of cheaper goods.

In the early development of the rural clothing industry an important part was played by gentlemen and peers. Minerals too were often found under aristocratic land – coal in Nottinghamshire, iron in Kent – and big landowners found it easier to obtain credit. But the results of their predominance were not wholly beneficial. Too often landowners who happened to possess mineral wealth were interested only in quick returns, to be squandered in an ostentatious standard of living. There are many sad stories of intelligent entrepreneurs with ideas to sell, unable to get adequate backing from landowners who were not interested in investing capital in long-term improvements. It was only after the revolution that smaller men with less extravagant tastes were able, more slowly, to build up these industries.*

In rural industry the relationship of employer to employee was more often that of creditor to debtor than one expressed in payment of wages. Merchants made advance purchases of lead, tin, coal, from small miners; they made advances to wire-makers, pin-makers, nailers, etc. A merchant clothier had little use for his accumulated capital except to extend his credit operations. The Cornish Stannaries offer a classic example of exploitation by credit. The labourer borrowed money and goods, pledging in return the tin when it was produced. Capitalists bought up tin in advance for £15–16 per thousand weight, re-selling it to the pewterers at £20–30 per thousand: the rewards of waiting! This ultimately undermined the position of the free tinners and brought the industry under the control of big capitalists. A nailer of Handsworth who died in 1588 left total property valued at £10 13s. 1d., and debts to the tune of £32 3s. 4d. 'The Manchester capitalists,' said Mr Wadsworth, 'not only financed the credit system of the [clothing] industry, but their loans and mortgages were the mechanism of a minor social revolution.' The effects on debtors were eloquently described by the Puritan preachers Dod and Clever:

Albeit that villeinage and bondage be not now in use among us, yet imprisonment [for debt] is not altogether out of use. . . . And everyone is so far in servitude, and in the creditor's power, as he wanteth ability to pay his debts. He may well be said to be another man's servant, whose state and liberty doth stand at another man's courtesy.

We should certainly not be sentimental about guilds in our period, whatever they may or may not have been earlier. They were usually controlled by oligarchies, and were often employers' rings. Apprentices supplied these oligarchies with cheap and docile labour. In almost every important London industry there were from the beginning of our period quarrels between big merchant capitalists and small craftsmen, the yeomanry, often organized or anxious to be organized in separate companies.

* I owe this point to the unpublished Nottingham D.Phil. thesis of Dr R. S. Smith.

These conflicts came to a head during the revolution, when the Levellers associated themselves with the cause of the yeomanry.

5

The policies favoured by governments, except for the interlude of Edward VI's reign, were restrictionist, aimed at checking the rapid development of capitalist relations. Their effect was to divert capital from industry. A statute of 1533 limited to 2,400 the number of sheep which one man might own. A law was passed against gig-mills in 1551–52, and confirmed by proclamation in 1633 – an action which delayed the clothing industry's recovery from the slump of the sixteen-twenties. Another act of 1552 tried to restrict the activities of all middlemen in wool except the Staplers' Company, to the benefit of a powerful pressure group rather than of the general public. The Weavers' Act of 1555 forbade country clothiers to own more than one loom, weavers more than two. The government intended the expansion of the clothing industry, if it must expand, to be confined to the towns – though backward Yorkshire, Cumberland, Northumberland and Westmorland were exempted from the Act.

The Statute of Artificers of 1563 extended guild regulation to the whole nation. It was trying to keep national industry and world trade squeezed into the Procrustean bed of the old urban organization. It excluded from industry all who had not undergone a seven years' apprenticeship. In the most skilled crafts, including weaving, it limited apprenticeship to the sons of those owning land worth more than £2 per annum (£3 if the prentice came to a corporate town). On paper at least, three-quarters of the rural poor were thus excluded, though in Wales and the North the cheapest household cloth could be woven in villages without apprenticeship. An act of 1576 limited to twenty acres the amount of land which clothiers in Somerset, Gloucestershire and Wiltshire might purchase – a clear manifestation of what Dr Ramsay calls the 'increased class consciousness' of the gentry in these clothing counties. It is hardly surprising to find that in Somerset in the sixteen-forties 'a people of inferior degree, who by good husbandry, clothing and other thriving arts, had gotten very great fortunes ... were fast friends to the Parliament' (Clarendon).

In Europe's other great sheep-farming country, Castile, wool was still grown principally on large estates marketing their own produce, without middlemen or middle-sized producers – as in thirteenth-century England. After the defeat of the towns in the Comuneros Revolt of 1520–21 there was no threat to the supremacy of the landed class, so Castile's trading classes could be made to pay for the government's wars by crushing taxation – which made capitalist industrial development impossible. The feudal landowners who were still the only wool producers were sheltered by the vast monopoly of the Mesta, fixing prices, monopolizing exports, pooling profits, preventing the conversion of land from pasture to tillage. The lesser gentry became *conquistadores*, plunderers of the New World; there was no economic future for them in their own country, where commerce was a despised occupation. So Spain never knew that alliance of a section of the gentry with a prospering commercial interest which was so decisive in preparing for the seventeenth-century revolution in England.

One of the most important developments of this century, but one which we can only dimly perceive, was the rise of a new group of peddling traders, middlemen, who for instance supplied domestic industry clothiers with their raw materials and who carried consumer goods from market towns to outlying villages. Such middlemen were harried by authority and vested interests, and disapproved of by traditional moralists. One aspect of the Cokayne Project of 1614 was a prohibition of the activities of middlemen in the wool trade. The government tried to check the activities of those who supplied food to London. But such men performed functions far too useful for government prohibitions to be fully effective. Professor Everitt has described 'the community of wayfaring merchants' as 'transforming elements in the Tudor and Stuart economy'. 'The rapid ascendancy of that community' between 1570 and 1640, he continues, 'was certainly not unconnected with the rise of the revolutionary party during the Great Rebellion.' Professor Everitt suggests 'a parallel between the vagrant life of the wayfaring community and the vagrant religion of the Independents'.* After 1640 the attempt to limit the activities of middlemen broke down.

The myth that Tudor governments supported a 'planned economy', or had any wish to promote social or economic welfare, has long been exploded. Elizabethan economic policy, if policy is not too strong a word, should be attributed less to 'depression economics' or 'war finance' than to fear of social disorder, especially from the lower classes. Governments had no objection to luxury industries, like silk, glass or the manufacture of fine paper; and of course none to armaments. They were open to bribery from pressure groups. But there was no considered policy of protecting English industry or furthering English trade. Governments were unsympathetic to the country's major industry, except in so far as cloth exports brought in customs revenue. Even agricultural innovations associated with the clothing industry were discouraged, as by a proclamation of 1585 which forbade the breaking of fresh ground for the sowing of woad. In the late sixteenth and early seventeenth centuries many corporate towns were reconstructing their guild systems, as the Statute of Artificers clearly intended, and tightening their bye-laws in an attempt to ensure full employment for their own citizens by suppressing the enterprise of others, including those living immediately outside the city walls.

The fifteen-nineties were years of bad harvests and high prices, of near-famine conditions. They ushered in half a century of exceptional hardship for the wage-earning classes. The great age of Elizabethan and Jacobean literature trembled on the verge of social breakdown. As the unemployed, vagabonds and beggars crowded into the capital in increasing numbers, neither trade, industry nor charity could relieve them. The ensuing decades saw a great effort at a state-controlled policy regimenting the able-bodied poor. They also saw a much greater effort of private charity to relieve poverty more constructively by endowing apprenticeships and scholarships, marriage portions for spinsters, almshouses for the aged. Others, like Hakluyt, advocated emigration to America. This policy was put into practice on a

*Thirsk, 1967, p. 573; cf. p. 463. Cf. also pp. 128–9 below.

mass scale in the sixteen-thirties, though not by the government. And – ironically – at the same time Francis Bacon was seeing visions of a scientifically industrialized community in which poverty would be abolished.

In 1624 the government ordered the destruction of a needle-making machine, together with the needles which it had made. Nine years later Charles I prohibited the casting of brass buckles and in 1635 the use of a windmill for sawing wood. At best government policy would have perpetuated a small-town economy in England. If the system of regulation and control had been effective, England's industrial development would have been irreparably ruined. But fortunately the government's power of enforcing its regulations was inadequate to its will. Whereas in France the king was able to build up a bureaucracy dependent on him alone, in England, despite attempts to follow the French model, the government remained dependent on J.P.s to enforce statutes and proclamations – and J.P.s had a habit of enforcing only those parts of the law which suited their interests. They were gentlemen and merchants themselves, increasingly (in the southern and eastern counties at least) drawn into capitalist industrial development. They were forced into working the system of regulation only by fear of social disorder, especially after the revolts of 1549 and 1628–31. In the clothing areas apprenticeship regulations were simply not enforced. New industries grew up outside the regulations of the 1563 Statute, with the help of free-trade common lawyers and judges who whittled it away. A decision of the King's Bench in 1615 treated the Statute as inapplicable not only to new industries but also to industries carried on outside boroughs, to freemen of London, and to unskilled labour. This was very far from the act's original intention. Nevertheless, there remained a great deal of confusion and dislocation which did nearly as much harm as enforcement of the law would have done.

In 1604 the Commons tried, unsuccessfully, to repeal the clause in the Statute of Artificers which restricted apprenticeship to sons of sixty-shilling freeholders. In 1624 Parliament did repeal a whole heap of regulating statutes which it regarded as obsolete, including those designed to prevent the movement of industry into the country. But enough remained, and from 1631 onwards the government issued a series of new orders and directions which it insisted on having enforced. In 1640 a threat of prosecution for breakers of prentice regulations caused wild alarm in Yorkshire, where 'not one clothier in the county but is guilty of the penalties of the said statutes', which were 'never observed in the county, and cannot be for many reasons'.

Monopolies were not bad in themselves: they were a form of protection for new industries in a backward country. The earliest monopolies were concerned with national defence – the Elizabethan Mines Royal aimed to make England independent of foreign copper for the manufacture of cannon. There were similar monopolies for saltpetre and gunpowder. But monopolies rapidly became noxious when they were used for fiscal purposes by governments hostile to capitalist development. In the seventeenth century monopolies were created in order to be sold, and in addition to those connected with an industrial process there were monopolies for licensing, giving permission to break the law, etc.

Monopolies, James I admitted in 1621, exhausted his subjects' purses more than Parliamentary taxation would have done. The wine monopoly, Pym told the House of Commons, cost the public £360,000 a year, of which the king got only £30,000. To the argument that monopolies were intended to protect English industry, their opponents had two finally damning answers. First, monopoly regulation was a check on production, whereas freer production would increase the wealth of the nation as a whole, and so equip England for the struggle for the markets of the world. Secondly, monopolies, far from achieving the social objectives claimed for them, were in fact more harmful to consumer, wage-earner and Exchequer than free production would be.

In such an atmosphere, with no government bureaucracy, informers thrived, 'seeking rather to nourish than to abolish offences'. At least two-thirds of the prosecutions for non-observance of apprenticeship were due to informers. They also did a brisk trade in denouncing or blackmailing middlemen and those who took more than the legal rate of interest. One informer collected £200 from tradesmen in Wiltshire in 1637; another, a Londoner, demanded £3 cash down and a life annuity from his victims, who, as Bacon noted, were likely to be of the wealthier sort; but all were exposed to blackmail:

> So that the best is always to agree
>   Although they have offended in nothing,
> And give a crown to save forty;
>   Yea, rather than fail, smaller offering,
> Sometimes I take a capon or a goose.

So said the Informer in Francis Thynne's *Debate between Pride and Lowliness* (published 1592, written earlier).

With growing financial difficulties in the seventeenth century, governments actually traded in the sale of exemptions from their own laws. There were informers to inform against informers. Just as guild regulations were extended to the nation, so the system of tale-bearing which sufficed in the manor court and guild was extended until it became a national profession.

Parliament disliked informers, and a statute of 1624 reduced the efficacy of the London professional by insisting that cases must be tried in local courts. (It was the expense of coming up to Westminster, the uncertainties of justice there and the loss of working time that enabled informers to blackmail smaller craftsmen. In any case local juries would always be sympathetic to breaches of government regulations of which they were no doubt themselves guilty.) So Parliament reasserted the control of J.P.s and juries over economic processes and reduced the influence of court-bred patentees. But in Charles's reign there seems to have been an increase in denunciations of middlemen, so essential to business society.*

Stuart paternalism ultimately broke down, despite the most favourable possible circumstances of peace and absence of Parliaments. The consequence of the collapse of the old régime was the triumph in politics of the economically dominant new forces, the acceptance of their morality – that men have a right to do what they will with their own, that the benefit of the capitalist is also

*M. G. Davies, *The Enforcement of English Apprenticeship, 1563–1642* (Harvard University Press, 1956), pp. 25, 31, 60, 75–6, 100.

the benefit of the community, that poverty is a crime, that the devil should take the hindmost. The alternative to these unattractive virtues would have been economic stagnation. Margaret James observed:

> Modern enterprise in industry, commerce and agriculture had made rapid strides before 1640, but its progress had been hampered by the theory and practice of paternal control, which at its worst had been corrupt and obstructive, and even at its best had interfered considerably with the free action of individuals. Puritanism was strongest among those classes who were best able to take care of themselves, and had nothing to gain and all to lose by the interference of church and state in economic affairs.

The destruction of the royal bureaucracy in 1640–41 can be regarded as the most decisive single event in the whole of British history.

6

In this backward economy, with labour permanently under-employed, where English laziness was a bye-word with foreigners, the problem of labour discipline, of making the poor work, was one that greatly exercised social thinkers. Some men were becoming more conscious of scarcity as the possibility of overcoming it began to open up. I have discussed elsewhere Puritanism's contribution to the evolution of an ideology of self-help.* The problem was to establish a regular rhythm of labour (abolition of saints' days, emphasis on the Sabbath rest, establishment of regular meal-times). The importance of this regularity, and of saving time, seems to have been accepted by the middle class during the seventeenth century. An alarm clock appears in a poem of 1654. But the lower classes were more resistant. On them the pressures of starvation must have been even more potent than Puritan sermons and the floggings ordered by J.P.s. One reason for the flourishing of the Yorkshire and Lancashire clothing industries was the rise of a cottage industry there. There was still uncultivated land on which cottagers – 'housed beggars',

*See Hill, 1964, especially Chapters 4 and 5.

Bacon called them – could squat. They and their families formed a convenient pool of the cheapest labour. 'A minor social revolution' this has been called. But economic pressures could not produce skilled labour. The Virginia Company in the early seventeenth century had to go to the Continent to find the skilled workers needed to establish sawmills, a silk industry and glass-making etc. in the colony.

In part it was a matter of organization, communications, as well as of abolishing restrictions in order to loosen up the economy. In 1610 Rowland Vaughan of Herefordshire described how the five hundred poor who lived within $1\frac{1}{2}$ miles of his home passed the year 'in idleness and beggary'. They lose a day's work to go to Hereford to buy flax (on credit). They have to go 3–4 miles to buy corn, and wait for it to be ground. 'If a better customer come, they are sure to be served last. . . . They spend one day with the weaver, and after it is wove, before they can sell, they make many journeys to markets.' Vaughan's proposed remedy was to bring the workers within one building, with meals provided. But short of such drastic reorganization, a simple increase in the number of middlemen would have helped.

Contemporary attitudes towards labour diverged. Puritans and others exalted the dignity of *free* labour at the same time as small artisans and husbandmen feared nothing more than to fall to the status of landless wage-labourer. When Drake said that the gentleman must haul and draw with the mariner, he was expressing the important truth that sailing-ships, unlike Mediterranean galleys, must be manned by free men, with some technical skill. In his assertion of the rights of those who worked, as well as in executing the gentleman Thomas Doughty to encourage the others, he looks forward to the seventeenth-century revolution. At the other end of oceanic voyages, the existence of free land in America soon came to have an attractive power for the unfree in England, like that which the Ukraine offered to Russian peasants, and so helped to enhance the dignity of labour.

Servants were as rightless politically in New as in old England; but hard work and craft skills were of more use there than blue blood. For many of the early settlers servitude was a temporary phase through which one worked one's way to freedom and landownership. 'We are all freeholders,' said a joyful letter from New England in the sixteen-twenties. 'The rent day doth not trouble us.' A token of 1647 was inscribed 'In Virginia land free and labour scarce; in England land scarce and labour plenty'. At about this time Hugh Peter returned to England to tell of the promised land across the ocean in which there were no beggars. Both the navy and the colonies developed thanks to private enterprise, yet in each sphere the opposition ultimately had to force its policies on governments. Both would promote a respect for the dignity of free labour that looks forward to Cromwell's preference of a 'plain russet-coated captain' over 'that which you call a gentleman and is nothing else'.

6

FINANCE

It is the common opinion that the King [James I] has not a
sou, for the late Queen sank a great deal of money in her wars
with Ireland and Spain, and it is a wonder that she did not
leave debts rather than cash. – *From* THE VENETIAN AMBAS-
SADOR *to* THE GOVERNMENT OF VENICE, *1607*

THE Tudor peace, and the lack of a standing army in England,
meant that taxation was relatively light by the standards of the
Continent, where crown and aristocracy combined to lay
crushing burdens on the peasantry. The flourishing of trade,
industry and yeoman farming in England in the century before
1640 owed much to this relatively light incidence of taxation; the
small sums collected contributed in their turn to the failure to
evolve a bureaucracy of comparable strength to that, say, of
France.

At the beginning of our period income from crown lands was
the most important part of royal revenue, greatly increased by
the accession of monastic lands in the fifteen-thirties. But by
renewing the obsolete French wars Henry VIII soon dissipated
the magnificent patrimony which Thomas Cromwell had given
him. The wars of 1542–46 against France and Scotland are estimated to have cost over £2 million, those of 1547–50 another
million or more. Crown lands were not merely or indeed chiefly
a source of revenue.

The crown had a great estate over all England [Burnet wrote], which
was all let out upon leases for years, and a small rent was reserved. So
most of the great families of the nation were the tenants of the crown,
and a great many boroughs were depending on the estates so held. The
renewal of these leases brought in fines both to the crown and to the
great officers; besides that the fear of being denied kept all in a dependence on the court.

Inflation thus put the monarchy in a cleft stick. The more
importance was attached to influence over tenants, the less hope

was there of exacting the full economic rent. In any case the crown suffered the difficulty of all great landowners in rationalizing its estate management; profits of crown lands went to stewards as well as to courtiers.

Lord Treasurer Middlesex attributed the fact that 'some counties of England did never oppose the King in anything, but were always conformable to his will', to the presence of many tenants-in-chief in those counties. The old feudal custom by which the heirs of any tenant-in-chief who died before they came of age became wards of the crown had been turned to fiscal advantage by the Tudors. The right to manage the estate of a ward during his or her minority, and the right to arrange his or her marriage, might each be worth a considerable sum of money. The wardships of rich heirs and heiresses were eagerly begged and bought by courtiers. The Court of Wards became an instrument of financial exploitation. In Bishop Goodman's words, it 'was such a tie upon the subject as no king in the world ever had the like'. Its revenues rose four times between the accession of Elizabeth and the meeting of the Long Parliament. They were used as 'perquisites' for civil servants, but the system got out of control: the unofficial profits were at least three times the official ones. A last attempt to end 'fiscal feudalism' in the interests of revenue was made in 1610, but negotiations with Parliament for the abolition of feudal tenures and the Court of Wards in return for an annual grant of £200,000 broke down. There followed a period of reaction under the influence of the Howards. The Court was abolished in 1646.

Meanwhile the business sector of the economy was getting richer, and the government was unable to tap this wealth by taxation. Royal revenue consistently failed to keep pace with prices, rising from about £200,000 a year in the late fifteen-thirties to over £600,000 in the early sixteen-thirties. But all the time the real costs of government were going up. So long as Elizabeth avoided war she could balance her budget; but the Spanish and Irish wars necessitated subsidies voted by Parliament, and even so the government had to sell capital in the shape of crown lands. There were thus financial as well as social reasons for James's appeasement of Spain – and he still had to sell lands. Government commitments were continually extending – in the maintenance of law and order, the subjugation of Ireland, the maintenance of the navy. Costs were also going up in traditional spheres of expenditure – muskets and cannon were replacing bows and arrows, ships were getting bigger, the civil service was expanding. Under Elizabeth and James the court still went frequently on progress, when the whole royal household could be maintained at the expense of some great courtier. From Charles's reign the court ceased to be peripatetic. By the seventeenth century the effects of the price revolution were making themselves felt on the aristocracy. It was more difficult to get peers to serve on embassies at their own expense. On the contrary, they were coming to expect perquisites from the court, to help them to survive economically.

Quite apart from this considerable rise in expenditure with no comparable increase in real revenue, government was becoming more bourgeois and bureaucratic: a matter of regular routine calling for regular income. The contemporary way of putting it was to say that the king could no longer live of his own: the alternative was the creation of a system of regular taxes. But this raised the question whether crown or Parliament was to control the reorganization.

Till 1588 Elizabeth's normal revenue was of the order of £250,000 a year; James I's was some £500,000. In the four years 1599–1603 the Irish war alone cost £1,131,000; the army in 1639 cost more than Charles I's total normal revenue, and crown lands had to be mortgaged again. It was a continuous process of living upon capital, to which there could be no end without an overall financial reorganization. Once that had taken place, government expenditure in the sixteen-fifties frequently exceeded £2,500,000.

It was difficult to reorganize the existing system of taxation, or to levy new taxes. Vested interests at court opposed any attempts at economy or rationalization: Cecil, Cranfield, Laud, all failed. Extraordinary revenue was traditionally voted by the House of Commons. Under Elizabeth, as earlier, taxes were voted almost without question in time of war. But James was unable to make ends meet even in peace-time; when war came in the twenties it coincided (as in the fifteen-nineties) with a run of bad harvests, and a condition of near-famine returned. Unlike Elizabeth's wars, those of her successors were uniformly and shamefully unsuccessful. Parliament began to demand some control of collection and expenditure of taxes, and in effect control of the foreign policy for which taxation paid. Similarly in Bate's case (1605) the question at issue was not merely whether Mr Bate should pay an extra 6*d.* on imported currants, but whether the king should have the sole right of raising the rates of customs – an action which could have serious effects on the whole economic life of the country – or whether Parliament should share this right. Apparently technical questions veiled the issue of political power to control the economic life of the country.

In France the government salt monopoly, the *gabelle*, by 1641 was producing twice the total English national revenue. The English monarchy tried in vain to establish any such overriding monopoly, or effective claim to mineral royalties. In the absence of a civil service it was more efficient to farm the customs to businessmen who took their own profits from them, to let Parliamentary taxation be assessed by the gentry who paid it. Widespread evasion and corruption naturally followed. To keep pace with inflation, inadequately paid officials relied on fees – which shaded off into bribes. Royal finances may have suffered, but successive Lord Treasurers did not. In the last two years of Salisbury's tenure of the office he had an income of at least £25,000 a year. In 1619 his successor, the Earl of Suffolk, was convicted of large-scale peculation. Cranfield's disgrace in 1624 is a more ambiguous case, but in 1636 Lord Treasurer Portland thought it necessary to obtain the king's pardon for misappropriating some £44,500. Nor indeed was graft of this kind universally reprobated. Sir Hamon L'Estrange wrote of the first Duke of Buckingham: 'for his study to advance his near relations, he might most worthily have been counted a monster and an extravagancy in nature had he cut off all regard of those to whom he was by consanguinity so near annexed'.

In raising extra revenue governments tried to keep within the letter of the law, so as not to force the issue of power. But keeping within the letter of the law led to straining of what many thought to be its spirit. Government came to be based on historical research. It may have seemed a small matter when in 1631 the government tried to fine the city of Leicester £300 for not sending representatives to Charles I's coronation; but such small items added up when men compared notes.

Another feudal survival which caused great annoyance was purveyance – the right of the crown to purchase goods well below the market price. In Elizabeth's reign over four million eggs, 13,000 lambs, 32,000 chickens, 600,000 gallons of beer were so bought each year. Purveyance hit production for the market and spared the great households. It was not to be taken, a judge said, from what 'a man hath provided for his own provision, but of that which is to be sold'. In 1597 purveyance was compounded at a flat rate on counties, but in 1610 James increased the rate. What could hinder him raising it a dozen times? Chamberlain was asking in 1614.

From the reign of Henry VIII to that of James I customs duties brought in half the ordinary state revenue. Customs were traditionally justified as the means of paying for the royal navy which defended merchants: but the Stuart navy did this very inadequately. Sir John Eliot in 1624 pointed out that in the Netherlands customs revenue was far greater because rates were lower, and so trade was encouraged. The advantage to the government of farming the customs was that a certain revenue, known in advance, was secured; there was no need to worry about peculation resulting from inability to pay customs officers properly. On the other hand, the customs farmers had to be allowed a very large profit, and it was a confession of the weakness of the royal bureaucracy that private enterprise could do its job so much more efficiently. There was a financial case for reorganization. But the government became increasingly dependent on the customs farmers for advances of revenue.

In the sixteen-thirties the government could no longer borrow from the Corporation of London, since its record as a borrower was so bad. A small group of London businessmen – those most influential in City government – advanced money on terms very favourable to themselves, and so became uniquely well placed for obtaining other perquisites. The alliance was to prove fatal to both sides. Loans from the customs farmers gave an illusory appearance of solvency to Charles I's government in the sixteen-thirties. In fact, although revenue rose by fifty per cent the future was always seriously mortgaged.

In sequestering the leases of the [customs] farmers in 1641 [Professor Ashton wrote], the Long Parliament was in effect launching an attack on the old régime which was no less important than its impeachment of Strafford. . . . The farmers had hopelessly compromised themselves in the eyes of Parliament which, by destroying the one permanent source of loans whose fortunes were inextricably bound up with those of the crown, succeeded in crippling irreparably the independent power of the crown to borrow.

We have here (and in the similar relations between government and aldermen) the explanation of the narrow ruling group in the City, and of the ease with which in the coup of December 1641 the overwhelming pro-Parliament sentiment of the mass of the citizens of London triumphed.

In the subsidies voted by Parliament, the richer landowners were fantastically under-assessed. 'Many be twenty times, some thirty times, and some much more worth than they be set at,' said Lord Burghley. With his own income assessed at £133 he came into the last category. This was the price which the government had to pay to its servants and to the classes on whom it depended for unsalaried (but not unrewarded) services in local government. 'The poor are grieved by being overcharged in taxation,' Fulke Greville said in 1593. 'If the feet [i.e. the poor] knew their strength as well as we know their oppression, they would not bear as they do.' Reassessment was threatened by Elizabeth in 1588 and was discussed again in the Parliaments of 1626 and 1628, but it at once raised questions of power – who would reassess, who would control the expenditure of the money so raised – which could not be amicably settled under the old régime.

Since Parliament could not or would not increase taxation to meet the mounting deficit, governments were forced into expedients which heightened tension between court and country, and brought comparatively little in revenue. A pattern emerges.

'Industrial feudalism' – monopolies, and the whole system of regulation – whatever the theoretical justification for it, became in Professor Tawney's classic phrase, 'smeared with the trail of finance'. The cost to the consumer was high; yet, apart from perquisites to civil servants and courtiers, the relief to the government was slight. The profits of revived fiscal feudalism also went to courtiers. Less than a quarter of what was paid for wardship and purveyance reached government coffers. The failure of the Great Contract in 1610 meant that the exactions of the Court of Wards increased, and with them the hostility of the landed class. The whole system of fees and perquisites was tolerable only when confined within limits. But as the government's financial need became more desperate, and the breach with Parliament became absolute, it became a burden on the whole economy. The £1 million borrowed by the government between 1624 and 1628, it has been suggested, may have been an important factor in retarding the rate of recovery from the slump of the early sixteen-twenties.*

Offices and titles were sold in the desperate search for funds – £10,000 for a peerage, £20,000 for the office of Lord Treasurer. James I having sold knighthoods until they were hardly worth having, his son then fined gentlemen £173,537 in five years for refusing to buy the discredited honour. Between 1615 and 1628 there was a fifty-six per cent increase in the peerage, nearly all of it by purchase. The price fell to £4,000. Charles I stopped the sale of honours, but perforce started it again in 1641. Many royalists agreed that the sale of honours brought the monarchy into disrepute. Between 1603 and 1629 the sale of peerages brought in, at a minimum calculation, £620,000, of which however only a small proportion came into the Exchequer; most went to courtiers. But between 1603 and 1641 James and Charles distributed among the peerage alone gifts and favours worth at least £3 million.†

The only long-term solution was a reassessment of regular taxation, so as to tap the real wealth of the country. After failure to do this by agreement with Parliament, Ship Money – assessed

*Ashton, pp. 42–4, 162.
†Stone, pp. 81–2, 116–27, 268.

on the 'true yearly value of rents, annuities, offices' – nearly became a settled annual tax, which would have made the government independent of the will of Parliament and the tax-payers. 'I conceive by the common law and the fundamental policy of the kingdom,' said Justice Finch in Hampden's case, 'that the King may charge his subjects for the defence of the kingdom . . . when it is in danger, and ought to direct the means of defence.' But the nobility and gentry, Sir John Bramston tells us, 'took it as the overthrow of the fundamental laws or constitution of the kingdom, and of Parliament, and of all property'. So did City companies. The Founders' Company of London seems to have paid no Ship Money after 1637, the Society of Apothecaries none after 1638. Refusal to pay became general. By 1640 some branches of the customs revenue had been anticipated for years ahead. There was a partial economic recovery in the late thirties, but it brought little alleviation for the lower classes, who by then were beginning to suffer from the fiscal policy of a desperate and nearly bankrupt government.

The collapse of personal government in 1640 meant that the overdue financial reconstruction was carried out by Parliament. Their measures laid the basis for the financial organization of England during the next century, in which government expenditure was to expand beyond the wildest dreams of the early Stuarts.

7

RELIGION AND
INTELLECTUAL LIFE

It is the church which supports the state, it is religion which
strengthens the government; shake the one, and you overthrow the other. Nothing is so deeply rooted in the hearts of
men as religion, nothing so powerful to direct their actions:
and if once the hearts of the people be doubtful in religion, all
other relations fail, and you shall find nothing but mutinies and
sedition. Thus the church and the state do mutually support
and give assistance to each other; and if one of them change,
the other can have no sure foundation. – BISHOP GOODMAN,
The Court of King James I (*first published 1839, written between 1650 and 1656*)

I

IT is impossible to discuss economic and social history without
discussing religion. The Reformation, as we have seen, had vast
social and economic consequences.* The parish church was still
a social centre for those nine out of ten English men and women
who lived in villages and small towns. It was the place where
elections were held, poor relief distributed, public and private
announcements made; it could be an amusement hall, a school, a
library, a storehouse. In a society without radio, television and
daily press, still largely illiterate and with a strict censorship
(except in the revolutionary decades), the pulpit was almost the
sole source of ideas on economics and politics. Popular opposition ideas tended to take a religious form, whether protestant
nonconformity or adherence to one of the old religions, the
witch-cult or catholicism.

We should never forget how insecure life still was. Overseas
trade faced the perils of piracy, shipwreck, the hostility of distant
powers, scurvy, etc. But life at home also was affected by natural
catastrophes, the fires to which wooden buildings were so liable,

* See pp. 34–41, above.

unstable prices, arbitrary taxation, famine, pestilence, sudden and early deaths. All this with no insurance, or insurance at fantastically high premiums. The margin between success and failure was very narrow; a man might obtain a windfall by, for example, a prudent marriage; but he could be ruined by factors quite outside his control. It is difficult for us, living in a world where everything is insured, where prices are uniform and not liable to violent fluctuations, where the weather is not a matter of life and death, where we can telephone for fire engines or the doctor and where expectation of life is more than twice that of the sixteenth century, to recapture the profound emotional instability of our forefathers. Naturally they believed in theories of predestination (man's fate is in God's hands, not his own; success justifies). Naturally they wanted to propitiate this very relevant God – whether by ceremonies or by virtuous conduct. We should always take seriously the religious professions of sixteenth-century men and women, for many of whom eternity might seem much more real than this brief and uncertain life on earth.

But to these traditional insecurities new ones were being added. In the sixteenth century, 'perhaps for the first time in all civilized history, an absolute majority of the population ceased to find their lives circumscribed by an immemorial round of traditional agricultural tasks. Instead, they faced the troubling ups and downs of an unpredictable market economy in which some few grew rich, some prospered, while many became paupers; and all, rich and poor, suffered inescapable uncertainty as to the future.'* It is hardly surprising that there was a spiritual crisis all over western Europe.

There had been a lot of popular heresy in the Middle Ages, whose continuous history down to the Reformation is just beginning to be retraced – the men of the sixteenth and seventeenth centuries were well aware of continuities. But there had been nothing like the outburst of popular independence of mind which the Marian persecutions revealed in England. Only nine of the 300-odd victims were described as gentlemen; the vast

*W. H. McNeill, *The Rise of the West* (Chicago University Press, 1963), p. 585.

majority were artisans or craftsmen. Their stand against persecution, at a time when their betters cowered or fled into exile, foreshadowed the radical movements of the sixteen-forties. Indeed the Imperial ambassador in London anticipated popular revolt in the capital against Mary's burnings. It was impossible for Elizabeth's government to ignore this popular feeling, though the Queen herself had little sympathy with it.

The propertied classes indeed faced a dilemma after the Reformation. In catholic times, as John Aubrey put it, 'the consciences of the people were kept in so great awe by confession'. This means of control was lost, just at a time when the ecclesiastical changes were unsettling men's minds, and indeed seemed to be taking over much of the programme of the lower-class Lollards. About the mid-century there was a panic fear of Anabaptists, who in 1536 had defended a communist régime in Münster for a year against the whole strength of the Holy Roman Empire. This fear is vigorously expressed in the Thirty-Nine Articles of the Church of England, and still more in Edward VI's forty-two Articles which preceded them. The introduction of parish registers in 1538, so invaluable to the historian, may have been aimed against Anabaptists, in England as it was in Zwingli's Zürich. In the later sixteenth century, Robert Browne and others initiated congregationalism. Where respectable Puritans would 'tarry for the magistrate', Brownists who advocated reformation without tarrying for any had a more menacing because immediately practicable programme. In 1613 we hear of 'wandering brethren', Brownists, who go 'hither and thither to and from England, abiding in no certain place'. Against them the vagabond laws were invoked, or in time of war they might be conscripted into the armed forces. In 1614 a well-informed Scottish observer commented on the strength of sectarianism in England. These lower-class groups came up from below the surface after the breakdown of ecclesiastical power in 1640. We must remember this third force of popular sectarianism when we are tempted to think of the religious disputes of the sixteenth and seventeenth centuries as though they were merely between orthodox protestants and catholics.

In these circumstances, control of the pulpit was of the greatest social and political importance, comparable to control of radio and press today. 'Those who hold the helm of the pulpit always steer the people's hearts as they please,' said Fuller. There would be 'a perpetual disaffection,' Bacon tells us, 'except you keep men in by preaching as well as the law doth by punishing'.

Elizabeth's *via media* in religion – protestant doctrine for the intellectuals, catholic ceremonies for the masses – was parallel to her *via media* in foreign policy, and both were related to society as well as to more abstract intellectual considerations. Her first Archbishop, Matthew Parker, had a wholly traditional view of the rôle of church and state in a hierarchical society. He had preached resignation to the Norfolk rebels in 1549, and opposed the principles of John Knox because he believed that the relation of a ruler to his subjects, of a lord to his tenants and of a master to his servants should all be governed by the same rules.

Parker's successor at Canterbury, Grindal, had been a Marian exile, and under him the radicals still hoped for a further instalment of reform. In Leicester and Walsingham Puritanism had powerful patrons at court. Puritanism was a social as well as a religious phenomenon, flourishing, as John Taylor the Water-Poet pointed out, in the ports as well as in industrial areas like East Anglia and the western clothing counties. Under Elizabeth it received strong support from market towns and a section of the gentry, expressed in the House of Commons. But the Queen resolutely opposed them, overruled and suspended Grindal, and in 1583 replaced him by an Archbishop after her own heart, John Whitgift. Whitgift used the High Commission to counteract secret support in high quarters for the Puritan gentry. 'The essence of the problem was social – the bishop against the gentry,' says Dr Collinson. The new ecclesiastical policy forced bishops to lean on 'crypto-catholic elements', with unfortunate long-term consequences. Lord Chancellor Hatton and his protégé Richard Bancroft helped Whitgift to break the Puritan movement in the fifteen-nineties, by methods 'which may recall [those] of Senator Joseph McCarthy'. The more prudent James appointed another Grindal-like figure, George Abbott, to Canterbury. But his opposition to James's 'crypto-catholic' foreign policy* led inevitably to his disgrace and ultimately to the triumph of Laud and the high-flying Arminians.†

The Elizabethan radicals felt that their reformation had been betrayed. But they were on the horns of a dilemma. Many of them had expected Elizabeth's restoration of protestantism to be only a brief interlude. 'The time requireth an unity and perfect agreement,' said the Puritanically-minded Walsingham, 'rather in them that make profession of that truth which is elsewhere so impugned and hath so mighty enemies.' This enforced unity, however, did not survive the nineties. For many of the middle class, Puritanism was a knife and fork question. Throughout the reigns of James and Charles church courts were proceeding against men for working on saints' days. Thomas Rogers, chaplain to Bancroft, attacked the Puritan view that 'the church cannot take away this liberty of working six days in the week'. 'The discipline of penance,' wrote Archdeacon Cunningham, 'and the canons which were enforced in the ecclesiastical courts were framed not with reference to burghal prosperity, but in the hope of detecting and suppressing the greed for gain.'

2

Any established state church needs ceremonial, even a protestant church which started by a revolt of the individual conscience against popish ceremonies. The naked erastianism of the Elizabethan church brought a natural clerical reaction as soon as the political situation eased with the defeat of the Armada and the Dutch victories of the nineties. Bancroft's emphasis on the divine right of bishops (1589), Hooker's great work *Of the Laws of Ecclesiastical Polity* (1593) and controversies in the universities about predestination contributed to the building up of a revisionist party (which came to be called Arminian) that aspired to recover some of the catholic traditions of the church. Professor Knights long ago drew attention to the over-production of

*See pp. 78–9, above.
  † The preceding paragraph draws heavily on Collinson, Parts IV and VIII, *passim*.

graduates and consequent graduate unemployment in England in the late sixteenth and early seventeenth centuries.* As a Cardinal in Dekker's *The Whore of Babylon* (1607) pointed out,

> 'All scholars that do eat
> The bread of sorrow, want and discontent,'

were potential converts to catholicism. The same point was made in the Parliament of 1610.

The bishops had long been regarded as yes-men of the court, and the high-flyers were rightly suspected of being hostile to Parliament and sympathetic to royal absolutism. 'Have we not sermons made every day to rail upon the fundamental laws of the kingdom?' an M.P. had complained as early as 1610. Another in 1621 said that the bishops, 'if we look not to them, . . . will encroach upon all men's rights and lands in England'. As the Laudian party came to occupy more and more bishoprics and deaneries under Charles I, 'Arminianism' began to have political implications. When a poet applied for permission to reprint in 1637 a poem written twenty years earlier against Gunpowder Plot, he was refused with the ominous words, 'We are not so angry with the papists now as we were 20 years ago.' Yet for saying that Laud was a treasonable papist, in the same year, a man was fined £3,000, exhibited with his ears nailed to the pillory, burned in the forehead with the letters L and R and condemned to hard labour for life. Nor should we leave out of account the economic idiocy of Laud's persecution of foreign protestants, which nearly wrecked the New Draperies. 'The restoring of the property of goods and freedom of the subject is a chief means to maintain religion and obedience to his Majesty,' the future royalist Edmund Waller argued in the Commons in 1641.

The intensity of feeling against popery, Professor Stone points out, worked to the further discredit of the House of Lords, since many peers were, and more were believed to be, papists. The fundamental impossibility of a resolutely pro-papist policy, to which I referred earlier,† was illustrated during the civil war by

---

*L. C. Knights, *Drama and Society in the Age of Jonson* (1937), pp. 324–5.
† See pp. 78–9, above.

Charles I's desire and fear to use Irish Roman Catholic support. He flirted with it sufficiently to get the worst of both worlds. But the complete fiasco of James II's reliance on Ireland forty-five years later suggests that a more resolute policy by his father would not have been more successful. 'To cherish the war under the notion of popery,' John Saltmarsh is alleged to have said in the early forties, 'is the surest means to engage the people.'

Of the strong and passionate popular hatred of bishops any amount of evidence could be brought from the five or six decades before the revolution. Bishops were unashamedly royal nominees. To take away their votes in Parliament, the great lawyer John Selden accurately observed, 'is but the beginning to take them away; for then they can be no longer useful to the King or state'. For their part the bishops, from Whitgift onwards, appealed to 'the self-interest of the property-owning laity',* arguing that those who called for parity in the church would soon call for a like equality in the state; that those who had conscientious scruples about paying tithes would soon have like scruples about paying rent. It was a valid argument: many of those who rallied to the defence of episcopacy in 1641 did so for explicitly social reasons.

3

At the beginning of our period sorcery and witchcraft probably played as big a part as Christianity in the lives of most English men and women. For centuries the church had been satisfied with a formal acceptance of Christianity by the mass of the population, and many pagan practices had been subsumed into catholicism. Older gods became saints, who still protected those who worshipped them: their shrines continued to work wonders and to be objects of veneration and pilgrimage. A great deal of magic was simply taken over and Christianized, since an overwhelmingly agricultural society still craved for the old fertility rituals. (Robert Burton made some of these points in his *Anatomy of Melancholy*.) But when our period begins the increas-

*Collinson, p. 314.

ing importance of urban culture, based on the rational techniques of craftsmen, had set up new tensions. We may think of
the fifteenth to seventeenth centuries as a period in which, all
over Europe, Christianity was going over to the offensive against
paganism, trying, perhaps for the first time, to eliminate its hold
on popular feelings. Persecution of witches started well before
the Reformation, but for a time it was no less fierce in protestant
countries than in catholic. Protestantism was itself a product of
the more rational urban culture, and was hostile to all forms of
magic, black or white, pagan or catholic. In Milton's *Nativity
Ode* Christ drives out demons just as protestants had driven out
saints and fertility gods.

Our period saw the rise and fall of witch persecution. The
first act making witchcraft a capital offence was passed in 1542.
Repealed under Edward, it was re-enacted under Elizabeth, and
more stringently under her successor. But the spread of urban
ways of life and thought, the expansion of the clothing industry,
of fen drainage and of the national market, all undermined the
rural isolation which fostered witchcraft: the new scientific
spirit made even believers in witchcraft, from James I to Increase
Mather, more critical of the evidence in particular cases. By the
eighteenth century witchcraft need no longer be taken seriously
as a threat to the values and so to the cohesion of society. The act
against it was repealed in 1736. Both Bishop Joseph Hall and
John Aubrey dated the decline of belief in spirits, ghosts and
witches from the interregnum. Thomas Edwards in 1646
recorded his horror at hearing 'a sectary plead for toleration of
witches'. The last recorded executions of witches in the home
circuit took place in 1657, a generation or more later in the outlying areas. In Essex, Dr Alan Macfarlane tells us, execution of
witches declined steadily from the sixteen-twenties; prosecutions fell off very sharply after the end of the civil war. The
lesser gentry who formed the majority on grand juries had
ceased to believe in witches.* (In the Dutch Republic there were
no witchcraft trials after 1610.)

Witches, Dr Macfarlane argues, were the victims of a community racked with economic tensions, as well as disease, suffer-

*Cf. p. 123n., below.

ing and sudden death.* (Hence the brief recrudescence of persecution in the political crises of the civil war and just after the restoration.) Belief in the malevolent power of witches, in collusion with Satan, was one of the ways in which evil was explained and yet the goodness of God preserved. Abandonment of this belief in the seventeenth century, at least among the educated, was part of an intellectual revolution, the emergence of a more scientific view of the world. Those parsons who argued that scepticism about witchcraft would lead to atheism had a point. For if witches and the devil were not the cause of evil, either God was to blame, or else a universe had to be conceived in which God and the devil did not intervene directly. Either seemed atheism to those who held the traditional anthropocentric view. 'No spirit, no God,' wrote Henry More in his *Antidote Against Atheism* of 1653. Francis Osborn thought this scepticism a triumph of lay common sense over the clergy. But it was also part of a religious revolution. The feelings of sin and guilt to which a hostile and uncontrollable environment gave rise were no longer purged communally by ceremonies and scapegoats: they were internalized. So they generated the driving moral energy and sense of individual responsibility which alone made it possible to begin to control that environment. Puritan self-accusations, the Puritan sense of guilt, were part of the price paid for a more rational and scientific view of the universe.†

Witches were normally found among the poorer members of their communities. 'Such as are in great misery and poverty,' declared a pamphlet of 1612, 'such the devil allures to follow him.' Richard Baxter made a similar observation towards the end of the century. Some believed that witches could not harm those who were generous to the poor. Many leaders of peasant revolt in our period claimed to be sent by God. Some of them may have been sent by the God of the witches rather than by Jehovah. Quakers were often alleged by their enemies to be witches, and so was John Bunyan: similar accusations had been made earlier

---

*I am most grateful to Mr Macfarlane for permission to draw on his Oxford D.Phil. thesis, 'Witchcraft Prosecutions in Essex, 1560–1680: A Sociological Analysis' (1967), which I hope will soon be published.

†Cf. pp. 204–6, below.

against the Waldensians, the Lollards, German Anabaptists, Familists, and by episcopal propagandists against Elizabethan Puritans. Charges of sexual promiscuity made against some left-wing sects during the interregnum recall similar accusations against witches. But witchcraft was equally often associated with popery, and a Parliamentarian newspaper of 1645 declared that all witches were pro-royalist; we should not make too much of any of these suggestions. Nevertheless, the successes of early Quakerism in the North of England, as later of Wesleyanism in Wales and Cornwall, may have owed something to the decline of magical religion in those areas. It is an interesting coincidence that May Day, which Puritan preachers hated for its pagan orgies and the City fathers feared for its prentice riots, is today celebrated by international labour. It began in America, in whose revolution 'liberty poles', descended from the maypole, had played a symbolic part.

8

FROM PEASANTS' REVOLTS
TO REVOLUTION

> The growth of the people of England, since the ruins . . . of
> the nobility and the clergy, came in the reign of Queen Eliza-
> beth to more than stood with the interest or indeed the nature
> or possibility of a well-founded or durable monarchy. . . .
> There remained nothing to the destruction of a monarchy, re-
> taining but the name, more than a prince who by contending
> should make the people to feel those advantages which they
> could not see. . . . The dissolution of this government caused
> the [civil] war, not the war the dissolution of this government.
> JAMES HARRINGTON, Oceana (*1656*)

IN our period England was notorious throughout Europe for the
violence of its politics. The modern sociologist, Pitirim Sorokin,
has calculated that between 1450 and 1640 there were more
internal disturbances in England than in any other European
country. He may exaggerate; but between 1558 and 1688 the
only English sovereign who had not lost one of his parents at the
hands of the executioner was Charles I; and Charles himself was
to suffer his grandmother's fate. In the eighteenth century there
were the 1715 and the 1745, and a succession of lesser riots.

As late as the fifteen-nineties the rich still feared that rogues
and vagabonds would embolden the poor to say 'they must not
starve, they will not starve', and proceed to direct action. 'What
can rich men do against poor men if poor men rise and hold
together?' a labourer asked in Essex in 1594.* But the prolonged
depression of the twenties and thirties left a cowed and dispirited
populace. The Poor Law, flogging and houses of correction had
broken the spirit of the poor.

In the countryside, as we saw,† the peasantry had ceased to be
a homogeneous class. Well-to-do yeomen and husbandmen

---

* I owe this quotation to the kindness of Dr Alan Macfarlane.
† See pp. 70–71, above.

shared the economic interests of the gentry rather than of the very poor. They went to the same schools as gentlemen, came to share their outlook and were prepared to follow their lead. This split in the peasantry, and alignment of the richer peasants with the gentry and merchants, was to be of crucial importance when the revolution came. After 1660 conservatives looking back thought that the grammar schools were the breeding ground of Parliamentarians. But not of Levellers: at the vital turning-point of the revolution, 1647–53, the gentry retained a leadership which it may have learnt, literally, by going to school.

In *Arcadia* Sir Philip Sidney had shrewdly observed that 'the peasants would have the gentlemen destroyed; the citizens . . . would but have them reformed'. Relieved of fear of lower-class revolt, splits within the propertied class became less inhibited. Elizabeth had managed to retain within the Privy Council spokesmen of two alternative policies – the conservative and the radical, Hatton and Leicester. But the growing dependence of the aristocracy on court pickings intensified the struggle for a monopoly of court favour. Essex carried his quarrel from the Privy Council down to the House of Commons, and in 1601 Cecil complained that 'Parliament matters are ordinarily talked of in the streets'. Essex's fatuous attempt to win a monopoly of patronage by *coup d'état* ended the balance within the Privy Council: henceforth control of patronage was normally monopolized, first by Cecil, then by the Howards, then by Buckingham. Driven out of the Privy Council and the hope of capturing the sovereign's ear, the 'outs' necessarily turned to Parliament. After 1629, when this forum for criticizing the king's advisers was closed, they had to contemplate even appealing to the people at large.*

As the social basis of the court narrowed, so its policy changed. It is no accident that the system of industrial regulation and control was tightened up from the fifteen-nineties. With it the opposition of the J.P. class, increasing in self-consciousness and awareness of their own cohesion, grew too, with the Commons as its forum. (Memories did not need to be so very long. Sir Francis Knollys, who sat in the Reformation Parliament of 1529–36, was

* I owe this point to my friend and former pupil Mr Peter Clark.

still an M.P. in 1593, when he could have met men who were to sit in the Long Parliament of 1640.) The men of property were reconstructing their country in a way the government was powerless to do. They were endowing schools and colleges, in order to open careers to the talented; they paid vast sums towards relief of the poor, though they resented being rated for this purpose; they subsidized lecturers, though they refused to pay increased tithes;* they opposed Ship Money because not voted by their representatives in the House of Commons, though they were soon to pay far larger sums to the Long Parliament; with a minimum of government encouragement they invested their savings in building an overseas empire.

James and Charles had Tudor precedents for collecting benevolences, exploiting the Court of Wards, fining for breach of obsolete statutes, using legal technicalities against individuals. But the social context had changed. 'The balance of the constitution' had also been a social balance, between the absolute power of the crown (to be used against feudal or peasant revolt) and the absolute rights, especially property rights, of the men of substance. This balance had been based on a convergence of interests and views.† As the social balance tilted, first James and then Charles had to produce theoretical defences of their prerogative, which laid them open to criticism. Wentworth emphasized that the king was the keystone of the social arch precisely because this aspect of the monarchy as the defender of property and privilege was being forgotten. Shakespeare in *King Lear* and *Timon of Athens*, Burton in his *Anatomy of Melancholy*, call the whole basis of the state and its justice in question. Hostility between court and City is amply documented in the drama of the period; it became more intense after about 1614, with the decline of the popular theatre and the ascendancy of the very class-conscious coterie theatre.

In 1622 the High Court of Chivalry was revived, to protect the privileges of the ruling class. Its activities in prosecuting rude remarks about peers intensified under Charles I's personal

*See Hill, 1964, pp. 89–90.

†B. Manning, 'The Nobles, the People and the Constitution', *Past and Present*, IX, pp. 50–64.

government, when proprietary colonies were deliberately used to subsidize the aristocracy. The game laws were more fiercely enforced in the sixteen-thirties, at least by the Council in the Marches: 'concern for the landowning class would seem to have triumphed over any interest in social justice'.* At the same time the government sought to co-operate with a narrow circle of financial capitalists, much as the Emperor Charles V had used the Fuggers. The merchant Lionel Cranfield was given a chance to rationalize government finance after 1616; he was disgraced in 1624. The sixteen-twenties have been called the era of Burlamachi, the Italian financier: he was bankrupt by 1633. The customs farmers followed.

In this decade the government came to rely more and more on the church, the nearest thing to an independent bureaucracy. Hence in 1641 we find even future royalists attacking bishops. The Root and Branch Petition said that bishops had encouraged the clergy to 'despise the temporal magistracy [i.e. J.P.s], the nobles and gentry of the land'. The monarchy was thus striving to win independence of the class whose interests it had so successfully represented in the preceding century. In 1638, for instance, Sir Thomas Wiseman – for slandering the Lord Keeper and the Court of Star Chamber – was fined £10,000 with £7,000 damages, deprived of his baronetcy and degraded from the order of knighthood; his ears were cut off, he was pilloried and imprisoned during the king's pleasure. This was not the way in which gentlemen expected to be treated. There was no longer any single way of defending the old order to the satisfaction of the whole ruling class. Charles's was one way, but it alienated a section of the aristocracy and gentry. When they revolted, they had the support of those wider sections of the population who felt that Charles's personal government endangered 'religion, liberty and property'. So successful was this support that ultimately it forced most of the aristocracy and some of the gentry back to the monarchical fold. But by then the floodgates were open.

We cannot often see individual members of the gentry reacting

*Penry Williams, 'The Activity of the Council in the Marches under the early Stuarts', *Welsh Historical Review*, I, p. 141.

to the new emphasis in government policy, though the reaction of the class as a whole is clear enough. But in one instance we can document a personal change of heart. Some time between 1597 and 1600 Sir Francis Hubert, moved by the famine and starvation of those years, denounced corn-hoarding and called for government action against it:

> 'But neither fear of God nor love of men,
> Nor common care of public misery,
> Can cause compassionate respect in them;
> For they are branned in their iniquity,
> And must be bridled by authority.
>> And therefore they that wield the state at will
>> Must by coercive means restrain such ill.'

But when revising his poem for publication in 1629 he had become aware of the danger that government intervention would frustrate private initiative; and he inserted a stanza to make this clear:

> 'But now I must not be misunderstood;
> I do not pass a heavy censure here
> Upon such men as for the general good
> Store up the plenty of a fruitful year
> And keep it safe till more cause doth appear
>> To vent the same; and when such cause shall be
>> As they were frugal, so they must be free.'

Thirty years earlier he had happily envisaged state action against free trade; by 1629 he had become more concerned with the freedom of the 'frugal'.* Many men had followed the same intellectual path, by 1640 if not by 1629.

---

*Ed. B. Mellor, *The Poems of Sir Francis Hubert* (Hong Kong University Press, 1961), p. 288. A similar fascinating change is the deletion of two stanzas in which Hubert made Edward II accuse Piers Gaveston and his mother of witchcraft, and six stanzas in which the poet speculated on the nature of witchcraft (pp. 58–9, 283). Hubert was an Essex man, living in the county until he sold his estates and settled in London in 1614. His growing doubts seem to have been shared by the Essex gentry (see p. 116, above).

Part Three

THE REVOLUTION

I

THE CIVIL WAR

> What will not an oppressed, rich and religious people do to be
> delivered from all kinds of oppression, both spiritual and tem-
> poral, and to be restored to purity and freedom in religion, and
> to the just liberty of their persons and estates? – RICHARD
> OVERTON, A Remonstrance of Many Thousand Citizens,
> *1646*

> Commissary-General Ireton: The liberty of all those that have
> the permanent interest, . . . that is provided for. And liberty
> cannot be provided for in a general sense if property be pre-
> served. – *Putney Debates in the Army Council, 1647*

I

THE English revolution, like the revolt of the Netherlands
eighty years earlier, and the French revolution one hundred and
fifty years later, started with a revolt of the nobles. Even the
ruling class was dissatisfied with the way Charles I ran the
country. By 1640 his government had broken down. It had the
greatest difficulty in finding money to pay the troops levied to
oppose the Scots, and the army itself proved most unwilling to
fight. An assembly of peers at York in September 1640 urged
Charles to call another Parliament. This meant surrender, as
Charles very well knew: in May he had dissolved the Short
Parliament after a three weeks' session because it put forward
demands which he found intolerable. The King still hoped to be
able to outwit and outmanoeuvre the opposition when he finally
summoned Parliament to meet in November 1640. Faced with
the stubborn refusal of the King to compromise, the equally
uncompromising Parliamentary leaders had to look for support
outside, in the country at large.

The Long Parliament impeached and executed Charles I's
ministers, Strafford and Laud. Others fled into exile. Star
Chamber, High Commission, the Councils in the North and in
Wales, the Court of Wards, were all abolished. Taxation without

Parliament's consent was declared illegal. The government's whole repressive machinery and its censorship collapsed. In November 1640 William Prynne and other victims of Charles's tyranny made a triumphal entry into London on return from prison: no magistrate dared control the rejoicing crowds, 'so low,' said Clarendon, 'the reputation of the government was fallen'. There were now two centres of power in the country. All the tensions of the preceding decade were suddenly released. Religious sects emerged from underground and assembled publicly; an orgy of pamphleteering began; there were riots against enclosure in many areas, riots against papists. All who had grievances looked to Parliament for redress: the petitions of this period may be compared with the *cahiers* which expressed popular dissatisfaction at the beginning of the French Revolution. As long as Parliament had neither confidence in nor control over the King it could not afford to alienate any potential friends in the country. So there was a unique period of liberty.

The use that the lower orders made of this liberty helped the king to get a party, to fight for the traditional, ordered, hierarchical society in which the king was keystone of an arch whose pillars were the gentry and the church. Many M.P.s who in 1640–41 opposed the royal system of government of the preceding decade swung round to support him when they faced the alternative. The maintenance of monarchy was essential: there were hardly any republicans among the propertied class. But there was no constitutional machinery for controlling the king: Pym appealed to the people, stirring up popular pressure on Parliament to force Charles to agree to specific measures. Votes were printed and sent down to constituencies: the Grand Remonstrance of November 1641 was from the first designed for distribution to the general public. In the heightened state of public excitement this was very dangerous. Many M.P.s decided, when they had to decide, that it was better to trust an untrustworthy king than to risk the even less known dangers of continued popular unrest. Parliament was able to fight a civil war because enough M.P.s felt confidence in their ability to lead the movement of revolt; but always this anxiety remained.

During the war, the quarrel between 'Presbyterians' and 'Independents' was between those who wanted to rely on Scottish help to bring about a compromise peace with the king, and those who wanted all-out victory even at the price of religious toleration and arming the people. The Independents forced the Self-Denying Ordinance through Parliament, which deprived peers and M.P.s of their military commands (though Oliver Cromwell and a few others kept theirs) and gave the opportunity for a reorganization of the army (the New Model Army, 1645). Many local quarrels were summed up by the divisions in the House of Commons. A 'Presbyterian' M.P. said of his 'Independent' rivals: 'the mean and beggarly followers on the other side were those who undid us, for they commonly ... having been merchants and being men of mean fortunes were not so sensible of the destruction of the kingdom as we who had estates to lose'. 'Very mean men' have been entrusted with the government of the county, complained the gentry of Glamorganshire in February 1646. There were similar complaints from the 'natural rulers' everywhere. In 1648 the gentry of Dorset demanded 'that our ancient liberties may not lie at the mercy of those that have none'; and they contrasted with Parliamentary committee men who had no liberties 'men of visible estates', by whom they wished to be governed. Parliament's appeal to the people and the Independents' advocacy of religious toleration had borne bitter fruit for the men of property. 'God uses the common people and the multitude,' Hanserd Knollys wrote, 'to proclaim that the Lord God omnipotent reigneth.' The democratic possibilities of such doctrines are clear. But some thought it was John Pym rather than God who was using the common people.

The quarrel which followed between 'Independents' and Levellers was between those who were satisfied with the traditional political institutions of the country provided Parliament's control over the king could somehow be enforced, and those who wanted a considerable extension of the franchise, the abolition of monarchy and House of Lords. A subsequent quarrel between Levellers and Diggers was between those who were satisfied with traditional property relations provided small men were protected against the powerful, and those who wanted private property ultimately to be abolished.

Since the Levellers never came to power their quarrel with the small group of Diggers was on paper only. But in the other disputes the opposition had always to appeal for popular support, and so the society remained uniquely 'open' and free until 1649, when the generals first seized political power from their 'Presbyterian' and royalist rivals, and then forcibly suppressed the rank and file movement which sympathized with the Levellers. Important changes were still to be brought about under army rule, and there was still greater liberty for more people than before 1640 or after 1660: 'those halcyon days of prosperity, liberty and peace,' said a Baptist looking back to the fifties, 'those Oliverian days of liberty'. But by 1649 the main problems had been solved, though the solutions were conservative rather than radical. 'The Protectorate showed that the English Revolution had stopped half-way,' as Miss Coate put it.* Once opposition from right and left, from royalists and Levellers, had been suppressed, the army itself became superfluous, expensive and potentially dangerous. After repeated attempts the generals failed to find an electorate which would support them.

So the monarchy was restored with the old problem of how the king was in the last resort to be controlled still unsolved. Charles II was clever enough never to force the issue: when his more foolish brother did force it, the immediate and overwhelming response of the men of property showed how completely the problems had *in fact*, if not in constitutional theory, already been settled. We must see the period 1660–88 as one in which the balance was tilted to the right, as in 1646–60 it had been tilted to the left. In 1688–89 stable equilibrium was reached, all the more successfully in that by then the democratic movement, still active in 1659–60, had been pulverized into submission, and barely raised its head in 1688. But on many occasions earlier it seemed as though something like the 1688 solution might be arrived at – in 1641, if Charles had agreed with Parliament, in 1647 if he had agreed with the army, in 1654 or

*M. Coate, 'The Social Theories and Action of English Dissenters in the 17th century', *The Way*, III (1941), p. 56.

1657 if Cromwell had accepted the offer of the crown, in 1679 if limitations had been placed on a popish successor.

Within this broad framework we can see how the civil war which began with a revolt of the nobles ended with a struggle between opposed social classes.

2

The causes of the demand for a Parliament in 1640, a royalist account tells us, were (1) Court jealousies of Laud and Strafford: (2) The 'country nobility, long discontented with their court banishment', wanted access to office, which they thought they could attain through Parliament. (3) Gentlemen, freeholders and all sorts of people wished to be eased of monopolies, taxes and tyranny. (4) 'The lecturing, house-creeping ministers' wanted the lands of the hierarchy to be confiscated and used to finance better payment of the clergy and the establishment of a new discipline. (5) Sectaries and (6) common lawyers both opposed ecclesiastical discipline. The lawyers in Parliament were 'most of them recorders, and so servants to incorporations'. (7) The country people generally fancied that a Parliament would free them from paying tithes. (8) London merchants hoped for some increase of trading, and hated monopolies. (9) 'All sorts of people dreamed of an Utopia and infinite liberty, especially in matters of religion.' The interest of that account is its many-sidedness: it shows a society ripe for revolution, for a complex series of inter-connected reasons. It is much less over-simplified than the analyses of some historians.*

If we look at the years 1640–41, when a nearly united House of Commons faced the crumbling royal government, we see a division between court gentry and country gentry. But this will not explain why men who opposed Strafford in 1641 fought for the King in 1642. Nor should we look only at the Commons. In 1640 a majority of the electorate was united in opposing the personal government of Charles I. The borough of Newcastle returned two M.P.s who were to fight on opposite sides in the

* [Anon.], *Persecutio Undecima* (1648), pp. 7–8, 33.

civil war; but in 1640 they cooperated against Strafford.* By 1642 a split in the gentry had been forced from below; when M.P.s had to choose sides, individual, personal and psychological as well as religious considerations came into play.

It was, as the Duke of Newcastle put it, 'neither the church nor the laws that kept up the King so long, but part of the nobility and gentry'. 'The strength of our party,' wrote a Parliamentarian pamphleteer, 'consists mainly in honest tradesmen, the gentry are naught, and the country people are for the most part blinded and misled by their malevolent hedge-priests.' In Somerset 'all the prime gentry' were for the King; only clothiers and freeholders for Parliament. In Essex the cloth workers, 'being poor and populous', were 'naturally mutinous and bold'. Their employers were 'sordid men', who equally naturally supported Parliament, 'whose constant style was tenderness of commerce. . . . The clothiers through the whole kingdom were rebels by their trade.' 'For 'tis notorious,' said a bishop after 1660, 'that there is not any sort of people so inclinable to seditious practices as the trading part of a nation. . . . The quarrel was chiefly hatched in the shops of tradesmen, and cherished by the zeal of prentice-boys and City gossips.'

Such accounts of social divisions could be multiplied indefinitely: townsmen, yeomen, freeholders and middling men, plus some gentry, against the nobility, most of the gentry, their tenants and 'the rabble'. Even more interesting are the reasons which contemporaries gave for the divisions. The King, said one, was supported by those of 'the nobility and gentry . . . whose honour is predominant over their reason and religion', and by 'men of implicit faith, whose conscience is much regulated by their superiors'. Parliament had the allegiance of men 'of a lower state', 'men of industry and labour, that love labour, that love freedom and to be something themselves'. Gentlemen, said an account of Gloucestershire, 'for the most part care not to render themselves the slaves of princes, that they might also rule over their neighbours as vassals. . . . The common people addicted to the King's service,' he added, 'have come out of blind Wales and other dark corners of the land.'

*Howell, *Newcastle upon Tyne and the Puritan Revolution*, pp. 126–7.

Parliament's main backing came from towns and rural industrial areas. But there were also struggles within towns (London, Bristol, Norwich, Newcastle and many others) between oligarchies (usually royalist) and rank-and-file citizens, often in alliance with yeomen and artisans outside their walls. In Cambridge the town was Parliamentarian, the university royalist. The government of the episcopal town of Chester, a port slowly decaying as the Dee silted up, was royalist, though there was much support for Parliament among citizens: Liverpool, which was to replace Chester as a port, was overwhelmingly Parliamentarian. Even in distant Carlisle 'the rascal rout' tried to capture the town for Parliament. 'We inland tradesmen,' said one of them, 'ventured all we had for the Parliament.' He contrasted this with the more lukewarm attitude of greater merchants. After 1660 town corporations were purged by commissions nominated by the neighbouring gentry, and dissenting ministers were excluded from corporations by the Five Mile Act. In the navy the rank and file declared for Parliament and chased away the few royalist gentlemen captains even before Charles raised his standard at Nottingham.

In explaining the formation of a royalist party, the official historian of the Long Parliament admitted that 'another thing which seemed to trouble some who were not bad men was that extreme licence which the common people, almost from the very beginning of the Parliament, took to themselves of reforming without authority, order or decency'. 'The common people,' the Earl of Clarendon agreed, 'were in all places grown to that barbarity and rage against the nobility and gentry ... that it was not safe for any to live at their houses' who opposed Parliament. There are many examples of bitter hostility to the new aspirations of ordinary people voiced by royalist aristocrats. Lord Poulett nearly got himself lynched by the people of Sherborne for saying that after a royalist victory no yeoman should be allowed to possess more than £5 a year. 'The meaner sort of people,' thought the royalist Sir John Oglander, 'are always apt to rebel and mutiny ... and if you give them an inch they will take an ell.'

One fear which beset gentlemen, on either side, was that their divisions might be the occasion for the setting up of something like a democratic third party. Once the prerogative courts were abolished the battle for the commons was on. The commoners gained an initial advantage in many areas by simply helping themselves. Men broke down the Earl of Suffolk's fences in Essex in April 1643, crying that if they took not advantage of this time they should never have the opportunity again. The outbreak of civil war stimulated a great peasant movement against enclosure.* In November 1643 a gentleman of Kent feared lest 'the multitude (that senseless and furious beast), ... would destroy all government both in church and state', or bring in one in which they 'may be able to tyrannize over their betters, whom naturally they have ever hated and in their hearts despised'. It was therefore, he thought, high time for 'all gentlemen ... to maintain episcopal government', since presbyterianism would 'equalize men of mean conditions with the gentry'. By 1644–45 in several south-western counties Clubmen rose up who aimed to keep both armies out of their counties, and the dreaded revolt of the common people seemed to have started. 'This third party,' a Parliamentarian newspaper wrote in 1645, 'hath peeped for many months in many corners. . . . They will have an army without a king, a lord or a gentleman almost.' The fears that the Clubmen aroused certainly helped to get the New Model Army accepted by Parliament in 1645 as the lesser evil, since it would end the war more quickly.

*So far studied seriously only by the Soviet historian S. I. Arkhangelsky, whose work has not been translated.

2

THE REVOLUTION IN GOVERNMENT

All relations were confounded by the several sects in religion, which discountenanced all forms of reverence and respect. . . . Parents had no name of authority over their children, nor children any obedience or submission to their parents; but everyone did that which was good in his own eyes. This unnatural antipathy had its first rise from the beginning of the rebellion. . . . The relation between masters and servants had been long since dissolved by the Parliament. . . . In the place of generosity, a vile and sordid love of money was entertained as the truest wisdom, and anything lawful that would contribute to being rich. – EDWARD, EARL OF CLARENDON, Life

I

THE sixteen-forties and fifties marked the end of medieval and Tudor England. The state which Thomas Cromwell had reconstructed in the fifteen-thirties was swept away in 1641 – the central government's power to rule without Parliament, its control over the localities. This revolution in government was much more important than that of a century earlier: the old state was not restored in 1660, only its trappings. The prerogative courts did not return, and so the sovereignty of Parliament and common law remained. The Privy Council henceforth had no effective control over local government. Taxation and therefore ultimately policy were controlled by Parliament. The government of the country for many years by the House of Commons and its committees was an experience that could never be forgotten: so were the execution of Charles I, the abolition of bishops and House of Lords, the existence of an English republic whose foreign and imperial policies were as impressively successful as those of the Stuart monarchy had been inglorious.

In 1658 a pamphleteer, looking back, said that if the Commonwealth had survived it would have surpassed Sparta, Athens,

Carthage and Venice, and would have required 'not less than the whole world for its portion'. Curiously enough this estimate had been anticipated by Cardinal Mazarin, who in 1646 said that an English republic would be

> an evil without comparison for France, and it would be much better for us if the King of Great Britain was re-established in his former authority, even if he was certain to be our enemy. . . . For . . . in a republic, taxation being voluntary and coming by consent and by agreement of everyone for a policy unanimously agreed, they will pay without murmurings or regrets whatever is necessary to make that policy succeed.

Mazarin was clearly thinking of the Dutch republic; but the military and naval strength of the English Commonwealth must have confirmed him in his economic interpretation of republicanism. France certainly did all she could to encourage the revival of monarchical forms under Cromwell, and then the even more satisfactory restoration of Charles II. But memories of the Commonwealth remained. 'England is become a warlike nation,' a pamphleteer wrote in 1660, 'furnished with gallant men both for sea and land, is courted by great princes, is a terror to our enemies, a protection to our friends; and, if we could agree among ourselves, it is a happy nation.'

'If Aristotle . . . were to come again to the world he could not find words to explain the manner of this government,' the French Ambassador in Charles II's London wrote to Louis XIV. 'It has a monarchical appearance, and there is a king, but it is very far from being a monarchy.' In the next decades the appearances sometimes deluded kings into thinking them realities. But the settlement of 1688–89 reasserted the supremacy of the non-monarchical elements in the constitution. The result confirmed all Mazarin's worst fears. The financial power of the community was concentrated in the hands of men – now agreed among themselves – who used it to carry out a ruthlessly aggressive commercial policy – against France.

2

The revolutionary decades completed the unification of England. The Tudor policy of eliminating local franchises was completed by razing the castles of great lords like the Marquis of Worcester during or after the civil war, and the walls of towns in 1662. Close military and financial relations between Parliament and its county committees were followed by the overriding of county authority by the New Model Army. Centralization was maintained in the years of military rule. The abolition of the Councils in the North and in Wales, and the military conquest of these royalist areas, made possible a final unification of the English legal system around the common law, the economic dominance of London over the privileges of local corporations and the spreading of Puritanism and other London ideas to the North and West. New inns grew up on the main roads to London, for gentlemen coming up to town and for migrant craftsmen. In 1653 the House of Commons at last was made representative of all England by the inclusion of members for the city and county palatine of Durham (re-enacted 1673). The Union with Scotland in 1652 – envisaged over a century earlier by Thomas Cromwell and the Edwardian radicals – extended this Londonization to the northern kingdom: dissolved in 1660, union returned in 1707, and with it Scottish M.P.s at Westminster. The Cromwellian conquest of Ireland, and the expropriation of Irish Catholic landowners, was not reversed in 1660, though it needed to be confirmed by the Williamite wars of the nineties, after which a separate Irish Parliament ceased to exist too.

This victory of South and East over North and West in the civil war led, paradoxically, to a reversal of the growing economic dominance of London, against which the outports had been struggling at least since 1604. During the civil war the monarchy could no longer protect the companies, and a period of virtual free trade ensued. (This was one reason why London companies were anxious for an early peace with the King, even if by compromise.) But under the Protectorate the East India Company and the Merchant Adventurers recovered government support, in return for loans. All accounts agree on the flourishing state of

London's trade in the early fifties. Yet the fillip given to colonial trade by the Navigation Acts undoubtedly promoted the prosperity of outports like Exeter, Plymouth, Bristol and Liverpool in the late seventeenth and eighteenth centuries; just as its stimulus to ship-building helped the shipyards of Whitby, Scarborough, Hull and Newcastle. The percentage of English shipping tonnage owned by Londoners was 43·3 in 1702, 29·9 in 1788.

As water communications improved, from the mid-century, the shift of industry and population to the North and West which we associate with the Industrial Revolution was already beginning. Darby transferred his ironworks to Coalbrookdale in Shropshire in search of fuel, Crowley in 1684 shifted to Sunderland in search of cheaper labour for his naval contracts. Worcestershire and Cheshire salt-mining developed apace in the later seventeenth century. The silk and hosiery industries moved from London to the Midlands. Coal, iron and lead mining expanded in Wales from the mid-century, the tin-plate industry after 1700. The West was particularly well placed for industries processing colonial raw materials and supplying colonial markets.

As clover brought marginal land in the North and West under cultivation,* squatters were attracted from all over England, as well as migrants from Wales, Scotland and Ireland. Nearly all the peasant houses which survive in the North and West of England date from after the revolutionary decades; many of those of West Riding weavers date from immediately after, though as late as 1698 Celia Fiennes commented on the paucity of stone buildings in the North. (In the later seventeenth century much better stone housing, and some brick houses, began to appear in the South and East too: the historian of rural housing sees in the forties and fifties a more complete break with the past than anything since the Reformation.†) The demand for labour in the North seems to have stimulated a population explosion there, which itself contributed to making the Industrial Revolution possible.‡ In the eighteenth century London's exclusive

*See p. 152, below.

†M. W. Barley, *The English Farmhouse and Cottage* (1961), pp. 184, 239.

‡See pp. 254-5, below.

political influence recedes with the rising importance of centres like Birmingham, Liverpool, Manchester, Bristol, Glasgow and the West Riding of Yorkshire.

3

Between 1649 and 1660 the House of Lords was abolished, and privileges of peers were in abeyance. They were liable to normal legal penalties. In 1653 two peers were sentenced to be burnt in the hand. At the restoration peers recovered their immunity from corporal punishment and arrest for debt, their right to be tried by one another. But privileges derived merely from peerage were slowly whittled away. The Test Act of 1673 imposed the first statutory oath demanded of peers: hitherto their word of honour had sufficed. After squabbles in the sixties the Lords lost their right to act as a court of first instance. The old crime of *scandalum magnatum* was falling into abeyance by the end of the century with the decline of the High Court of Chivalry. Towards the end of our period, which is often thought of as the heyday of the Whig aristocracy, Arthur Young contrasted 'the honours, power and profit derived to the nobility from the feudal system' in France with 'anything known in England since the Revolution or the Long Parliament of 1640'.

Feudal state declined too in this new commercial world, where successful peers were men of business too. 'In times past,' a Deputy Postmaster General grumbled in the seventies, '(before the wicked rebellion), a nobleman or a great officer of state or court would have half a score or a dozen gentlemen to attend him, but now all is shrunk into a *valet de chambre*, a page, and five or six footmen; and this is part of our cursed reformation.' The Cavalier Parliament rejected a bill to restore the Heralds' College's coercive jurisdiction; henceforth the right to bear arms depended on social consent, not law. The last Heralds' Visitation took place in 1686. The attempt to preserve a fictitious blue blood against the invasion of commercial wealth could no longer be kept up now that dukes were marrying merchants' daughters. Many traditional Parliamentary families disappeared from national politics in the forties and fifties and after, owing to impoverishment or failure to produce a male heir.*

The most important feature of the restoration for our purposes was its anti-democratic character. Lords came back to reinforce social snobbery, bishops to enforce religious inequality. The restoration put paid to the possibility of any extension of the franchise, any widening of the pale of the constitution. The extrusion of nonconformists from local government by the Clarendon Code intensified the dominance of the landed oligarchy and its hangers-on. The political and social disabilities imposed at the restoration have left their mark upon English dissent to this day. Puritans ceased to be a revolutionary party and became a group of pacifist sects, sectarian and provincial-minded. The educational reforms of the revolutionary decades, at all levels, were reversed, except in so far as the Royal Society conserved something of the scientific tradition which had been the glory of Oxford in the fifties. 'Probably no event in English history,' wrote the historian of dissenting academies, 'has had so far-reaching and disastrous an effect upon education as the restoration.'

The breakdown of royal government had left the natural rulers of the countryside unmolested by the driving force of the Privy Council. During the interregnum, control of county committees had been seized by men of lesser rank, who did not shrink from radical measures, and this was followed by the rule of low-born major-generals. But in 1660 the reunited gentry were left in complete control of the militia, the only effective armed force in the country, and of rural local government, with none of the supervision from Whitehall that Laud and the major-generals had exercised, though there were unpleasant moments under James II when nearly half the J.P.s in England and Wales were replaced and Judge Jeffreys tried to reassert the authority of the central government. J.P.s succeeded to many of the powers of the moribund church courts – e.g. in compelling the lower orders to attend church on Sundays. 'Now we may do what we will,' a Quaker makes a J.P. say in 1660, 'and who shall control

*D. Brunton and D. H. Pennington, *Members of the Long Parliament* (1954), p. 18.

us? . . . Now will we build our decayed churches and restore our fallen worship: now will we repair the broken fences of our parks, that we may have game to the full.' In fact the iniquitous game laws date mainly from the restoration period. They established new privileges and disarmed the lower classes. An act of 1671 forbade anyone below the rank of £100 freeholder to kill 'game' on his own lands, and gave gamekeepers the right to enter and search houses of the lower orders, and to confiscate unauthorized weapons. During the civil war deer parks had been thrown open: soldiers and villagers had enjoyed unaccustomed feasts of venison. Many parks were never effectively restored: the gentry no longer confined hunting to their own land but chased the fox across country, regardless of ownership. The tyranny of the squire over his village, reinforced by the sycophancy of the parson, was virtually unchallenged for the remainder of our period. 'As J.P.s the gentry put down the riots of their labourers,' wrote Mr Harding, 'and as M.P.s they passed the statutes which allowed them to do so.' 'The honour of being trusted and the pleasure of being feared,' wrote Petty ironically in 1662, 'hath been thought a competent reward' for unpaid J.P.s. Sir John Oglander, more frankly, told his son that the office of J.P. was 'a place that may be a means to raise thy fortunes, being a place of gain'. All this did nothing to increase respect for the law among the lower classes.

In 1668 the Parliamentarian town of Liverpool, in which 'riches and pride is so predominant', had 'a perfect antipathy' against 'all gentlemen'. Nevertheless, the neighbouring gentleman who said this was shrewd enough to realize that 'if they prosper you must thrive, and if the town sink you must drown. . . . Therefore in the name of God let them love you,' he urged his son, 'and you them, and twenty of the greatest men in the county cannot wrong you.' It is an unusual use of the word 'love'; but it helps to explain how the gentry used an alliance with the burghers whom they despised to free themselves from their feudal superiors; and how they battened on and profited by the sordid economic activities of the towns. It throws a flood of light on late seventeenth- and eighteenth-century society. The relationship differed markedly from that of the sixteenth century, when towns could get privileges only through patrons.

4

Attempts had been made during the interregnum to eliminate rotten boroughs: no corporations were represented in the radical Barebones Parliament, and the Instrument of Government greatly reduced their number, as well as disfranchising poorer freeholders. It established an electorate of £200 men, independent middle-class voters. The old franchise was restored in 1659, and confirmed at the restoration. Charles II concentrated on re-modelling corporation charters, always in the interests of a narrow oligarchy; and James II tried to pack or influence corporations as the most hopeful way of obtaining a favourable Parliament, though he also influenced county electorates by wholesale dismissals of J.P.s, lord-lieutenants and deputy-lieutenants. These efforts were apparently so successful that in 1688 William summoned the members of Charles II's Parliaments, not of those which had been called after the great purges of 1681–85. In 1679 the Whigs proposed reviving the £200 franchise, but after 1688 no further attempt to reform the electorate was made: the new firm took over the old institutions. Corporation oligarchies were susceptible to pressure from *any* government: their narrow electorates were the basis on which the eighteenth-century system of Parliamentary corruption was reared. The monied men stepped in to control this system, made safe against democracy. 'Nothing is now more common,' remarked a letter-writer in 1675, 'than for members first to buy their [i.e. the electors'] voices and then sell their votes, which are grown very good merchandise at court.'

After 1660 the sects abandoned politics, many of the old revolutionaries emigrated. Those who remained were slowly weeded out as unsuccessful plot succeeded unsuccessful plot. Nevertheless, some continuities can be traced. Under Charles II and James II Whigs seem almost invariably to have had more popular support than Tories: Whigs always favoured the wider franchise in disputed elections. At Windsor in 1640 the vote was extended to all inhabitants. In 1661 it was restricted to mayor, bailiffs and burgesses; in 1679 the Whig Commons resolved that it should be restored to all inhabitants. In London in 1682 the Whigs were supported by the 'rascality and meanest of the people', the Tories by 'the substantiallest and ablest citizens'. Shaftesbury's Green Ribbon Club and the rebel Duke of Monmouth (like the Chartists a century and a half later) had colours of Leveller green. Monmouth's main support came from the clothing areas of the south-west, former Clubmen areas. But after 1688 both Shaftesbury and Monmouth seemed in retrospect, to the victorious Whigs, dangerous radicals who had played frivolously with popular passions.

We perhaps take too much for granted the ease with which the propertied class, thanks to a front-bench agreement between leading Whigs and Tories, painlessly reasserted its control in 1688–89. In part this was due to the pusillanimity of James II, who ran away earlier than he need have done, leaving England without a government; in part it was due to the utter demoralization of the radicals after the defeats of 1685. Yet even at the end of 1687 Gilbert Burnet supposed that 'a rebellion of which he [William] should not retain the command would certainly establish a commonwealth'. In fact social disorder was not far from the surface in 1688–89. There were riots and plunder of the rich in London, Norwich and many other cities, at Brill in the peaceful countryside of Buckinghamshire. Fortunately for the men of property they invited William in time, and he prudently brought a large professional army with him: so there was no danger from the people of England this time. 1689 marks the end of the Good Old Cause as well as of monarchy in the traditional sense of the word.

But memories of the revolution died hard. In 1679–81, and again in 1709–10, the Tory cry was 'No 1641!' In 1690 a lord-lieutenant wrote to another earl that the mayor of Nottingham was not to be trusted with arms. He was an obscure man, formerly a servant of Oliver Cromwell, one of 'a crew of Independents, Presbyterians, Anabaptists and Family of Love' who had been intruded into local government by James II. Such men were henceforth to be kept firmly in their place. Elections were dominated by 'the brawling noise of drunken country curates, bellowing to take care of the churchmen and of the Church of England. "Gentlemen, remember the Roundheads of 41." Forty-one indeed was a scurvy year to 'scandalous clergymen,' added the *Memoirs* of the Newcastle merchant Ambrose Barnes nostalgically. But by 1769 it was safe for Burke to use fear of the lower orders not in order to maintain the *status quo*, but to demand reform. When the gentry 'deserted the freeholders' under Charles I, he argued, 'the body of freeholders got up, and gentlemen were trampled down: they were made slaves to draymen and brewers'.

From 1688 onwards England was, for the propertied class, an exceptionally free society by contemporary European standards. 1688 ensured that henceforth it would be impossible to govern without Parliament, as Charles had done between 1681 and 1685, in contravention of the law, and as James had done after 1686. There were to be no more standing armies, whether radical or popish. The supremacy of common law emerged with the abolition of prerogative courts, but – just to make quite sure – the common lawyers from the interregnum, through new uses of the writs *certiorari* and *mandamus*, developed remedies for the citizen against arbitrary government. The *Habeas Corpus* Act of the Whig Parliament of 1679 protected from arbitrary arrest anyone who had the money and the social confidence to use the writ. After 1701 judges were no longer dependent on the government: juries were not accountable for their verdicts. There was no administrative law; J.P.s administered their own areas in accordance with their conception of local needs. The press was the freest in Europe. But few of these advantages were available for the lower fifty per cent of the population. The abolition of feudal tenures guaranteed the property of landlords; the failure of attempts during the interregnum to win legal stability of tenure for copyholders ensured that the property rights of the poor should not stand in the way of the improvements of the rich.* The defeat of the radicals during the revolution thus helped to harden the formation of England into two nations. Before 1640 the major social division had been between privi-

*See p. 147, below.

leged and unprivileged: now it was between rich and poor, free and unfree, the armigerous and the disarmed, those who commanded the militia and those who were conscripted to fight overseas, those paying for and those subject to the Poor Law. The unfettered sovereignty of J.P.s drawn from the employing class was hardly liberty for their employees.

Liberties were for men of property, and Englishmen of property were in fact freer mentally as well as physically. Sprat in his *History of the Royal Society* spoke of 'men of freer lives' (than artisans), who could approach the technological problems of industry in a more detached and scientific way, since for them they were not 'dull and unavoidable employments'. (Sprat was arguing that there would have to be a great deal of unsuccessful investment in new technological devices before success was realized.) A similar point had been made about politics by Moses Wall, writing to Milton in 1659, to account for the failure of the radical revolution: 'Whilst people are not free but straitened in accommodations for life, their spirits will be dejected and servile.' Industrial and agricultural advance to 'give the body of the nation a comfortable subsistence' was needed before liberty for the mass of the population could be won.

3

THE AGRICULTURAL
REVOLUTION

Do not all strive to enjoy the land? The gentry strive for land,
the clergy strive for land, the common people strive for land;
and buying and selling is an art, whereby people endeavour to
cheat one another of the land. – GERRARD WINSTANLEY,
A New Year's Gift for the Parliament and Army (*1650*)

Seeing we have with joint consent of purse and person conquered [William the Conqueror's] successor Charles, and the
power now is in your hand, the nation's representative, O let
the first thing you do be this, to set the land free! Let the
gentry have their enclosures, . . . and let the common people
have their commons and waste lands quiet to themselves. –
WINSTANLEY, An Appeal to the House of Commons (*1649*)

I

IN agrarian relations the Middle Ages were brought to an end in
1646 by the abolition of feudal tenures and the Court of Wards.
When in April 1660 the Convention Parliament agreed to the return of Charles II, the next business it turned to was confirma-
tion of their abolition.

The importance of this was fourfold. First, landowners were
freed from dependence on the crown,* and governments were
deprived of a source of lucrative perquisites for courtiers.
Secondly, landowners gained absolute ownership of their estates.
During the abortive negotiations of 1610 for abolition of feudal
tenures, Salisbury had promised M.P.s 'you may return into
your counties and tell your neighbours that you have made a
pretty hedge about them'. Thanks to the revolution, this hedge
was now secured. Land was freed from the arbitrary death
duties and spoliation of wardship, and so long-term planning and
investment of capital in estate management were made possible.

The strict settlement, a legal device for entailing land on to the

*See pp. 101–2, above.

eldest son, which we can first trace from 1647, would have been pointless for most landowners without the abolition of feudal tenures the year before. The strict settlement helped land-owners to survive periods of indebtedness without resorting to sale. It led on to the great consolidations of landed property which made the Whig oligarchy of the eighteenth century, and which set younger sons looking for careers in business, in the civil service, the army, the navy, the colonies. It also contributed to the relative depression of the lesser gentry. Harrington and the Levellers during the revolution had attacked primogeniture, and wished to prevent the concentration of landed property. Again we see how decisive for future development was the defeat of the radicals. Entails, said John Aubrey, are 'a good prop for monarchy'.

Thirdly, feudal tenures were abolished upwards only, not downwards. The act of 1660 insisted that it should not be understood to alter or change any tenure by copyhold. Copy-holders obtained no absolute property rights in their holdings, remaining in abject dependence on their landlords, liable to arbitrary death duties which could be used as a means of evicting the recalcitrant. The effect was completed by an act of 1677 which ensured that the property of small freeholders should be no less insecure than that of copyholders, unless supported by written legal title. So most obstacles to enclosure were removed: the agricultural boom of the late seventeenth and eighteenth centuries redounded to the benefit of big landowners and capitalist farmers, not of peasant proprietors, whose extreme poverty, however hard they laboured, was commented upon by observers from Richard Baxter to Arthur Young. The century after the failure of the radicals to win legal security of tenure for the small men is the century in which many small landowners were forced to sell out in consequence of rack-renting, heavy fines, taxation and lack of resources to compete with capitalist farmers.*

*On the importance of the abolition of feudal tenures for English eco-nomic development see H. J. Perkin, 'The Social Causes of the British Industrial Revolution', *Transactions of the Royal Historical Society*, Fifth Series, No. 18, pp. 123–43.

Fourthly, compensation for the Court of Wards came not from a tax on land (as had been proposed in 1610) but from an excise, to which the main contributors were not the gentry, the beneficiaries from the abolition, but the poorer consumers, its victims. And the crown got not the £200,000 compensation which James I had thought inadequate in 1610, when prices were lower, but £100,000. So the dependence of the monarchy on those who voted its taxes was ensured. In yet another respect Thomas Cromwell's state was being dismantled within a century of its construction.

2

During the interregnum lands worth at least £5,500,000 were confiscated and sold, and nearly another £1,500,000 was raised by fines on royalists, many of whom had to sell land in order to pay. Add the effects of heavy taxation, especially on landowners, and we can see what the total result must have been. Tenants had become landlords and landlords tenants, declared a pamphlet of 1654; servants masters and masters servants. But there was no permanent agrarian revolution to the advantage of the really small men, such as Levellers and Diggers wanted, and such as occurred during the French and Russian revolutions. Instead, the interregnum accelerated economic divisions which had been forming in the preceding period. A number of lesser gentry families disappeared, now or in the ensuing century. In the north of England at least the century after 1660 'saw the liquidation . . . of scores of ancient families, lesser gentry and freeholders, and the rise out of the ashes of vast new agglomerations of landed estates'. Hence, Professor Hughes adds, the absolute necessity of a place in the revenue services or the armed forces for the sons of many a declining gentle family, which accounts for much of the politics of this century. Reinvestment in land in the eighteenth century, Professor Ashton reminds us, was sometimes undertaken specifically to regain the footing which a family had lost during the revolution, when merchants had usurped the position of landowners.

Land transfers and heavy taxation led to a significant redistribution of wealth, to profiteering by lawyers, scriveners and bankers engaged in buying and selling land, as well as to its purchase by merchants and government contractors. Interregnum purchasers were understandably anxious to secure quick returns on their highly speculative investments. Winstanley, among others, referred to the 'new (more covetous) gentry'. Close attention to estate management was forced on those landowners who survived, including many royalists, some of whom even profited by a period of quiet recuperation on their estates, immune from heavy court expenditure. Others had losses to recoup when they recovered their lands in 1660 or earlier. All this helped to break down traditional agrarian relationships and substitute those of the market place. On ecclesiastical lands a new leasing policy was deliberately introduced after the restoration: 'The committee for sequestration under new management,' wrote Professor Hughes sardonically.

The abolition of feudal tenures and the whole atmosphere of the interregnum favoured a rational, scientific approach to economic problems. We should not suppose that sentiment had ever overruled economic considerations for the vast majority of landlords. But now such considerations took first place, with the approval of contemporary moralists. The difference between the traditional, feudal attitude and the modern, capitalist one was made clear in 1656 when a peer told his tenants that if they would not carry themselves with justice and affection towards him they would have their rents and entry fines raised. '£10 will do more than most men's love,' the royalist Sir John Oglander advised his son. A peer who did not attend closely to estate management, but left it to 'the government of his servants, by whom he is . . . cheated' was described by Samuel Butler as 'a degenerate noble'.

3

Charles I's government had striven to prevent corn export, even on occasion from one county to another: nothing like that happened after 1641. What Professor Hoskins calls 'a revolution

in corn production from about the middle of the century'
resulted in the supply of corn now being adequate to feed the
towns. The bulk of the landed class was producing for the market, and the activities of middlemen were now probably less
impeded by the government. The Parliament of landlords which
took over political control after 1640 was not interested in preserving a peasantry engaged in subsistence production. From
1654 onwards corn export was permitted when prices were low
in England; from 1670 regardless of price, except in time of
dearth. From 1673 to 1681, the years of resurgent Whiggery in
Parliament, and after its ultimate triumph in 1689, there was a
bounty on the export of corn. By the end of the century corn
exports were worth over £250,000 a year. This stimulus to
export increased the price to home consumers, but it was very
profitable to landlords and farmers. England joined the Baltic
area as the corn-supplier of Europe. To quote Adam Smith:

That security which the laws in Great Britain give to every man that
he shall enjoy the fruits of his own labour, is alone sufficient to make
any country flourish; . . . and this security was perfected by the Revolution [of 1688] much about the same time that the bounty on corn
was established.

Contemporaries attributed to the revolutionary decades a
number of agricultural improvements. Sainfoin, clover, lucerne,
asparagus and artichokes all date from this period. The development of market-gardening and intensive fruit-farming, especially
for the London market, brought about a minor revolution in the
diet of ordinary citizens. Turnips were being grown as a field
crop, and more potatoes. Tobacco too was cultivated in the
fifties, but was prohibited in the interests of colonial production.
Many of the improvements of the later seventeenth and eighteenth centuries were proclaimed in Blyth's *English Improver*
(1649) and the vastly increased literature on agriculture which
began to appear from the forties. Already the crop yields of the
Low Countries and England were well ahead of the rest of
Europe. As historians push the Industrial Revolution forward to
the later eighteenth century, so they pull the agricultural
revolution back into the seventeenth century.

Connected with propaganda for agricultural improvements was a new attitude towards enclosure. Fitful and ineffective as the approach of governments before 1640 had been, they did sometimes try to check enclosure: no government after 1640 ever did so. All questions affecting property were henceforth left to the common law. Changes in interpretation of the law helped to weaken the position of tenants *vis-à-vis* landlords, to the advantage both of enclosers and of landowners with mineral deposits under their lands. These changes resulted from a shift of opinion in the propertied class. At the beginning of the seventeenth century it had been noted that land increased in value by fifty per cent as a result of enclosure for pasture: in the fifties enclosed pasture was worth three times as much as enclosed arable. But in 1663 Fortrey thought that *arable* trebled in value by the intensive crop cultivation which enclosure made possible. 'Everyone by the light of nature and reason,' wrote a clergyman in the year in which the last enclosure bill was defeated in Parliament, 'will do that which is for his greatest advantage,' and will plough up pasture if corn is in short supply. So the impersonal workings of the market came to be relied on to achieve what Charles I's personal government had failed to do. Opposition to enclosure was associated with the Levellers and other radical movements. In 1682 Houghton included enclosure of commons and disparking of parks among the principal benefits from 'his Majesty's most happy restoration'.

'There are fewest poor where there are fewest commons,' observed Samuel Hartlib. Enclosure of common land not only increased corn production: it also deprived the poor of a source of fuel and pasture, and so by increasing their dependence on wages forced them to work harder and more regularly than they otherwise would have done. 'This will give the poor an interest in toiling, whom terror never yet could enure to travail,' said another clergyman. Again the market would achieve what the Poor Law had failed to do: the poor would gain morally, the rich financially. Enclosure for pasture would *increase* employment in the clothing industry, at the same time as it reduced the number of those who lived off the commons without working, and so released labour for industry. Enclosure had always been profitable, but in the sixteenth century most moralists had disapproved of it. It now became a pleasurable religious and patriotic duty in the eyes of all but disreputable radicals, whose views could no longer be published and could safely be ignored. 'It is a very strange principle and unheard-of paradox,' wrote the Rev. Joseph Lee, 'that nothing can be done to God's glory which tends to men's profit. Do not tradesmen in following their vocations aim at their own advantage, do none of them glorify God thereby?' Clergymen had not put it quite like that in the sixteenth century: but now the market had triumphed over the community.

The new attitude to enclosure was justified by a pamphleteer of 1653 from the need to grow more food for the rising population. Together with the defeat both of the old monarchy and of the radical movements of the revolution, it made possible a great extension of the cultivated area. 'England affords land enough for the inhabitants,' wrote Adolphus Speed in 1659, 'and if men did but industriously and skilfully manure it, we need not go to Jamaica for new plantations.' Thanks to enclosure and the new root crops and artificial grasses, land need no longer be left fallow. Thanks also to the floating of watermeadows, the number and quality of animals could be increased, and they could be kept alive through the winter to fertilize land and increase yields. Farmers could break the manure barrier which had for so long held back production. The export bounty on corn also acted as a stimulus. Resistance to marsh drainage, voluble before 1640 and in the fifties, became ineffective thereafter. The completion of Vermuyden's scheme for draining the Fens increased England's arable land by some ten per cent. Royal forests were sold during the interregnum and came under cultivation; they were not recovered at the restoration, when even so good a royalist as the Duke of Newcastle used highly dubious methods to get royal forests into his possession. The forest laws ceased to be enforced during the revolution, and were never effectively revived. Clover revolutionized the cultivation of heath and hitherto marginal land. This was especially important in the North and West, to which population was migrating as industry followed low wages and cheap food. Disafforestation included driving squatters from their cottage holdings.* Cottagers and commoners could no longer find protection for their rights in the waste. Winstanley's vision of the commons and wastes of England (together with confiscated church, crown and royalists' lands, royal forests and former monastic lands) being cultivated by and for the poor, 'that there may be no beggary nor misery among mankind', remained only a vision.

All these factors led to a great increase in output and a downward trend in agricultural prices from the end of the seventeenth century. The Royal Society in 1663 took very seriously a suggestion that famine could be prevented by extending potato cultivation all over England, and asked all landed members of the Society to set an example. The seventeenth-century agricultural revolution opened up the possibility not only of feeding the existing population more adequately but also of meeting the great expansion of urban populations which provided both the home market and the labour force for the Industrial Revolution. The new agriculture incidentally contributed to England's defeat of their Dutch trading rivals in the seventeenth century. Dutch wealth was largely built up on spices (for seasoning dried meat) and fishing (to produce an alternative winter diet). Spices and herrings were the nearest the Dutch came to possessing commercial raw materials. Fresh meat all the year round reduced English dependence on these imports, and so fitted in with the policy adumbrated in the Navigation Acts. The landed class thus made its contribution to England's commercial victory over the Dutch.

But the agricultural revolution disrupted a traditional way of life. Tell the fenmen, Fuller said, 'of the great benefit to the public, because where a pike or duck fed formerly, now a bullock or sheep is fatted; they will be ready to return that if they be taken in taking that bullock or sheep, the rich owner indicteth them for felons; whereas that pike or duck were their own goods, only for their pains of catching them'. This too was a loss of freedom for the poorer classes.

The fall of prices and rents in the early eighteenth century

*Cf. pp. 62–3, above.

accelerated the substitution of leasehold for copyhold and freehold. The land tax completed the process. It financed colonial
wars at the landowners' expense, in the sixteen-fifties and
nineties. It could be defended by reference to the abolition of
feudal tenures and a steep rise in rents. The corn bounty of 1673
was justified as a measure to help the gentry to pay the land tax.
But again we must not be deceived by averages. Big landowners
leasing to the most efficient farmers profited more by the boom
than the lesser gentry, who still had a traditional standard of
living to maintain and could not plough profits back into the
land. Just as the yeomanry's victory in the civil war heralded a
process of social differentiation in which all but the toughest
capitalist peasants went under, so the victory of the gentry in
1688 led to increasing disgruntlement of the Tory squires as the
land tax which paid for the French wars eliminated the economically unfit.

'One begins to suspect,' wrote Professor Hughes, 'that the
last civil war in England, the Jacobite Fifteen, was due, in no
small degree, to the desperate poverty of the northern Catholic
gentry. Not that bankruptcy was a monopoly of adherents of the
old faith. . . . Jacobitism was the occasion rather than the cause
of the final liquidation of scores of lesser gentry and freeholders
in these parts. . . . Before 1745 the new men were completely in
the saddle.' So the seventeenth-century revolution was completed.*

---

*In a book published after this was written, Dr Kerridge argues with an
overwhelming mass of evidence that 'an agricultural revolution of unparal-
leled achievement' took place mainly before 1673. Its main components were
the floating of water meadows (1629–65 – all these dates are very rough and
concern the high point of the movement), the substitution of ley husbandry
for permanent tillage or grass (1590–1660), the introduction of new fallow
crops and grasses (turnips, clover, sainfoin, 1650–73), marsh drainage (1590–
1653), manuring (the new industries helped to produce fertilizers), and stock
breeding. All this led to greatly increased production of corn, fodder, meat
and dairy products at lower costs (Kerridge, Chapters III–X *passim*). Dr
Kerridge suggests that by 1700 three quarters of English enclosure had
already taken place (p. 24).

4

THE COMMERCIAL REVOLUTION, EMPIRE AND FOREIGN POLICY

It is trade and commerce alone that draweth store of wealth along with it, and that potency at sea by shipping which is not otherwise to be had. – ANTHONY ASHLEY COOPER, *First Earl of Shaftesbury*

We might be without a King, but not without a trade. . . . Though the executive part was in the King, yet they were to see what was fit to be done if he failed. – JACK HOWE *in the House of Commons, 1695*

I

IN trade, colonial and foreign policy, the end of the Middle Ages in England came in 1650–51, when the republican government was free to turn its attention outwards. The Navigation Act of 1651, 'perhaps the wisest of all the commercial regulations of England', as Adam Smith called it, laid down that the colonies, chartered or proprietary, should be subordinated to Parliament, thus making a coherent imperial policy possible; and that trade to the colonies should be monopolized by English shipping. As modified in 1660, the act laid the basis for England's policy over the next century and a half. Merchants, Sir Lewis Namier pointed out, need more positive state action than do landowners or agricultural labourers; and from the revolutionary decades they began to get it. In 1651 the Venetian Ambassador had reported that 'merchants and trade were making great strides, as government and trade are ruled by the same persons'. These rulers first offered union to the Dutch, on terms which would have given English merchants free access to trade with the Dutch empire and transferred the entrepôt trade from Amsterdam to London. When the Dutch government (equally responsive to the interests of commerce) refused, war was declared. Union had been proposed under Elizabeth, by the Dutch, and offered again on terms very favourable to Dutch merchants in 1614–19. In 1651 the terms which the Commonwealth put forward were equally advantageous to English merchants.

The Dutch wars (1652–74) broke the Dutch hold on trade in tobacco, sugar, furs, slaves and codfish, and laid the foundation for the establishment of English territorial power in India. English trade to China also dates from these years. Oliver Cromwell's policy of aggressive commercial and colonial war looks back to Hakluyt, Ralegh and the Providence Island Company, forward to William III and the elder Pitt, Cromwell's admirer. The capture of Jamaica in 1655 provided the base for the slave trade on which English merchants were to wax rich. From the time when Blake's fleet bombarded Tangier and forced a treaty upon the Barbary corsairs and Cromwell's troops captured the privateering centre of Dunkirk, British ships received better protection than those of any other nation. The bill of 1661 annexing Dunkirk and Jamaica to the English crown had 'the most universal consent and approbation from the whole nation that ever any bill could be attended with'. The continuation after the restoration of the Navigation Acts and the policy of trade wars marks, in the words of Mr Godfrey Davies, 'a turning point in European history'. With the Navigation Act of 1651, Professor Wilson confirms, 'we have arrived at a fully fashioned conception of economic policy in an essentially national form. . . . Henceforth the merchant was here to work out his destiny, free of formal organization, within a general protective framework of national legislation.' Economists and government advisers had been feeling their way towards such a solution from the depression of the twenties; but it was not adopted until merchants had a full share in the framing of government policy. It could never be put into effect until the English state was strong enough to challenge and defeat the Dutch republic; and this was impossible under the old monarchy.

The main exponent of the new policies was Maurice Thompson, who had financed buccaneering by the Providence Island Company. He was a former interloper who had crashed his way into the East India Company, but had no use for its traditionalist policies.* Thompson was also interested in the Gold Coast slave trade, and had a vision of England as a great power combining the slave and East India trades to bestride the world. The Navigation Acts marked a transition from an organization based on monopoly companies to a total integration of the country's trade based on national monopoly, with the state playing a leading role. The Navigation Acts and Blake's fleet made the companies superfluous, with their two-way trade, their limitations on output and maintenance of high standards of quality and high prices for exports. Henceforth England was one great staple. By the mid-seventeenth century the companies had done their job of focusing trade on London and promoting a capitalist oligarchy there, just as the monarchy had done its job of destroying feudal liberties and monopolizing force.

The Navigation Act of 1651 represented the victory of a *national* trading interest over the separate interests and privileges of the companies. It was naturally disliked by some members of the old companies, though the Levant and Eastland Companies favoured it. It contributed to the victory of the English New Draperies over their Dutch rivals. The navigation system also benefited England's artisans by protecting the home market from Dutch competition and by increasing colonial and overseas markets, at the same time that any colonial industrial development which would compete with England's was prohibited. We may contrast the other great colonial empire, that of Spain, where a sixteenth-century industrial revolution was frustrated by the competition of South American industry, by failure to encourage shipping and produce a coherent imperial policy. The Navigation Acts realized a Baconian vision towards which men had long been groping: that state control and direction could stimulate material progress.† England's customs revenue increased over three and a half times between 1643 and 1659. By the end of the century it was ten times what it had been at the beginning.

---

*What follows is based on J. E. Farnell, 'The Navigation Act of 1651, the First Dutch War and the London Merchant Community', *Economic History Review*, Second Series, XVI (1964), pp. 439–54.

†See pp. 159–61, below.

The coalition of interests which had supported the Dutch war broke down under the Protectorate. Maurice Thompson and others still backed Cromwell's anti-Spanish policy and the attack on the West Indies. Thomas Povey, Thompson's associate, thought that the effective implementation of the Navigation Act demanded the conquest of Jamaica. There was little opposition from commercial circles to the Spanish war in its early stages, except from those who traded to Old Spain. But by 1659 the trading community had come to dislike a war in which merchant vessels were lost without compensating advantages, whilst customs dues and excise remained high, and the Dutch began once more to pick up trade with parts of Europe from which they had been excluded in the early fifties. Down to 1651 the Dutch had been out-trading England to the Baltic; between 1654 and 1656 only two Dutch ships a year went from England to the Sound. But in 1657–58, thanks to the Spanish war, Dutch and Lübeck ships began to recover ground.

Compensation for loss of trade to Spain was found in the Portuguese alliance of 1654, by which English merchants forced their way into the Portuguese colonial monopoly in America, Africa and Asia, in return for protection by English sea-power – something which England had never been strong enough to offer before. In 1650, four years before the Portuguese treaty, James Howell said, 'Portugal affords no wines worth the transporting'. Within a few decades port had become the English gentleman's drink *par excellence*; consumption of French claret suffered.

The 1660 Navigation Act virtually abandoned the Baltic carrying trade to the Dutch. This had become possible because England no longer depended on Baltic corn, and hoped to cease to depend on that area for naval stores. At various times bounties were introduced on American imports of pitch, tar and masts. Thanks to the strength of the English navy, no power ever threatened to close the Sound to English shipping between the Commonwealth's victory over the Dutch and 1780.

Cromwell allied with Sweden to balance the alliance of the Netherlands with Denmark, but he was careful to allow no Baltic power to become strong enough to hamper England's free access to this area. When Charles X asked for English help in 1657, the

Protector demanded the cession of Bremen. If this had been secured, England would have gained the foothold in northern Germany which possession of Hanover by the English crown in the eighteenth century, and of Heligoland in the nineteenth century, allowed her to occupy as long as Germany was disunited.

Although formally the economic legislation of the interregnum was annulled in 1660, in fact the ensuing years 'saw a vigorous reconstruction of this apparatus of economic control and stimulation. Its principles were not new.' In this sense we can agree with Professor Wilson that 'the restoration has a better claim than most dates to be regarded as the economic exit from medievalism'. The promoter of the Navigation Act of 1660 was Sir George Downing, Cromwell's Ambassador at The Hague, who personifies the anti-Dutch party and the continuity of its influence after 1660.

The Navigation Acts closed the British empire to foreign shipping, and established a monopoly area of privilege for British merchants. The Dutch colony of New Amsterdam was first out-traded and then annexed. The Dutch wars and the act of 1660 made London Europe's entrepôt for colonial produce. Between 1638 and 1688 English exports and re-exports trebled or quadrupled. Initially the colonies were important as sources of raw materials, like cotton, sugar and tobacco, which were processed in England and re-exported. But in time the colonies became even more important as markets for British manufactures, for the mass production of which the New Draperies had been a harbinger. There was no limit to the North American market.

By the end of the century fifteen per cent of England's overseas trade was with the colonies; by the end of our period thirty-three per cent. The alternative to the navigation system would have been acquiescence in the surrender of the carrying of England's trade to the Dutch, with consequent weakening of the navy. The profits of trade with East and West Indies would have gone to Dutch merchants. The imperial monopoly created by the Navigation Acts allowed merchants to buy English and colonial exports cheap and sell them dear abroad, to buy foreign goods cheap and sell them dear in England. This increased merchants' profits, and forced national income from consumption into capital, especially into the artificially stimulated ship-building industry, which boomed. Thanks to new building and prizes captured in war, English shipping tonnage is believed to have more than doubled between 1640 and 1686. Shipping became one of the three or four greatest industries in the country. Even sailors benefited from England's monopoly, their wages rising sharply and permanently between 1650 and 1670.

In 1673 the Baltic trade was thrown open to all English merchants; in 1689 the Merchant Adventurers lost nearly all their privileges, so that cloth export was free to most areas; in 1698 the African trade was opened, in 1699 trade to Russia and New-foundland. The Navigation Acts created a monopoly big enough to be open to the whole merchant class, as against the privileged cliques to whom the trading companies had been restricted. Joint-stock companies, especially after 1688, absorbed capital from the whole country. When the economist Sir William Petty had a conversation with James II in 1686, he was as anxious to be reassured about the King's intention to maintain the Navigation Act as about arbitrary taxation, the Irish land settlement or religious toleration.

Industries other than shipping and those associated with colonial trade were relatively starved of capital by the navigation system, until by the mid-eighteenth century England had so far surpassed the Netherlands that Dutch capital was pouring into England. Accumulation through monopoly trade was more rapid than in industry; by the late eighteenth century large sums of capital were available for industrial investment, and the navigation system itself became superfluous. This 'Commercial Revolution', as Bolingbroke* and Professor Davis call it, was a necessary precondition of the Industrial Revolution.

After 1660 the crown took over a number of colonies. This was, however, something very different from the royal colonial policy of the years before 1640, for now the real authority over the colonies was that of Parliament and the permanent civil service – apart from a dangerous period when James II was preparing to

*Plumb, 1967, p. 3.

abrogate all colonial charters in order to make the colonies (with Ireland) bastions of royal absolutism. The meeting of the Long Parliament had saved Massachusetts from direct subjugation to Charles I: 1688 achieved for the colonies much of what had been won in England in the forties, but at the price of confirming the sovereignty of the imperial Parliament. Proprietary colonies, with trifling exceptions, came to an end soon after 1688.

Henceforth the state had a dual function: war and order. It was strengthened in its external relations, vastly greater sums being voted for war under William and Anne than ever before; and it had a generally recognized internal function of preserving the subordination of the lower classes, and of holding the ring between the landed and monied interests. In 1696 the Board of Trade was set up as a permanent government department. It was, says Professor Andrews, 'in the main a defender of the mercantile classes in England – that is, the capitalists of their day'. It was set up at the instance of Parliament, and given the task of promoting trade and industry. Its members 'acted with minds open to everything except fundamental ideas'.

Politics ceased to be ideological: the job of government was to increase the wealth of the country, and to furnish lucrative employment for the ruling families and their adherents. Locke's philosophy, observed Dr Roll, 'is a symptom of the decline of state power which commercial capital had created at an earlier stage of its war against feudalism. . . . The new state was . . . the creation of economic power no less than its master.' Locke's philosophy sanctioned a freedom based on property, a freedom with which the state must not interfere: a freedom which, like the doors of the Ritz Hotel, was open to rich and poor alike. 'The clash and ferment of economic ideas,' said Professor Wilson, 'reflected the freedom of a society where trade was allowed to fight its case against the surviving remnants of feudalism: neither the freedom nor the ideas should be under-rated as a formative influence on economic growth.' It was the end of medieval and Tudor conceptions of regulation and control.

2

'The commercial interest had never enjoyed so much weight in politics' as in the years after the revolution: the words are Dr Williamson's. The three Dutch wars were fought to establish England's independence of the Dutch carrying trade, to win the slave and Far Eastern trades; the nucleus of all later settlements in India had been won before 1670. Between 1660 and 1685 the value of a holding in East India Company stock increased ninefold: between 1672 and 1682, for the first time since 1617, the aggregate dividends of the English East India Company were higher than those of the Dutch Company.

Crucial to the new foreign policy was the Anglo–Portuguese alliance. Charles II's marriage to Catherine of Braganza has been described as virtually a condition of his restoration. Charles's aunt thought it a misalliance, but had to admit that it would be good for trade. With Catherine came Bombay, direct trade (slaves) with Portuguese West Africa and with Brazil (sugar, partly for re-export, and gold). With her also came Tangier, England's first base in the Mediterranean, though Charles may have valued it more as an excuse for building up a standing army. The English republic had for the first time used sea-power in the Mediterranean to put pressure on Spain; Cromwell used the threat of it to bring persecution of the Vaudois to an end in 1655. Charles II ultimately abandoned Tangier (as well as selling Dunkirk to France), and, under the complaisant James II, Louis XIV forced a renewal of the persecution. But after 1688 the Cromwellian policy was resumed, and England's prestige on the Continent revived when the Vaudois returned home to Savoy, symbolically under William III's flag.

Cromwell's charter of 1657 gave the East India Company government support against interlopers. Henceforth the company had a permanent joint stock and was in the closest financial association with whatever government happened to be in power at Westminster. It needed government support to get its charter renewed: governments needed the company's financial help. The company was ruled by a very rich oligarchy, attacks on which were denounced as 'levelling'. After 1688 the company came under fire, since its dependence on the government in the eighties had given it a Tory colour. One of the earliest acts of the Convention Parliament was to charge Sir Josiah Child with high misdemeanour for arresting an interloping ship. But a company was still needed to perform semi-state functions in the Far East. The Tory company was outflanked by a new East India Company. By 1709 the two were ready to join hands and share the booty, symbolizing the end of effective Toryism in the City. Toryism sank to be the policy of a group of backwoods squires, with support from the lesser clergy and the oligarchies of formerly privileged urban corporations.

The united company was one of the greatest holders of the funded state debt. The East India trade stimulated navigation and shipbuilding: it demanded ships of great burden. The company's imports were at first mainly pepper; calicoes and silks from the later seventeenth century; coffee and tea in the eighteenth. England's superior sea-power enabled the company's ships to acquire a quasi-monopoly of the port-to-port trade, squeezing out local Indian traders. By 1732, when statistics first become available, the company's goods were selling for nearly £2 million a year.

The Netherlands, England's most dangerous commercial rival, had been beaten by 1674. The Whigs and the monied interest already saw France as England's main competitor for world trade and world power. But Charles and James persevered in pro-French policies, for political, financial and religious reasons, regardless of commercial interests. Only after the expulsion of James II did English policy become resolutely anti-French. France was formidable in that, though far less developed economically than the Netherlands, it was a larger and stronger state, infinitely less vulnerable to the war against commerce to which the Dutch had succumbed. It took a much longer series of wars to defeat France after the Dutch empire had become a virtual English protectorate. The War of Spanish Succession (1701–13), despite its name, was for England mainly a commercial war. It was not until Louis XIV made it clear that he intended to exclude English merchants from the whole Spanish empire, and open it to French merchants, that public opinion in England favoured war. England seized Minorca and Gibraltar as naval bases in the Mediterranean, retaining the latter permanently. The Portuguese empire, like the Dutch, was taken under British protection, which guaranteed its survival.

3

After negro slaves,* Ireland was the principal victim of the navigation system which gave England her world hegemony. The brutal Cromwellian conquest and transplantation of the Irish was at least accompanied by attempts to incorporate Ireland within the English economic system. The Navigation Acts of 1651 and of the Convention Parliament in 1660 put Ireland on an equal footing with England; the Cavalier Parliament demoted her to the status of a colony, and a colony whose raw materials competed with those of the mother country. Irish ships were not permitted to trade with the colonies direct, and Ireland was near enough to England for the laws to be enforced against her traders with a vigour that could not be shown across the Atlantic. The import of Irish sheep and cattle into England was forbidden (1667) and of Irish butter and cheese (1681), in the interests of English graziers. After a brief experience of independence in 1689–90, the unhappy country was again brought under England's heel. The Irish woollen industry was killed by the prohibition in 1698 of export of Irish wool or cloth except to England, enforced by a regular naval blockade. Landed and monied interests in England were agreed that it was to their mutual advantage to destroy the Irish cloth industry, as well as to keep the cost of wool low by prohibiting its export from England or Ireland: so closely allied did the two interests now believe themselves to be.

After the Cromwellian and Williamite conquests three-quarters of the soil of Ireland belonged to Anglo-Irish protestants or absentee Englishmen; by the mid-eighteenth century £750,000 in rent left Ireland each year, tribute from the poverty-stricken peasantry to their English overlords. Absentee land-

*See pp. 227–30, below.

owners took little interest in estate management: there were few improving landlords. The Roman Catholic majority of the population was deprived of all political rights. The one compensation allowed to Ireland was English encouragement of the linen industry after 1696. It had proved impossible to manufacture linen in England itself which would compete with the Dutch industry. Fortunately the protestant Ulster area proved suitable, and the Dutch industry was killed, to the satisfaction of English merchants.

The effects of the navigation system on Ireland, a lord-lieutenant said as early as 1666, would be to reduce the country to 'barbarism and poverty'. Locke grimly commented on 'Boyle's cure for nose bleeding with a dead man's skull' that the latter was 'more plentiful in Ireland'. There were famines in Ireland in 1726–29 and 1739–41, 400,000 being estimated to have died in the latter, one in five of the population. Hunger and under-nourishment were rife even in 'good' years. Ireland was saved only by the rapid extension of potato cultivation. The Irish emigrated in thousands, to America and to England; they were to play a large part in the radical movements of both countries. So few were English protests against the ruthless exploitation of Ireland that we should remember with gratitude the individuals who spoke up against it, from the Leveller Walwyn in 1649 ('the cause of the Irish natives in seeking their just freedoms . . . was the very same with our cause here') to Swift in 1720 ('by the laws of God, of nature, of nations and of your country, you are and ought to be as free a people as your brethren in England'). But only under pressure of England's necessities in the war of American Independence did the régime of terror over Ireland begin to relax.

In Scotland, unlike Ireland, the English revolutionaries attempted to appear as liberators. Scotland too was included in the 1651 Navigation Act. Scots had long been asking for free trade with England; now they got it, together with uniform taxation, abolition of feudal tenures and of serfdom. Legal reforms included the substitution of English for Latin in the courts, the abolition of heritable jurisdictions, the creation of popular courts baron in every county, the institution of J.P.s. Attempts were

made to subvert the authority of the Kirk by encouraging break-
away movements.

Colonel John Jones set forward the radical English policy for
Scotland with remarkable clarity. 'It is the interest of the
Commonwealth of England to break the interest of the great
men in Scotland, and to settle the interest of the common people
upon a different foot from the interests of their lords and masters.
... The great men will never be faithful to you so long as you
propound freedom to the people and relief against their tyranny.'
But Jones also saw the weakness of this policy in the absence of a
strong Scottish bourgeoisie. 'The people will hardly compre-
hend the excellence of a Commonwealth, ... they having no
money to buy lands in England.'

The reforms were administered by an alien army. There was
little active resistance from the Lowlands in the fifties, but
repeated risings in the Highlands called for a large army of
occupation, and an assessment of £8,500 a month. Cromwell
thought that the 'middle and meaner sort' were becoming more
prosperous and less oppressed under his rule, but he apparently
referred to the middle class of the towns rather than to the
peasantry, from whom hostility continued. The towns were
deliberately taxed lightly, as most faithful to the English interest.
Burnet said, with some exaggeration, 'we always reckon those
eight years of usurpation a time of great peace and prosperity'.

Equality of commercial privileges was brought to an end at the
restoration. Legal decisions later in the century, however, re-
established the right of Scottish merchants to trade with the
colonies, and Scotland's economic growth seems to have continued. The Union of 1707 restored full rights of free trade with
England and its empire, thus further extending the area of the
London market and London influence.

4

Before 1640 aristocratic privilege and vested interests had in
many ways impeded the development of national communications. The corporation of Southampton in 1624 opposed the
improvement of water communications with Winchester. The

city of Gloucester levied tolls on vessels passing up and down the Severn, under its charter of 1626–27. Landowners maintained weirs and mills which obstructed river navigation: we hear complaints of this from Kent in 1600, from the Wye Valley, Devon and Cornwall in 1610. Even after the restoration the town of Salisbury encountered resistance from Wiltshire landowners to its proposal to make the river Avon navigable. In the early seventeenth century coal came from Staffordshire to Birmingham by ox-drawn wagons; in the later years of the century it came by water. By Defoe's time water communications linked Warwickshire with Bristol, and the Stour brought coals to Kidderminster.

For after 1688 the national view began to prevail over sectional vested interests; there was a boom in the improvement of water communications. This boom seems to have ended by 1701, a year of economic crisis and Tory government. The Tory victory in 1710 again held up a project for making the Weaver navigable in Cheshire. The local gentry were 'apprehensive of destruction of their fish weirs and the trespass of bargees', who might become addicted to poaching. The Weaver Navigation Bill did not reach the statute book until 1721.

Similarly with roads. In 1633 a Worcestershire clergyman complained that 'by occasion of these ill-repaired highways' he had to sell his tithes 'far under value'. The development of a national market waited on communications. During the revolution surveyors of highways were first given power to levy rates and to hire labour to supplement the traditional unpaid statute labour. The first general act of Parliament for road improvement dates from 1663, the year in which engrossing of corn and bullion export were first permitted. Authority was given to the J.P.s of Hertfordshire, Cambridgeshire and Huntingdonshire to set up turnpikes on the Great North Road to pay for road improvements; but this development of the toll principle was not fully utilized until the eighteenth century. Yet by 1673 a conservative was denouncing coaches, because their passengers 'escape the wet and dirt which on horseback they cannot avoid'. Whereas in the good old days two or three journeys ruined one's clothes, now coaches will lead to unemployment in the clothing industry. Public carriages and stagecoaches penetrated as far as Westmorland only after the civil war. Already men were congratulating themselves on the fact that travelling was easier in England than on the Continent. By 1636 there were 6,000 private or public-hire coaches in London.* The Post Office, beginning just before the revolution as a private monopoly, emerged during it as an essential government service. A 1*d*. post was established in London in 1680. By the mid-eighteenth century there were many deliveries a day in London, and the whole country had a good postal service. This expansion of transport services must have created much employment.

*Kerridge, p. 179.

5

INDUSTRY

> It is one of the natural consequences of freedom that those
> who are left to shift for themselves must sometimes be reduced
> to want. . . . Manufactures and commerce are the true
> parents of our national poor. – SIR F. M. EDEN, The State of
> the Poor, *1797*

I

THE Middle Ages in industry and internal trade also ended in
1641, when the central government lost its power to grant
monopolies and to control the administration of poor relief.
Attempts to prohibit the activities of middlemen, whether in
industry or agriculture, now ended: London merchants extended
their unimpeded activities over the whole country. Guild regulations and the privileges of town oligarchies, long opposed by the
common lawyers, became far more difficult to enforce. The
townsmen of Blackburn set up a new fortnightly market in the
sixteen-fifties, and defeated all post-restoration attempts to
extract tolls from them: there were no doubt similar cases.*
Government-sponsored attempts to provide work for the unemployed ceased, for fear they might compete with private
enterprise. The prosperity of the Birmingham region, and of
Liverpool and Manchester, date from these decades. In the short
run the revolution and the civil war had an unsettling effect on
the economy, just as the French revolution had on the French
economy one hundred and fifty years later; but in the long run
England's economic liberty, unique at that time in Europe, had a
stimulating effect, especially noticeable after 1688 confirmed the
political gains of the earlier revolution.

The successes of the forties in removing hindrances to free
production led to a more naked and straightforward confronta-
tion of big capital and small producers. In many quarrels in

*D. Davis, pp. 58–9, 149.

London companies the Levellers made themselves the spokes-men of small masters and journeymen, fiercely resisting the en-croaching might of the big capitalists who were forcing them down to proletarian status. 'The poor clothier,' declared a group of wealthy manufacturers in 1650, 'had better be a journeyman to him that buys wool of the grower than trade for himself' by buying from middlemen. The Levellers' defeat removed yet another obstacle to the advance of capitalism.

The revolutionary decades shook the foundations of English society and loosened its cohesiveness. Armies were small by modern standards, and there was no devastation comparable to that which ruined Germany during the same period. But apart from the actual fighting, the amount of social dislocation must have been great, to say nothing of the intellectual and moral shake-up, the disintegration of traditional loyalties and certain-ties. Soldiers in the Parliamentarian armies were allowed on disbandment to take up jobs for which they had not the requisite apprenticeship qualifications, and there were proposals that all restraints on free access to industry should be abolished. The physical movement of armies across England, Scotland and Ireland, the social shifts following the redistribution of wealth – all this made the period one of unusual social mobility. In many obvious ways industry was stimulated by state and army con-tracts, notably ship-building and armaments. In 1653 the government ordered 1,500 cannon on a single day; there were thirty-four iron furnaces in Kent and Sussex, of which fourteen were permanent. The Second Dutch War caused eleven more to be relit. The beginning of the Northampton boot trade is dated from the interregnum. The cloth, leather, metallurgical, gun-powder, paper and brewing industries received similar en-couragement. The demands of the armed forces helped to push wages up. In the naval shipyards at Chatham, Woolwich and Deptford wages were deliberately raised by the Rump Parlia-ment. The timber shortage stimulated brick-making, and the building industry spurted after the Great Fire of London in 1666, when prentice regulations again went by the board.

Industrial advance had been delayed in pre-1640 England by lack of purchasing power. Those with money tended to spend it on luxury imports or on building, which was often done less by wage labour than by the semi-forced services of tenants. The interregnum increase in artisans' and yeomen's purchasing power and the continuing rise in real wages later in the century meant a break-through.* The historian of the Midlands industries sees these decades as a significant turning point, not only in this temporary stimulus to demand but, more important, in the evolution of 'a new philosophy' – away from thinking of trade and industry as dutiful servants of the state to thinking of the state as the servant of industry and trade.†

In the sixteen-eighties Adam Martindale, looking back to his youth in Lancashire in the twenties and thirties, wrote:

Freeholders' daughters were then confined to their felts [etc., etc.] . . . The proudest of them (below the gentry) durst not have offered to wear an hood or a scarf (which now every beggar's brat that can get them thinks not above her), no, nor so much as a gown till her wedding day. And if any of them had transgressed these bounds, she would have been accounted an ambitious fool.

That of course is the sort of thing most old men say about their youth. But Sir Josiah Child and many others made similar observations; and there is a precision about Martindale's remarks which fits in with other evidence. Freeholders, the middling sort, have the new purchasing power; the poorer classes are lucky if they can emulate them. Complaints of people, women especially, dressing above their station were frequent in London in the first two decades of the seventeenth century; by the mid-century they had spread even to an outlying area like Lancashire, thanks to the extension of the London market, the expansion of the Lancashire clothing industry, and the revolution's disruption of traditional standards of right and wrong. 'There are five times as many of most trades,' said a pamphlet of 1673, 'as were . . . twenty or thirty years ago, . . . and thereby . . . trade . . . more diffused.' In 1686 there were said to be 100,000 retail shops in London; and the village general store seems to have been a seventeenth-century innovation. In

*I owe this point to Professor F. J. Fisher.
†W. H. B. Court, *The Rise of the Midland Industries* (1938), pp. 45–7.

171

The Life and Death of Mr Badman Bunyan tried to keep small men in the paths of commercial morality in this fluid society where known standards were disintegrating.

The nationalization of the home market was a two-way process. From the interregnum the Ironmongers' Company of London lost to Midlands middlemen its control of retail trade in hardware articles, despite an attempted come-back in the favourable circumstances of James II's reign, backed by a new royal charter. The phrase 'Brummagen ware' expressed London's view that the Midlands did not maintain satisfactory standards of craftsmanship.

The tendency was towards larger units of production. In 1655 a salt-maker of Shields had a thousand workers, and there were similar large concerns in the glass-making industry. By the end of the century the silk industry was organized in large units, employing 500–700 workers. The introduction of slitting-mills into nail-making in the Midlands was a major technical advance, leading to expansion of production. The rolling-mill was used in the ironworks of South Staffordshire in the later seventeenth century. Die- and stamping-machines were another example of the ferment of mechanical invention that was going on in the Birmingham area before the age of steam. The manufacture of white paper on a significant scale dates from the sixteen-eighties, and by 1697 nearly half the white paper used in England was of home manufacture.

In the seventeenth century many of the independent lead-miners of Derbyshire ceased to own the mines they worked, and became wage-labourers employed by capitalists. The free tinners in the Cornish Stannaries also became more dependent on capitalists. The conditions under which disputes were settled in the coalfields, Professor Nef tells us, were after 1640 increasingly favourable to owners of large collieries, and unfavourable to manorial tenants wishing to work coal in a small way, or to obtain compensation for use of their land. The coal and iron industries, where heavy capital investment was needed, came to be dominated by large-scale units long before – e.g. the textile industry.

There were similar tendencies, however, in the clothing

industry. The old draperies needed, most of all, skilled and careful labour; the New Draperies above all needed capital. So in the New Draperies of south-western England and East Anglia the control of merchant capital developed most rapidly. The Yorkshire worsted industry, introduced relatively late, was capitalist from the start. Elsewhere in Yorkshire the clothing industry was dominated by small producers, of whom Defoe tells us that 'every manufacturer' keeps a cow or two and hens for his family.

The stocking-frame, invented at the end of the sixteenth century, had been discouraged by Stuart governments. Cromwell incorporated the stocking-frame weavers, and the industry expanded rapidly, especially around Nottingham. An export trade, notably to Portugal, developed as well as supply for the home market, squeezing out the handicraft knitters. Again this was a highly capitalized industry, since the frames and the raw material, silk, were both expensive. The Dutch ribbon loom had been prohibited by the government in 1638 because of the opposition of small craftsmen. Post-restoration governments helped to suppress those who rioted against it. Even though the older draperies were not expanding in the later seventeenth century as the New Draperies were, still exports of broadcloths rose in *value*, since they were now dyed and dressed in England. In 1688 Davenant estimated that the value of woollen manufactures was about £8 million a year, of which £6 million were taken by the home market.

The Glorious Revolution changed the whole political climate. 'Parliament,' wrote Mr Lipson, 'came directly under the influence of a capitalist régime which now demanded its liberation from the shackles of state control.' Two great Tudor companies – Mines Royal and the Mineral and Battery Works – lost their monopolies, as did the Merchant Adventurers and the Royal African Company. From 1689 – 'the *annus mirabilis* of the rights of property', Professor Stone called it – freeholders could mine copper or lead on their own lands (or sub-let the mining rights). Hitherto mines believed to contain gold or silver could be opened and worked by the royal monopolists, without compensation. In the nineties there was a rash of new companies in a rapidly expanding copper-mining and copper-working industry.

Since 1688, said Adam Smith, 'in Great Britain industry is perfectly secure, and though it is far from being perfectly free, it is as free as or freer than in any other part of Europe'. Parliament refused to enforce the Elizabethan machinery of industrial regulation, assisted in this by judicial decisions. In 1694 the clause in the Statute of Artificers which excluded the sons of poorer freeholders and copy-holders from the clothing industry was repealed. This allowed a proletariat of textile workers to exist *de jure* as well as *de facto*. In a case of 1704 the judges declared that the Statute of Artificers 'extends only to servants in husbandry, not to gentlemen's servants nor to journeymen'. The breakdown of apprenticeship regulations gave employers greater freedom to exploit juvenile labour. From the boom of the nineties all economic writers agree in lauding the virtues of freedom; and there is a new emphasis on English ingenuity, inventiveness and technical skill. English artisans, said John Puckle in 1697, are 'universally allowed as the best upon earth for improvements'. The change within the century in this respect is remarkable.* In 1701 England's wealth was believed to have increased by twenty per cent since 1688.

The prohibition of wool export, consistently pursued by governments from the fifties, was denounced by opponents as a legacy of the revolution, the work of the Commonwealth party, to the detriment of landowners. (Similar prohibitions had been issued under James I and Charles I, but apparently as a device to raise money by licences granting exemptions.) In 1666 the famous law for burying in woollen was passed, repeated more strictly in 1678. Some complained that protection of wool lowered its price, and so caused graziers to concentrate on mutton. Certainly the quality of English wool does seem to have deteriorated, and the best English cloth in the eighteenth century included a mixture of Spanish wool.

The freedom of cloth export established during the interregnum and re-enacted under William III had a reinvigorating effect on the clothing industry of the south-west: dyeing and

* Contrast p. 99, above.

finishing of cloth developed at Exeter, and by the end of the century no cloth was exported thence to London. But gradually the lower wages and more convenient water-power of the West Riding brought a shift of the serge trades to Bradford and Halifax, not without fierce disputes and riots over attempts to cut wages in the south-west. By 1774 Yorkshire worsted exports nearly equalled woollens; and total exports from Yorkshire were over half those of the entire country. The West Riding had won its way to pre-eminence before the great inventions. By that date, as a natural consequence, worsted workers were among the most militant in the county.

2

For most of the seventeenth century full-time wage-labourers were probably still a minority of the population. Spinning was normally a by-industry; so was nailing. Wages were very slow to advance in the clothing industry before the interregnum, and only in Lancashire is there much evidence that weavers still held land. The period from 1530 to 1640 had been one of active state intervention. 'The history of wage-regulation,' Mr Lipson tells us, 'more especially in industry, affords clear indication that the fall of the absolute monarchy was the turning point in the evolution of capitalism.' We enter an era of *laissez faire* which lasts till the late nineteenth century. The unstable conditions of the revolutionary decades, the competition of the armed forces for manpower, and the strength of the radical movements, seem to have resulted in a considerable rise even in wages assessed by J.P.s; wages well above those assessed were in fact paid. One reason for the ecstasy with which the propertied class welcomed the restoration was that it gave a chance to beat wages down again. But it seems likely that the real wages of all but the very poorest rose again later in the century.

Some economists, their eye on the home market, thought high wages a sign of prosperity: more agreed with Petty, that wages 'should allow the labourer but just wherewithal to live; for if you allow double, then he works but half so much'. A man who had tried to employ the poor in a Bristol workhouse said in 1696,

'We soon found that the great cause of begging did proceed from the low wages of labour.' Children in this workhouse could not earn half their keep. In the same year 1696 the Commissioners for Trade and Plantations were complaining of 'the dearness of labour', and arguing that labour costs must be brought down if exports were to prosper. There were no inhibitions in this period about recognizing that the interests of capitalists and wage-labourers were fundamentally opposed. It was Mandeville who said, 'Whatever procures plenty makes labourers cheap, where the poor are well managed, who as they ought to be kept from starving, so they should receive nothing worth saving.'

This degradation of the poorest of the labouring population helps to explain the hatred and horror of falling to complete dependence on wages which was able to express itself more freely during the revolution. The poor, wrote Winstanley, say '"We can as well live under a foreign enemy working for day wages as under our own brethren, with whom we ought to have equal freedom."' 'Rich men receive all they have from the labourer's hand.' Winstanley thought that hiring labour and accepting hire should equally be punishable by loss of freedom and a period of re-education. We recall the French observer who in 1694, noting the courageous behaviour of condemned felons at Tyburn, spoke of Englishmen's 'contempt of death and fear of labour'.*

The redistribution of wealth through taxation, which enriched some government creditors and contractors, and raised some wages, helped to intensify divisions among the peasantry, and to push more of them below the poverty line. Dr Hoskins dates the growth of the poor *as a class* from the revolutionary decades. The period from the breakdown of the royal government to the Act of Settlement of 1662 had, however, been a period of exceptionally free mobility for the lower classes. Some may have joined the armies, others travelled in search of work or God. The restoration put an end to this freedom. The preamble to the Act of Settlement said that 'poor people . . . do endeavour to settle themselves in those parishes where there is the best stock, the

*See pp. 260–65, below.

largest commons or wastes to build cottages and the most woods for them to burn and destroy'. That is an exact description of the class for whom Winstanley and the Diggers had made themselves the spokesmen: if private appropriation and cultivation of the commons was to proceed, some restriction on the freedom of movement of this class was necessary. The act of 1662, which aroused no opposition in the Parliament of landlords, gave just that.

It empowered two J.P.s, upon complaint made to the overseers, to eject any newcomer to a parish who had no means of his own, and return him to the parish where he was last legally settled. This was applying to the whole working population a principle hitherto applicable only to vagrants and rogues. 1661 had been a year of high prices and near-famine following on the disbandment of the armies of the repuolic. The object of the act was to immobilize the working population, in order to deprive political opposition of the chance of organizing itself, to protect London and corporate towns from a surplus of labour, and to keep labour cheap in the countryside. A conservative gentleman like Sir John Reresby of Yorkshire complained that London 'drained all England of its people, especially the North, our tenants all coming hither, finding by experience that they live here better in a cellar or a garret than they could live in the country of a farm of £30 rent'. Reresby was advocating a tax on new buildings in the City: his admission of London's liberating effect on the outlying regions is significant.

The prohibition on movement by the Act of Settlement was more efficacious against unskilled workmen, those most likely to become a charge on the rates, than against the skilled: it accounts in part for the influx of Scottish and Irish labour to fill unskilled jobs. Although smaller corporate towns enforced the law, newer industrial centres in the West Riding, Lancashire and the Midlands grew increasingly lax in the eighteenth century, and the law proved impossible to enforce effectively in London. If labour were known to be needed, an unmarried immigrant would be issued with a certificate which allowed him to move, though usually only for short distances. An act of 1697 reduced restrictions on mobility by licensing the issue of certificates of settlement. This made parishes willing to accept labourers and their families from farther away, when employment was available for them.* But there was no obligation on the parish of settlement to issue such a certificate: it could be refused, and a man be detained in a parish where he was unable to obtain work. The J.P.s' power of granting or refusing certificates to move was a real and bitterly-felt restriction on the liberty of movement of the poor, especially the rural poor. The laws, as the Hammonds judiciously summed up, 'did not stop the flow of labour, but . . . regulated it in the interest of the employing classes'. The act of 1662, following the abandonment after 1640 of any national policy of setting the poor on work, established a system of local *laissez faire*, run by Dogberry and Verges, under the supervision of Squire Western. 'High wages and insubordination in the towns – low wages and subordination in the country – was a common theme of early eighteenth-century writers,' says Mrs George.

This was far from being the only indignity the poor were subjected to. 'None are so servilely dependent,' said Baxter of poor husbandmen, 'as they are on their landlords. They dare not displease them lest they turn them out of their houses or increase their rents.' The Act of Settlement was ostensibly directed against cottagers and squatters on commons, and does seem to have been followed by a destruction of cottages erected in the freer times of the interregnum. Again J.P.s were re-asserting their control. From the restoration onwards J.P.s assumed the right to sentence to transportation condemned criminals, or even persons acquitted who could not find sureties for good behaviour. At Bristol the justices (almost all of whom traded to the American colonies) used to threaten petty malefactors with hanging in order to get them to pray for the mercy of transportation. They were then sold for money, together with more conventionally condemned felons. Chief Justice Jeffreys objected to this practice – not because of its inhumanity but because mere J.P.s ought not to exercise the royal prerogative of reprieve and transportation. But in 1718 J.P.s were given statutory power to

*P. Styles, 'The Evolution of the Law of Settlement', *University of Birmingham Historical Journal*, IX (1963), pp. 33–63.

transport, and used it widely. It is hardly surprising that the years after 1688, which saw the rise of the modern work-house, charity schools and societies for reforming the manners of the lower orders, also saw a burgeoning of trade union activity.

6

THE FINANCIAL REVOLUTION

The people were too hard for the King in property; and then in arms too hard for him. We must either lay the foundation in property, or else it will not stand. Property, generally, is now with the people; the government therefore must be there. If you make a single person, he must be a servant and not a lord. . . . All government is built upon property, else the poor must rule it. – CAPTAIN ADAM BAYNES *in the House of Commons*, *1659*

I

IN finance the Middle Ages in England ended in 1643, when two new modern taxes, the excise and the land tax, were introduced. Charles I's unparliamentary taxation had been condemned in 1641, and Charles II made no attempt to revive it. The Court of Wards was not restored in 1660. Instead Charles II received compensation for wardship and purveyance from the excise. This was a tax on consumption, modelled on Dutch practice, which had been contemplated in the thirties, but which the royal government had never dared to introduce. In 1643 Pym brought it in to pay for the civil war, and it remained an essential part of the English fiscal system. At first it fell on a wide range of articles of consumption, but after the restoration it was confined to beer and spirits, cider, tea, coffee, chocolate. Tea, coffee and chocolate were still luxuries, but beer was the principal drink of the poor. Duties on malt, hops, salt, candles, soap, leather, paper and other articles had been added by 1713.

The assessment, primarily a land tax, followed the model of Ship Money, reassessing taxation on the landed class. It thus replaced both the Parliamentary subsidy and the profits of wardship. The land tax paid not only for the civil war and for the wars of Oliver Cromwell, but also in part for those of William III and the eighteenth century. Crown lands, sold during the revolution, were partially recovered in 1660, but they ceased to be of any fiscal importance. They were mostly resold in Charles II's reign. Henceforth there could be no question of the king 'living of his own'. The taxes which had been peculiarly obnoxious to the monied interest – monopolies, impositions, arbitrary fines – were abolished and replaced by taxes controlled by Parliament and falling especially on the landed and poorer classes. The revolution also pointed the way ahead in local rating. An ordinance of 1647 practically consolidated the church rate with the poor rate.

From 1642, when Parliament imposed a new Book of Rates, the customs were used for the quite new purpose of helping an export drive. In the early fifties the export duty on cloth was reduced; in 1656 duties were lowered on a number of imported raw materials and manufactured exports, and raised on exported raw materials and imported manufactures which would compete with our own. In 1660, when Parliament voted Tunnage and Poundage to Charles II, it appended a Book of Rates as a tactful reminder that there were to be no more impositions without Parliament's consent. From 1665 onwards financial grants tended to be appropriated to particular objects. In 1677 Parliament refused to grant supply until the government had made known its foreign policy; and the Commons insisted on their exclusive right to initiate money bills since they regarded the upper house as too sympathetic to the crown. After 1688 merchants were sufficiently influential to ensure that the vastly expensive wars were financed by a tariff policy which protected English industries. The general level of duties on import trade roughly quadrupled between 1690 and 1704; in 1700 all export duties on woollen cloth were abolished.*

The excise and the land tax helped to transfer command over resources from landowners and the poor to contractors and money-lenders who were likely to use them as capital. The old principle of taxation had been status, sometimes measured by wealth; the new principle on which the excise was justified was

*R. Davis, 'The Rise of Protection in England, 1689–1786', *Economic History Review*, Second Series, XIX, pp. 306–11. A policy of industrial protection had been advocated in the manifesto of the Fifth Monarchy rebels of 1660, *A Door of Hope*.

consumption: wealth not consumed – i.e. capital – was exempt from taxation. Hence the importance of making the poor as well as the landed class pay: it was a form of forced saving. This is the sense to be given to the otherwise odd defence of the excise as the 'most equal' form of taxation. Acceptance of this new principle marks a transition from a hierarchical, functional, estates conception of society, in which the duty of the poor is to labour rather than to pay taxes, to a theory of society as composed of individual atoms, with rights to be recognized by the state which must be paid for: a Ritz Hotel view of society. Equality before the law and excise are expressions of the same mode of thought.* (Mun had indeed argued that the increase in food prices caused by excise would be offset by a rise in wage rates, following a simple subsistence theory of wages. Wages did rise during the interregnum, but there is no way of ascertaining whether Mun's explanation is the true or the only one.)

In the years immediately after the restoration – whether intentionally or not – revenue collected fell far short of what Parliament had anticipated, and even further short of the needs of government. Since taxation was now recognized to be the exclusive business of the House of Commons, this gave the lower house a lever which it did not fail to use. Danby complained that the Cavalier Parliament '(than which I never hope to see a better)' thought that 'they ought to meet often, and that (though they are convinced that the revenue is too narrow for the necessary expenses) the crown ought from time to time to be beholding to them for those additions which may be wanting at the year's end'. Charles II had to rely on Louis XIV for money because he dared not use such fiscal devices as his father had resorted to. He was aided by the growing prosperity of the country, which led to so great an increase of customs revenue that he became financially independent both of Parliament and of France.

*W. Kennedy, *English Taxation, 1640–1799* (1913), pp. 65–7, 83–8.

2

Another consequence of the post-restoration financial shortage was that the crown came to depend on loans from City merchants and bankers, often the men who had financed Cromwell. In 1675 it was even proposed that money to be voted by Parliament for new ships should be lodged with the City, and no payment be made without an order from the Lord Mayor and Common Council. The proposal was defeated only by eleven votes. Some lenders made great profits from the King's necessity: Sir John Banks increased his capital sevenfold in fifteen years, largely by this means. But there was of course a highly speculative element in any loan to Charles II: William Kiffin is said to have thought it cheaper to give the King £10,000 than lend him £40,000.

During the revolution a national bank was often advocated. The vast sums levied by taxation and by confiscation and sale of lands, the necessities of state finance and private creditors, had led to a big expansion of banking facilities. 'Somewhere between 1640 and 1675,' Professor Wilson assures us, 'the City of London came to know the three essential functions of the banks as a later age recognized them: to take deposits, to discount bills and to issue notes.' But despite this the revolution in public finance which had begun during the interregnum, and for which the old Cromwellian George Downing fought in the sixteen-sixties, could not be completed until after 1688. Under the Protectorate all revenues except the assessment were brought under the Exchequer. This created the possibility of real Treasury control of revenue and expenditure, a planned budget, and so planned raising of loans. But only under William III was confidence between government and taxpayers established, and a long-term public debt established.

Banks had been viewed with suspicion by the governments of Charles II and James II. 'Where there is a bank,' Harrington had said, 'ten to one there is a commonwealth.' Sweden was indeed the only monarchy in which a bank existed, and this was small and insignificant. The Stop of the Exchequer in 1672 brought to an end an attempt to develop a permanent fiduciary issue by Exchequer 'tallies of loan': some of the leading bankers were hit hard, and confidence evaporated. The government had to pay twelve to twenty per cent for loans at a time when the East India Company raised money at four to five per cent. 'The only chance for a bank was a revolution,' Thorold Rogers put it. He probably exaggerated when he argued that the principal founders of the Bank of England were all Independents; but certainly both Dr Hugh Chamberlen and Dr Nicholas Barbon were the sons of notorious interregnum radicals. After 1694 the corporation of London faded out as lender to the government in its corporate capacity, and was succeeded by the Bank, which could mobilize resources from all over the country. As in so many other spheres, the voluntary, joint-stock principle succeeded the corporate principle. 'Modern history in the sphere of government borrowing begins in 1694,' said Professor Ashton. The main opposition to the Bank came from the House of Lords, and there were only two peers among the 107 initial holders of large amounts of stock. But by the end of our period the Bank of England had become, in the words of Lord North, 'a part of the constitution'.

The Bank of England proved as important in attaching the men of property to the new régime as the dissolution of the monasteries had been one hundred and fifty years earlier. And whereas the dissolution made Henry VIII potentially independent of Parliament, the Bank brought government borrowing under direct control of the representatives of the propertied. Henceforth the monied interest played a decisive role in politics; no political group could hope for success without support in the City. When the prosperity of the South Sea Company in 1720 seemed likely to oust the Bank from its central position as chief lender to the government, a shrewd observer asked: 'What occasion will there be for Parliaments hereafter?' But the South Sea Bubble burst.*

The new fiscal system helped the accumulation and concentration of capital. The Bank of England lent money to the government at eight per cent, and was empowered to print bank notes which circulated as currency. Payment of interest on the National Debt, guaranteed by Parliament, necessitated heavy

*See pp. 220, 243, below.

taxes, which transferred wealth from the poorer and landed to the monied classes. A national debt is the only collective possession of most modern peoples: the richer they are, the more deeply they are in debt.

3

The new finance begat a vast extension of the middle and lower ranks of the civil service. In the interregnum new departments (the Committee for Compounding with Delinquents, the Committee for the Advance of Money, housed in the halls of the great City companies, and the commissioners for sale of confiscated lands), provided a host of new jobs, many of which were filled by merchants. Commissioners were appointed to collect customs and excise, though farming returned at the restoration, because it ensured a regular and dependable sum for the Exchequer, and facilitated borrowing. Only later, as the financial machinery improved, was it found more economical to revert to the Commonwealth system of collection by salaried civil servants (1671 customs, 1683 excise).

Many of the new civil servants survived the restoration. Samuel Pepys soon found that 'living as I do among so many lazy people ... the diligent man becomes necessary and that they cannot do anything without him'. He soon ceased to worry about the unseemly remarks he had made at the execution of Charles I. The financial civil service furnished jobs for destitute ex-cavaliers, and was later to be one of the main instruments of the organized system of Parliamentary corruption. No less a person than Secretary of State Morrice made his son Customs Collector at Dartmouth, Barnstaple and Exeter.

Bullionist theories of foreign trade declined sharply from the interregnum. In 1660 the Council of Trade summed up the wisdom of two decades when it declared: 'Money and bullion have always forced their way against the several laws; ... the trade of the world will not be forced, but will find or make its own way to all appearances of profit.'

The transition from bilateral to multilateral imperial trade*

*See pp. 155–60, above.

was accompanied in the generation after the first Dutch war by a revolution in the financing of international trade. Where previously the relatively rudimentary payments system required considerable transfers of bullion, after the interregnum more sophisticated techniques of short-term international lending and for the clearing of international payments were evolved. In England they were not perfected until after 1688 and the foundation of the Bank of England; but it has been suggested that 'no adequate explanation of the advent of the Industrial Revolution is possible which fails to take into account the financial aspects' of the Commercial Revolution.*

A series of technical devices facilitated the advance of capitalism. An act of 1662 limited the legal liability for debts of the shareholders of some big trading companies, and so encouraged investment. A permanent stock market in London seems to date from the sixties, if not earlier; it expanded rapidly with credit facilities, until by 1720 investors from all over the country were ready to lose their money in the South Sea Bubble. Cheques date from 1675. From the late seventeenth century purchasing power was increased by a new security given by act of Parliament to bills, which had been circulating since at least the mid-century. By the middle of the eighteenth century there were permanent bill-brokers in London. From 1697 rates of exchange for European countries were being printed twice weekly and displayed at a London coffee-house. And from the early eighteenth century the speculative element in overseas trade was substantially reduced by the development of marine insurance.

4

For nearly eighty years before 1624 the official rate of interest (when there was one) remained unchanged at ten per cent; in the next ninety years it halved. This revolutionary fall was the consequence of the advance of capitalism. In Jacobean Parliaments landowners opposed reducing the rate of interest, because it 'will

* J. Sperling, 'The International Payments Mechanism in the Seventeenth and Eighteenth Centuries', *Economic History Review*, Second Series, XIV, pp. 446–68.

bring down the price of land, no man will lend money, and so many mortgages will be lost'. In 1669 a government committee declared that 'in all monarchical and aristocratical governments the first pulling down thereof has been lowering of interest', as had been done in England in the wicked republican year 1652, when it was reduced to six per cent, confirmed alas in 1661. But merchants' opinion was very different. They and the economists regarded the rate of interest as the basic factor in the differences between the Dutch and English economies. Their attack on high interest rates was natural when liquid funds were scarce and banking undeveloped. Davenant reckoned that the total stock of wealth in England was twice that of Holland, but effective capital was less, because so much English wealth was tied up in land mortgages, law-suits, hoarding, unwieldy taxation and consumption of luxury goods. Sir Josiah Child said the wealth of England was great enough to lower the rate of interest if it could be brought into circulation, as witness the £1,500,000 paid annually in assessments during the Commonwealth. In the Cavalier Parliament, when the land market was no longer flooded, Colonel Birch stated the exact opposite of the earlier Commons' views: 'As interest goes up land goes down, like a pair of scales'; Petty and Child said the same thing in more theoretical terms.

After 1714 private capital could not offer more than five per cent return on loans, though the government could give as much as it pleased: the effect must have been to divert resources from industry and agriculture to the state – mainly to financing war. In 1727 the rate of interest on government stock was brought down to four per cent, in 1757 to three. This was reflected in private transactions, so that cheap capital was available by the mid-century for drainage, land reclamation and other agricultural improvements, for canal- and road-making as well as for construction of factories. This gave England the same kind of competitive advantage over France as the Netherlands had had over England in the seventeenth century. But the example of the Netherlands should remind us that interest rates in themselves do no more than offer the possibility of industrial expansion: they do not create it.

The development of the equity of redemption had comparable effects. Until the early seventeenth century landowners regarded raising money on mortgage as a desperate remedy. The lender's object was if possible to foreclose, the borrower's to use all the advantages of his superior social position to bilk. In the heroic early days of predatory capitalism there was a speculative windfall element in many forms of economic activity, whether overseas trade or privateering, mining or the purchase of a monopoly. The possibility of big gains often seemed more attractive than regular if modester income. But from the early seventeenth century, and especially after 1640, as it became clear that capitalism had come to stay, the importance for the landed class of raising capital which would not have to be repaid immediately, and by means which would not endanger landownership, became obvious. The difficulties in which many royalist landowners found themselves in the forties and fifties worked in the same direction. New purchasers and improving landlords also needed capital. At the same time lenders came to see the advantages of secure income over often hypothetical capital gains. There was enough land on the market for foreclosing to be an unnecessarily roundabout way of acquiring it. In the absence of banks, mortgages were a sensible form of long-term investment, since agricultural profits were reasonably certain given a modicum of prudence by the landowner. Despite attempts in 1653–54 to strengthen the hand of creditors foreclosing, the law in fact gave both sides what they wanted in the equity of redemption; scriveners emerged as middlemen in the financial market.

The combination of lower interest rates after 1624 with permanent mortgage contributed largely to the closing of the open land market and to the recovery of so many aristocratic families which is a feature of the period after the abolition of feudal tenures. They no longer needed to sell when in financial difficulties. The new situation made possible the evolution of the strict settlement during the revolution (cf. the ordinance of August 1654 reforming Chancery in order to protect mortgages). The development of the permanent mortgage was for landowners what a funded debt was for governments. Royal creditors lived in an uncertain twilight between opulence and bankruptcy under

Charles I and II, and a satisfactory permanent method of financing governments was evolved only after the establishment of the Bank of England. Landowners' creditors led a similarly speculative existence until the equity of redemption funded landowners' debts. And of course as mortgages became safer, so this too helped to lower rates of interest. Many landowners opposed the establishment of the Bank of England because they believed it would lead to a fall in rents and a disuse of loans upon mortgage. In fact the abolition of wardship, and the evolution of joint-stock companies, mortgages and a funded debt, all contributed to making possible long-term calculation, stable capital investment.*

*P. G. M. Dickson, *passim*. Mr Dickson's emphasis is on public credit rather than taxation.

7

RELIGION AND THE
INTELLECTUAL REVOLUTION

This country, where they are always talking about religion,
but where there's certainly less of it than you would believe
possible. – WILLIAM III to the ELECTRESS SOPHIA OF
HANOVER, *December 1689*

> The country poor do by example live;
> The gentry lead them, and the clergy drive:
> What may we not from such examples hope?
> The landlord is their God, the priest their pope.

D. DEFOE, The True-Born Englishman (*1701*)

I

IT is difficult to exaggerate the social significance of the religious
and intellectual revolution of the sixteen-forties and fifties. 1641
was no less a turning point for the church than for the state. In
that year the High Commission was abolished, and with it the
government's control over the parishes. Bishops and church
courts ceased to function, church lands were sold. Ecclesiastical
censorship ceased to exist, as did ecclesiastical control over
education. Burning for heresy was abolished in 1648, and though
Thomas Hobbes thought the bishops would have liked to burn
him after the restoration, they never did. For many years after
1640 there was effective religious toleration. Sects hitherto
illegal, whose members were drawn mainly from the lower
classes, now met and discussed in public, and their views were
printed. As between 1530 and 1560, we should be careful not to
read backwards into this period sectarian divisions which
crystallized later. Most Englishmen, including most parsons,
were content to remain members of the English church, whether
that church was episcopalian, presbyterian or more broadly
protestant. For a brief period Episcopalians, Presbyterians,
Congregationalists and Baptists worked side by side in a national

church whose broad base deserves more study from those interested in ecclesiastical reunion. The attempt after 1660 to reimpose a narrow Anglican uniformity failed, and henceforth it could never again be pretended that all Englishmen belonged to a single church. Whether or not religious toleration was legalized, the existence of organized religious bodies outside the state church was a fact of which account had to be taken. The long-term liberating effects of the competition of rival religious views, as against the monopoly which the established church had enjoyed until 1641, is impossible to calculate.

Before 1640 the struggle for control of the pulpit had been political as well as theological. Episcopacy could flourish in Scotland only with the strong backing of the English government, as was shown before 1640 and after 1660. In England the connexions were not less close. Puritans, wrote Sir William Dugdale, 'under a seeming devout and holy pretence . . . got in a number of lecturers into most of the corporate towns and populous places of this realm . . ., especially into the City of London, whom they maintained by voluntary contributions, to the end that they might be engaged to preach such doctrine as should (upon occasion) prepare the people for any disloyal attempt, and dispose them to rebellion when any opportunity served.' 'These lecturers,' the Duke of Newcastle told Charles II, 'have preached your majesty out of your kingdoms.' Hostile remarks like these help us to understand the popular hold of the Puritan clergy, and the ease with which traditional Anglicanism collapsed when it lost government support in 1640.

'Religion was not the thing at first contested for,' said Oliver Cromwell of the civil war. The initial dispute was about how church and clergy were to be brought under the control of the nobility and gentry, so that, as the later royalist Lord Falkland put it to his fellow M.P.s, they should 'not dare either ordain, suspend, silence, excommunicate or deprive otherwise than we would have them'. But would the nobility and gentry still be able to control the state without the help of the church? Defenders of episcopacy thought that the whole social order would be endangered if the ecclesiastical hierarchy fell. The nature of the constitutional crisis was transformed by the inter-

vention of the popular movement against the church. M.P.s
protested against 'turbulent spirits, backed by rude and tumul-
tuous mechanic persons', who 'would have the total subversion
of the government of the state'. What they most feared was that
the church might fall, and be seen to have fallen, to an assault of
the people. Those who scrupled to pay tithes might soon refuse
to pay rents.*

During the revolution indeed almost anything seemed possible. The Levellers and many sectaries advocated abolishing
tithes – as in New England, where the clergy were paid salaries
from public funds. But if tithes were abolished without compensation, this would mean the end of an English state church
(since tithes paid the established clergy), and also the expropriation of those gentlemen who at the dissolution of the monasteries
or by later purchase had succeeded to impropriated tithes. The
dissolution of the Barebones Parliament in 1653 was precipitated
by rejection of a proposal to declare tithes sacrosanct. The
Instrument of Government proposed to replace them by some
less contentious method of paying ministers. This was no doubt
mainly a tactical concession to the radicals; but it shows how
strong opposition to tithes still was. In 1653 Dorothy Osborne
attended a sermon by Stephen Marshall in which the preacher
affirmed that 'if there were no kings, no queens, no lords, no
ladies, nor gentlemen nor gentlewomen in the world, 'twould be
no loss at all to God Almighty'. 'I was near laughing,' she said.
Such opinions certainly contributed to the gentry's willingness
to accept a restoration of king and bishops in 1660: religion and
liberty seemed small things to sacrifice to economic confidence
and political subordination.

Bishops came back in 1660, but not to their old power.
Without the High Commission, said Bishop Sanderson in 1662,
'all the pains particular bishops can take will contribute but little
to the settlement of the church in peace and prosperity'. The
number of penances imposed by the Archdeacon of Nottingham's court in 1662 was less than a quarter of those in 1638.
'He cared not for the court nor power of it, it was but ex-

*B. Manning, 'The Nobles, the People and the Constitution', *Past and
Present*, No. 9, pp. 59–62.

communication,' cried a Wiltshire man in 1668. In 1675, when church courts were trying to help a Nottinghamshire rector to collect tithe on wages, employers urged their workmen to resist, since the worst penalty that could be imposed was excommunication, 'which was only their not going to church'. Here we have the key to the decline of ecclesiastical power after 1640. It had lost the support of those who counted among the laity; the church could never recover the place in society which Laud had tried to give it. After 1670 Chancery took over the jurisdiction over wills and intestacy which used to belong to the church courts. The licences granted to dissenting chapels under the Indulgence of 1672 made a mockery of presentments for nonconformity; and in any case dissenters were dealt with by J.P.s in secular courts, since their offence was political. Worst of all, a J.P. grumbled in 1677, 'the country people generally are so rotten that they will not complain of them, though they see and know of these seditious meetings before their eyes daily'.

The revolutionary associations of religion during the interregnum had a profound and lasting effect. The gentry, many of whom had been patrons of Puritans before 1640, rallied to the church after 1660, thus ensuring its survival. Henceforth the socially conservative function of the Church of England was recognized by all. It was 'best suited to monarchy', Charles II claimed: 'he that took one stone from the Church, did take two from his crown'. Religion was 'a necessary part of our government', though Presbyterianism was no fit religion for gentlemen. Indeed the church identified itself so closely with Tory nonresistance policies that its prestige suffered badly when they had to be rejected in 1688.

For dissenters the years after 1660 were a severe testing time. 'Heretofore at Parliaments,' wrote Henry Newcome sadly in 1661, 'we [the Presbyterian clergy] have thought it our duty to meet and frame petitions, and get hands, and send them up, etc.; now all this is wholly taken out of our hands.' Their enemies henceforth took the lead in forming opinion. Inevitably dissent became quietist, pacifist. The nonconformist clergymen who were extruded in 1662 were, in some cases, maintained by contributions from the City of London, or from a friendly but conforming peer or gentleman. Others taught in dissenting academies, which combined the functions of grammar school and university for those excluded by the Clarendon Code. They were much cheaper than Oxford and Cambridge, as well as providing far better teaching, including more science and modern subjects.

Class lines were drawn tighter after 1660. Dissenters 'are not excluded from the nobility', wrote John Corbet in 1667; 'among the gentry they are not a few, but none are of more importance than they in the trading part of the people, and those that live by industry, upon whose hands the business of the nation lies much.' They tended to trade perforce with one another, and this accentuated the split between nonconformist town and Anglican countryside.

Between 1662 and 1689 persecution was intermittent but often severe. Long periods in gaol, arbitrary fines, the general insecurity and sometimes sheer plunder of their goods ruined many of the small craftsmen from whom nonconformity's strength was drawn. On the other hand the exclusion of dissenters from state office and universities drove them into business. Much of the moral energy which had been devoted to politics was now turned to more material ends. The Lancashire textile trades appear to have been built up in the seventeenth and early eighteenth centuries by dissenters. Celia Fiennes in her tour of 1695-97 frequently noted the connexion between nonconformity and enclosure. That nonconformity led to business success was a commonplace by the end of the century. The Quakers indeed had reason to bewail a decline in religious zeal as members of their community prospered. Many before Wesley noted the disturbing cycle, that godliness led to hard work which led to wealth which led to ungodliness. English industry also benefited from the immigration of thousands of Huguenot craftsmen, especially silk-weavers, notably after Louis XIV's Revocation of the Edict of Nantes in 1685. Economic writers began to advocate liberty of conscience precisely because it would attract foreign immigrants and discourage emigration, as well as because of the economic importance of dissenters.

They were 'patient men', Sir William Petty argued, 'and such as believe that labour and industry is their duty towards God'. One argument against toleration, John Corbet noted, was that it was 'thought to give too great advantage to the citizens and the commonalty, . . . to make all sorts more knowing and less servile, and consequently less obsequious to the wills of great men'. Can 'the nobles and gentlemen of England . . . maintain their authority and splendour with the freedom of citizens and the common people?' 'The entire dissenting party' was believed in 1679 to be against 'the gentry and their interest'.

The democratic sentiments of the revolution indeed survived among the sects. The Quaker insistence on 'thou-ing' superiors and not removing their hats as a token of respect was one aspect of this; and there are ominous overtones in Bunyan's rebuke to the upper classes for being 'loath to receive those little ones of His, because they are not gentlemen, because they cannot, with Pontius Pilate, speak Hebrew, Greek and Latin'.

The sects played an important part in forwarding the Londonization of England. The Quakers began by evangelizing the hitherto neglected North and West, but all sects came to look to London for ministers, for guidance and financial support in time of persecution. After the Toleration Act their organizations, especially the Quakers, saw to it that legislation in their favour was uniformly observed and enforced all over the country. The central nonconformist pressure groups formed 'an important link between local and central government', Mr Hunt tells us, 'helping to promote administrative uniformity throughout the country', and thus tempering the local omnipotence of J.P.s.*

After the revolution, middle-of-the-road Calvinism was distasteful both to the ruling class and to lower-class radicals. Although some Puritan social attitudes were taken over by the Church of England – Sabbatarianism, the bourgeois virtues – an ideological cleavage set in between town and country. The gentry – with parsons in tow – re-established their pre-eminence in the countryside, except in rural industrial areas like the West Riding; but in towns dissent had come to stay. Those who set

*N. C. Hunt, *Two Early Political Associations* (Oxford University Press, 1961), pp. 25–6, 31.

the tone in villages tended to be unsympathetic to new ideas generally, and all too often to regard education for the lower orders as politically dangerous. A Tory gentleman opposed an amendment to the Schism Bill of 1714 whereby dissenters would be allowed to teach writing; for 'under the notion of writing they learn to read'.

In towns, and especially in London, the new Puritan and bourgeois morality triumphed, at least after 1688, when the dissolute and pro-French courts of Charles and James were replaced by the more humdrum Calvinist respectability of William and Mary, whose public image was so much more that of a happily married couple than their real life. Restoration comedy was the last irresponsible snook-cocking of those who would not accept Puritan-bourgeois morals. After 1660 there is an almost self-conscious anti-Puritanism in the Anglican-dominated country-side. Great propaganda emphasis was laid on the alleged kill-joy activities of the major-generals and Puritans generally during the interregnum, no doubt in part to blot out the memory of their attempts at social justice and protection of the poor. The propaganda was so successful that one still meets echoes of it in old-fashioned text-books today. After 1660 the phallic maypole became almost a symbol of the restored church and (more appropriately) of Charles II. As power was monopolized by the great landed magnates and the monied interest, so the lesser gentry found themselves isolated in their little islands of rural sovereignty. They became more and more resentful, nostalgic, Tory. The almost deliberate rural paganism, cakes and ale, hunting and open-air virtues which they cultivated, were contrasted with the book-keeping sordidness and pettifogging plutocracy of London. The opposing moralities have their apotheosis in the novels of Fielding and Richardson. In the eighteenth century the aristocracy at least attended church in their villages, if only to set an example. Sir Roger de Coverley popularized this new habit.

Another characteristic of the tired post-restoration days was a revulsion from ideological politics. This was particularly noticeable among the many ex-Parliamentarians who rapidly shed their Puritanism in 1660 and profited by serving the Merry Monarch.

But the same weary and wary desire to cultivate his own garden was expressed under James II by Sir John Reresby, a devoted royalist:

> I had seen so many changes, and so many great and little men re-moved in my time, that I confess it began to cool my ambition, and [I began] to think there was a time when every thinking man would choose to retire and to be content with his own rather than venture that and his conscience for the getting of more, and a little help to his family that way was better than more gotten by other means. . . . I was convinced that safety was better [than] greatness.

The passage shows, incidentally, what even relatively honest men of property expected from a political career in the late seventeenth century ('the getting of more'). The transition from ideological to non-ideological politics meant for many ordinary men of property simply that the winning of 'a little help to their families' was less risky and better organized. Here is an important key to what we call 'corruption' in the eighteenth century. It was no more 'corrupt' than the wealth gained through office by a Buckingham, a Strafford, a Danby; it was very much less dange-rous, and far more were consuming smaller slices of a much larger cake. The church too offered a career for younger sons of the gentry, especially necessary after the evolution of the strict settlement. In the eighteenth century bishops began to employ permanent administrative personnel on their estates, a job as good as a post in the civil service.

2

'On the 5th of July 1641,' says Dr Robert Birley, 'the England which we know today was born.' He refers to the overthrow of Privy Council, Star Chamber, High Commission, and the liberation of the printing press. The history of the press as a fourth estate in England, and as a vehicle for advertising, both date from the sixteen-forties. Very little capital was needed to set up a hand printing press worked by two men: the press could still be a democratic instrument, as was shown by the out-burst of pamphleteering during the revolution. In 1678–81 the

predominantly Whig press was an important counter-influence
to the predominantly Tory pulpit. In Defoe and Swift we soon
have political journalists of genius competing for the public ear.
In 1695 the Licensing Act was allowed to lapse – significantly,
not because it interfered with the public's right to knowledge,
but because it interfered with the right of booksellers to make
profits by publishing. Henceforth, though governments tried to
restrict the press's freedom of criticism and its circulation among
the poorer classes, liberty of the press for the well-to-do was
established – the Ritz Hotel principle again. The style of dis-
course was affected. In the sixteenth century men with new
ideas had normally propounded them in dialogue form – Sir
Thomas More, Thomas Starkey, Sir Thomas Smith, Sir Thomas
Wilson, Edmund Spencer – thus evading full responsibility for
them. But now political and economic ideas were presented in
straightforward pamphlet form. The decline of aristocratic
patronage, the extension of the reading public and the influence
of science all combined to produce a simplification of prose style.
New professions were opened up by the development of the
literary market. Fuller's *Worthies of England* (1662) was one of
the first serious works aimed at popularity *and* profit. The
theatre, the first capitalist entertainment industry, offered a
career open to the talents, even to talented women.

Above all we should emphasize the intellectual changes resulting from the revolution. 'The civil wars have left in this nation
scarcely any trace of more ancient history,' reflected Dr Johnson,
and if any turning point between medieval and modern ways of
thought can be found it was undoubtedly the rude intellectual
shock of civil war, regicide and republic. Evidence of an increasing historical sense is to be found in the appearance of the word
'anachronism' about 1646. 'Learning flourisheth,' wrote the
conservative George Lawson in 1660, 'matters in religion are not
so much taken upon trust and tradition as formerly. Arts and
languages advance; the light of the Gospel shines.' The revolution had shown that no institutions were eternal. The political
thought of the Levellers, Winstanley, Milton, Hobbes and
Harrington, opened up new vistas of speculation. Though
everything was done to obliterate the memory of that epoch,

ways of thinking could never be the same again. Professor Jordan suggested that greater tolerance was the main legacy of the revolution, and gave social reasons for this in the break-through of 'the thought of the poor and inarticulate', in which 'the stratum of tolerance seems firm and unbroken' as far back into history as we can go. The existence after 1689 of some degree of religious toleration and of competing sects forced a reappraisal of the whole subject of religious liberty, not least among Anglicans who found their church suddenly cast from its position of persecutor.

The Reformation had established the Bible as the supreme authority: the church had tried to insist that the clergy should interpret the sacred text. The sixteen-forties established the sovereignty of common law over its rivals, and lawyers were its interpreters. The incursion of the common man into politics during the interregnum overthrew priestly mediators, and tried to overthrow lawyers, who imposed an expensive and incomprehensible ritual between ordinary people and justice. It was not without reason that the radicals tended to link lawyers and clergy together as 'corrupt interests'. The radical attack on the law fitted in with the Leveller thesis that the old constitution had broken down during the civil war and that the state must be refounded. In this new state the Levellers wanted complete equality before the law, and 'as the laws ought to be equal, so they must be good'.

This appeal to conscience against authority is an appeal to the present against the past. For the society in which men live forms their consciences, whereas authority gets fossilized in a set of institutions or writings. The appeal to conscience was not – as its enemies alleged, and as logically it appears to be – an appeal to absolute individualist anarchy. In the revolutionary decades many men agreed in finding, either in their consciences or in the Bible, principles which were profoundly critical of existing social relations. For such men, never before able to discuss freely, or to get their views into print, religious toleration and the collapse of the censorship revealed an intoxicating amount of agreement, at least on a negative programme. Tyranny, Overton argued, is irrational, and therefore ungodly.

Thus all roads led away from authority and towards rational-ism. With the fall of church courts parsons abandoned the claim that they had a divine right to tithes; they continued to collect them because authorized by the law of the land. With Hobbes, sovereignty and political obligation were based on expediency. Divine right was dead here too. Biblical texts and historical pre-cedents yielded place to rational argument.

The Levellers were most explicit about giving up appeals to precedent. But events forced it upon others too. Thus Prynne wrote in 1644, 'Parliament, being the sovereign power in this realm, is not tied to any precedents, but hath power to make new precedents, as well as new laws.' Similarly Charles I in 1648, when pressed hard by Parliamentarians to agree to the sale of bishops' lands, said 'precedents in cases of conscience cannot satisfy; they only proving that such things were done, not the lawfulness of them'.

Milton went further still, assuming an agreement among all virtuous men on the rights and wrongs of politics. 'No man who knows aught', he wrote, 'can be so stupid to deny that all men were born free, being the image and resemblance of God himself, and were by privilege above all the creatures born to command and not to obey.' All men? Even those who previously existed only to be ruled? How alarming to the ruling classes must the theology of Quakers and others have seemed, who believed that something of the divine resided in every man. 'Where all are equals, I expect little obedience in government,' wrote a colonel about Quakers in 1657. The Calvinist doctrine that the mass of mankind was sinful, that the elect were a minority, fitted the needs of an oligarchical society much better than this democratic theology.

Man is 'created sick, commanded to be sound', cried Fulke Greville. Hamlet proclaimed the grandeur and misery of man. Marvell was continually facing

> '. . . the conjunction of the mind
> And opposition of the stars.'

The tension within what many besides Marvell called man's 'double heart', the contrast between desire and possibility, grace and sin, underlies much metaphysical paradox. The conflicts were often expressed in the imagery of civil war: 'set me at war with myself', said Joseph Hall, 'that I may be at peace with Thee'. Joseph Beaumont wrote:

> ''Tis time to fight. But oh! I am betrayed!
> These rebels are
> Already got so far
> Into my heart, no care
> Of man's will help: sweet Jesu lend me aid.'

Men were still surrounded by blind, uncontrollable forces, whether of nature or society. But some were becoming conscious of new possibilities of controlling these forces. The great geographical discoveries; scientific, technical and medical advance; the liberation of thought at the Reformation and after: all this offered quite new perspectives, which were intoxicating to a Marlowe, terrifying to a Donne. They called for fresh thought about the nature of man.

Francis Bacon, for instance, accepted the Fall as a fact. He believed that man, by the exercise of reason, and by intense effort, could build a new society on earth which would recreate the abundance of Eden, and eliminate much if not all of human sinfulness. Labour, the curse of fallen man, might be the means for him to rise again. This was theologically highly unorthodox, and Bacon made his points obliquely. His ideas, popular among the Parliamentarians, undoubtedly helped to reduce the shadow of original sin that had dogged humanity for so many centuries. Bacon could not exorcize this spectre, he could only ignore it. But he and others like him converted mankind's backward look to a golden age into hope for a better life here on earth, attainable by human effort. Hitherto the forward look had been the property of the wilder Chiliastic sects. But the English revolution enabled some thinkers to escape from mere millenarianism.

Gerrard Winstanley, for instance, inherited some of the Chiliastic revolutionary tradition, but he had also been influenced by Bacon's thought and by the technical developments which Bacon summed up. Winstanley (like Marlowe) denounced religion as a sham, priests as cheats: he demanded heaven for the poor on earth *now*. But he also believed that if men were freed from religion and private property, the possibility of using science for the relief of man's estate would be enormously accelerated. He saw the conflict within man's heart as cosmic and political as well as spiritual:

> There is no man or woman needs go to Rome nor hell below ground ... to find the ... power of darkness; neither to go up into heaven above the skies to find Christ the word of life. For both these powers are to be felt within a man, fighting against each other. ... And this is that day and night, the light and darkness, winter and summer, heat and cold, moon and sun, that is typed out by the fabric of the great world; for within these two powers is the mystery of all divine workings wrapped up. ... To know the secrets of nature is to know the works of God.

Milton is another example. The Reformation had widened the gulf between man and God by abolishing mediators, whether priests, saints or the Virgin; but it had increased the possibility of bridging the gulf by direct communion with God. This placed a strain on individuals, unsolaced by confession and absolution, which was new and intolerable for all but the toughest. Milton was tough. He was elated by consciousness of the moral dignity of individual man, free to choose between good and evil. Yet the problem of human sin worried him throughout his life. The paradox of the Fortunate Fall is as old as Christianity, but for Milton it was breathlessly new and immediate. The virtues which Milton most admired were those which arose after the Fall – self-reliance, courage in adversity, a restless, critical independence of mind. Some men were undeniably morally free: sturdy, independent fighting souls, capable of rational choice. To such men Milton appealed in his divorce pamphlets and in *Areopagitica*. At this stage his emphasis on the wickedness of human nature was historical: human traditions and authority handed down from the past were suspect, and must be criticized by right reason today. It was a Baconian emphasis.

But the mass of men, Milton found, increasingly as the revolution progressed, were steeped in prejudices and superstitions, swayed by priests and landlords, incapable of guiding their actions by what Milton regarded as right reason. There is an element of prejudice here: the virtues which Milton extolled were the bourgeois virtues: those of a free individual, economically independent, expensively educated. Milton's 'reason' was the rationality of bourgeois society. The more communal virtues, brotherly love and solidarity, which Winstanley extolled, played a subordinate part in Milton's scheme of things. But Milton was largely right on the facts. In centuries of class-divided society, the gulf between the educated and the masses had grown steadily wider, and there was now little common ground. The dreary round of agricultural toil left neither time nor energy for intellectual speculation. Where the economic changes of the sixteenth century had impinged on the village, they had torn peasants from their holdings, cast them into helpless, persecuted vagabondage; or left them insecurely clinging on: again no stimulus to rational thought.

Milton came up against these facts as a practical politician. He mixed with the Levellers, and – since he dissociated himself from their programme – he must have been keenly aware of the tragic dilemma in which they found themselves. The Levellers believed in the equality of man; they demanded a wide extension of the franchise: yet there was no guarantee, in an illiterate and land-lord-dominated society, that open voting would not lead to a restoration of the old order and the overthrow of all that the Levellers and Milton believed in. In the theological terms in which the age thought, there could be only one explanation of the failure of the mass of the population to respond to the manifestly rational appeals of Milton and the Levellers. This explanation was original sin, the Fall.

In the revolution, as Milton saw it, the prodigious efforts of the rational and the good, which came so near to success, had been frustrated by the depravity of the majority, and by evil in the hearts of some even of the seeming godly. Milton made it his task, after he retired from politics about 1655, to make historical sense of this failure, to justify the ways of God to men. *Paradise Lost* is deeper and more tragic than the poem which Milton would have written twenty years earlier. And yet the conclusion of the poem is not tragic, nor is hope deferred to an after life. Milton rejected Calvinist predestination. Grace is offered to all men 'at least sufficient for attaining knowledge of the truth and final salvation'. The old myth of the Fall was transmuted with a new content which expressed confidence even in defeat. The legend had summed up the sadness of oppressed humanity throughout the ages: Milton gave a new hope in creative effort. His golden age, like Bacon's and Winstanley's, is put into the future, here on earth. Fallen man is potentially capable of reaching greater heights than Adam. Potentially: for the process is still selective. Not all can yet realize their full capacities: the democracy of grace is not universal: some are more equal than others. But all are potentially equal: and the look is forward. By knowledge of good and evil, out of strenuous conflict, we can win to 'a Paradise within thee, happier far'. '*Happier far*': so values are transvalued.

3

The seventeenth century saw a decline of belief in hell. For centuries the fact that God had preordained the majority of his human creatures to an eternity of torture had been accepted, so far at least as we can tell from written records. Few seem to have detected any conflict between this and the beneficence of an omnipotent deity. The contradiction was pointed out by some lower-class medieval heretics; but the ordering of the after life so closely followed the ordering of life on earth, where a minority ruled and prospered and the majority toiled and suffered, that few indeed of the former questioned it. But in the sixteenth and seventeenth centuries, as greater possibilities of economic freedom began to open up before some of the lower classes, voices were raised against the monstrous assumptions of the traditional doctrine. Mr Walker in his *The Decline of Hell* has traced the shame-faced abandonment by the clergy (under lay pressure) of the grosser forms of the doctrine, and the emergence of a more democratic conception of the after life. What he does not sufficiently emphasize, however, is the part played by lower-class radicals in propagating these new views. Those who rejected the social subordination which the doctrine maintained had no inhibitions about questioning the doctrine. The forty-second of Edward VI's Articles denounced those – presumably Anabaptists – who did not believe in an eternity of punishment for the ungodly. The supreme and most obvious example of such thinkers is Winstanley, the most radical of all seventeenth-century political figures, who treated the doctrine of eternal punishment as a cheat, the aim of which was to maintain earthly inequality.

The breakdown of the censorship and of the repressive machinery of the state church set ordinary men free to say 'there was neither heaven nor hell except in a man's conscience'; 'if I should worship the sun or the moon, . . . no man has anything to do with it'; 'he would sell all religion for a jug of beer'. The 'atheism' of the post-revolutionary English attracted the attention of foreign observers, and certainly had much to do with the acquiescence of the men of property in the return of the ecclesiastical hierarchy in 1660. As a post-restoration bishop noted, it was especially 'the plebeians and mechanics' who 'have philosophized themselves into principles of impiety and read their lectures of atheism in the streets and the highways'. With the return of relative freedom of the press at the end of the century, Unitarians publicly rejected the doctrine of eternal torment: the eclipse of Presbyterianism in England by Unitarianism helped on the decline of hell. So a potent argument for religious persecution lost some of its weight, the argument that cruelty on earth may save the heretic (or others) from eternal punishment after death.

This moral revolution coincided with the abandonment of the use of torture in judicial proceedings, and with the end of witch-burning: it is evidence of greater sensitivity to pain in others. But it is evidence of something far deeper than that. Hell declined because men came to believe that virtuous actions performed for the sake of reward, or from fear of punishment, were not really virtuous at all; even more important, that these standards could be applied to the whole population. For long the defenders of hell as the great deterrent, and some of those who were doubtful about it, insisted that the lower orders could be kept within bounds only by fear of eternal torment. This view of course was not abandoned in our period: it is not extinct today; but it was beginning to be questioned as the greater common sense of the mass of the people began to be felt alongside the frightened ferocity of the ruling class. The rise of democracy and the fall of hell coincided in time. Those who look back nostalgically to the superior virtues of an aristocratic culture sometimes forget trivial details like eternity.

4

A number of important if gradual changes were taking place in the ways of life of the middling groups of the population. Higher incomes and technical improvements in building led to much more comfortable houses, with greater privacy, for all but the poorest classes. Houses began to have stairs, more rooms, including bedrooms, chairs instead of benches, brick chimneys, glass windows, locks on doors, mirrors; paper and books were cheaper; citizens moved out of London's smoke to the suburbs. Simultaneous economic tendencies were increasing the number of those who had at least some time for reading; especially middle-class women for whom it was now a mark of social status not to work, and who would have been intolerably bored but for the *Spectator* and the rise of the novel. The class to which the *Spectator* appealed was defined in its opening number: readers would have 'the satisfaction to find that there is no rank or degree among them who have not their representative in this club', since it included a gentleman, a lawyer, a merchant, a retired army officer and a gallant.

The individual family, the voluntary societies, whether dissenting chapels, coffee-houses or political clubs, began to replace the geographical communities of the Middle Ages, in which the church was everywhere the community centre. Something was lost of neighbourliness by this combination of suburban privacy with voluntary association: something was gained in intellectual stimulus by the congregation of large numbers, especially in and around London; men and women could find others who shared their interests and were ready to discuss them. A society of atomized individuals re-formed into communities: but its communities were voluntary, and its interests more diverse. (I speak here mainly of the propertied class, whose sons were coming to monopolize the grammar schools. The latter had originally been endowed largely for the poor; but by now their exclusive concentration on classical studies made them useful mainly to members of the leisured classes who could hope for a professional career.)

Scientific ideas received a fillip during the revolution, thanks to greater freedom of publication and discussion, to the introduction of scientists to Oxford by the Parliamentary Commissioners, and to the formation in London and Oxford of the groups which after the restoration took the initiative in founding the Royal Society. Again and again in his writings John Aubrey, F.R.S., refers to superstitions which prevailed before the civil war and had disappeared by the end of Charles II's reign. Hobbes too noticed the importance of change in making for intellectual stimulus: 'it being almost all one for a man to be always sensible of the same things, and not to be sensible at all of anything'. This intellectual stimulus came from the economic developments of the period as well as from the political revolutions. The attitudes of seventeenth-century science gave men a new confidence. Nature came to be thought of as a machine that could be understood, controlled and improved upon by knowledge. It is one thing to dominate nature through command of serfs and cattle; quite another to invent machines for the same purpose. The potentialities of cattle and serfs are given, limited: the potentialities of machines handled by free men are limitless. Bacon thought all sciences could be perfected in a few years; Petty believed that 'the impediments to England's greatness are but contingent and removable'. In 1549 Sir Thomas Smith had been remarkably precocious in using the analogy of a clock to explain economic causation. But mechanical analogies soon came to dominate discussions of society and the state, as against the traditional organic image of 'the body politic'. With them came the idea that governments might have a positive role to play in exerting man's control over things.*

*Ferguson, p. 293; cf. pp. 361–2, 377, 390–1, 408.

The difference between the England of Shakespeare [wrote Professor Tawney], still visited by the ghosts of the Middle Ages, and the England which emerged in 1700, . . . was a difference of social and political theory even more than of constitutional and political arrangements. Not only the facts, but the minds which appraised them, were profoundly modified. . . . The natural consequences of the abdication of the authorities which had stood, however imperfectly, for a common purpose in social organization, was the gradual disappearance from social thought of the idea of purpose itself. Its place in the eighteenth century was taken by the idea of mechanism. The conception of men as united to each other, and of all mankind as united to God, by mutual obligations arising from their relation to a common end, ceased to be impressed on men's minds.

Writers on science, from Bacon to Locke, slowly brought about an intellectual climate in which scientific laws, the laws of nature, were equated with the law of God, immutable rational precepts, and also with an equally immutable moral law. The social importance of this was seen when political economy began to arrogate to itself the position of a science. For Locke laws against usury were not so much harmful as foolish and ineffective. The laws of supply and demand regulated prices, including the price of labour: to combine to raise prices was wrong, morally wrong, for labourers no less than for monopolists. Already in the writings of Petty, Locke and Dudley North we look forward to the iron laws of the dismal science.

Science depends on economic development. As Lewis Mumford showed, the glass industry, in which England's predominance was acknowledged, made possible spectacles, the telescope, the microscope, the thermometer, the barometer, more accurate observation and measurement, and Newton's great synthesis, as well as less draughty houses, more intensive market-gardening and mirrors for introspection. The rapid expansion of the English paper industry (protected after 1688) contributed to greater cleanliness in the distribution of retail goods and to more tasteful and hygienic wall coverings for upper-class houses. It aided the spread of literacy and the emergence of a full-time civil service, rapid postal communications and dissemination of news, the preservation of accurate records. A great deal of time and money was saved. More accurate watches enabled doctors to count the pulse, once Harvey's discovery of the circulation of the blood had been accepted. The new scientific attitude pervaded life at many points. Governments after 1688 used statistics – for example, those collected on the balance of trade, on public revenue and expenditure, on the state of the coinage. The economist Charles Davenant was made Inspector-General of Imports and Exports, to supply statistical information to the Board of Trade and the Treasury. In the generation after 1688 English government was revolutionized by these new methods of rational calculation, applied by civil servants who were often Fellows of the Royal Society. In 1665 the Bills of Mortality were eagerly scanned to assess the progress of the plague. Life insurance dates from the end of the seventeenth century. Sir William Petty, who contributed so much to the development of 'political arithmetic', has also been described as 'the father of political economy'. At a lower but ultimately more important level, the mass of the population had by the second half of the seventeenth century become so accustomed to mental arithmetic that the abacus ceased to be used by adults, though it is still employed over large areas of the globe today.

In many smaller ways like this we can see the revolution as a turning point in the establishment of a competitive business society. It was then that general practitioners shook themselves free from control by the College of Physicians, whose monopoly had been protected by the Privy Council before 1640. Medical practice, Mr Roberts tells us, became 'a free economic activity like any other', its personnel and behaviour directed by the market, thanks to the existence of 'a numerous middle class, which not only expected adequate medical care but was also able to pay for it, provided that the fees demanded were not exorbitant', as the physicians had tried to keep them.* The first free public library in Europe to be run independently of the church or a municipality – Chetham's Library at Manchester – dates from 1653; though even earlier the Parliamentary Committee at York had thrown the Minster Library open to the

*R. S. Roberts, 'The Personnel and Practice of Medicine in Tudor and Stuart England, Part 2, London', *Medical History*, VIII (1964), pp. 217–34.

public. Hitherto unfamiliar imports – tea, coffee, chocolate, tobacco – together with cheaper spices and cheaper sugar, revolutionized diet and social habits. Coffee-houses, whose existence would have been impossible without the development of the Levant trade, established themselves from the fifties as 'market places of news', reflecting the new availability of political information and the new desire to discuss it; just as the description of them as 'lay conventicles' suggests the shift of political interests away from religion to more secular subjects. Coffee-houses were suppressed in 1675 as 'the great resort of idle and disaffected persons'; but they survived.

The noblest of the revolutionaries had envisaged England as a strong man rousing himself from sleep: 'a nation not slow and dull, but of a quick, ingenious and piercing spirit, not beneath the reach of any point the highest that human capacity can soar to'. This fine confidence evaporated in the fifties. But English social relations were profoundly modified by the revolution; so, less perceptibly but in the long run perhaps even more significantly, were the ways in which men and women thought about themselves, nature and society.

Part Four

FROM POLITICAL TO
INDUSTRIAL REVOLUTION

I

SOCIETY AND POLITICS

Stability comes from the balancing of tensions, not from
inertia. – DOROTHY MARSHALL (*1962*), *p. 3*

I

AFTER 1688 the heroic age of English politics is over. The violent oscillations of the preceding fifty years were succeeded by a
relative calm. Divine-right Toryism was dead: support for the
Jacobite rising in 1715 came principally from bankrupt northern
landowners and from the Scottish Highlands. The '45 got nearer
to military success, but the Jacobite force was a foreign invading
army, not an English rebellion. There was little enthusiasm in
England either for George II or for the Young Pretender. 1685
had seen the last organized revolt of the radicals; the heirs of
Shaftesbury and Monmouth had little influence in the Whig
party after 1688. The defeat of the two extremes coincided with
the consolidation in power of men of moderation, of property,
of compromise: the Whig oligarchy, the Bank of England. The
names Whig and Tory continued to be used, but gradually lost
all save a historic significance: the heroic figures of a Strafford, a
Laud, a James II dwindled to the Rev. Henry Sacheverell.
Where King Pym, Oliver Cromwell and the false Achitophel had
sown, Sir Robert Walpole and the Duke of Newcastle reaped the
golden harvest. 'The greater number of those who make a
figure,' said Swift in 1710, were 'a species of men quite different
from any that were even known before the revolution' of 1688:
army officers or 'those whose whole fortunes lie in funds and
stocks.'

As the Whigs increasingly became the party of big business, so
a democratic fringe was exploited by Tory leaders. Tory politicians out of office learnt to speak the language of earlier Whig
republicanism, sponsoring bills against placemen and defending
a wide franchise in boroughs. Sacheverell was cheered by church

and king mobs, much as Shaftesbury and Monmouth had been cheered by no-popery mobs. The Sacheverell mob tried to burn down the Bank of England. The weavers of Southwark, old-style craftsmen and nonconformists almost to a man, opposed the church and king mobs in 1709. In the debates on the Septennial Act of 1716 'the Tories talked like old Whigs and Republicans against monarchy and ministers etc., and the Whigs magnified the advantages of unlimited absolute power and prerogative, vilified the mob, ridiculed the people and exalted the crown'. Swift referred to Stephen College, the 'Protestant Joiner' who had been executed in 1681, as 'a noble person'. In the early eighteenth century Jacobites found support among the Derby-shire miners (whose ancestors had been Levellers in 1649) and among the weavers of the Monmouth area, who had not lifted a finger for William in 1688. What was an honest man to do in such a society?

Until the rise of true radicalism in the later eighteenth century, all opponents of the Whigs had to call themselves Tories. 'Tory radicalism' was an uneasy and wholly negative alliance of the two defeated classes of the seventeenth century – the back-woods gentry and the urban poor – against their bourgeois and aristocratic rulers. The majority of provincial newspapers in the early eighteenth century proceeded on the assumption that most of their readers were 'Tory' in the sense that they were against the government, hated political corruption and looked back to a mythical golden age of social stability.* This kind of democratic Toryism, of which Bolingbroke tried to make himself the spokes-man in *The Craftsman* of the thirties, would pass easily into the radicalism of the seventies. Even the rather unattractive John-Bullishness of freeborn, beef-eating Englishmen, hating popery, wooden shoes and Frenchmen, went with a certain independence *vis-à-vis* social superiors.

The heroic age of religion was over too. The Toleration Act of 1689 was in many ways an unsatisfactory compromise: it did not extend to Roman Catholics, Unitarians, Jews or atheists, and it left protestant dissenters excluded from public life unless they

*See p. 267, below. Cf. L. M. Munby, 'Politics and Religion in Hertford-shire, 1660–1740', in *East Anglian Studies* (1968), pp. 138–42.

were prepared to communicate with the Church of England at least once a year. The latter retained its property and its social dominance, but at the price of abandoning the social ideals of Laud. The frustrated, tormented life of Swift shows how difficult it was for the noblest Anglicans to accept the position of Erastian chaplains to the monied interest: the Vicar of Bray found it easier. But eighteenth-century England was far from stagnant, even though religion and politics had lost much of their excitement. Trade was expanding rapidly, under government encouragement; agriculture was depressed in the twenties, thirties and forties, but cheap food lowered industrial costs. Industry was slowly gathering strength for the great explosion which was to come after 1780. The financial system of the country was being reorganized to meet the needs of a modern commercial community.

Political and religious ideals faded, as both right and left, Jacobites and republicans, came to recognize the permanency of the revolution settlement. Bolingbroke, great-grandson of Cromwell's Lord Chief Justice and himself brought up under dissenting influences, led the High Church Party under Anne. The Duke of Newcastle illustrated the debasement of political terms when in 1720 he thought his efforts on behalf of the South Sea Company would serve 'my friends and the Good Old Cause, neither of which I will forsake while I live'. Fifty-seven persons had a better hereditary claim to the English throne than George I: it was impossible to take divine right monarchy seriously after his succession.

As long as the propertied class was divided into opposing landed and monied interests, and as long as the House of Commons regarded its function as criticism rather than government, the monarchy retained considerable powers of manoeuvre. Swift seems genuinely to have believed in 1735 that 'without some unexpected assistance from heaven, many thousands now alive will see government by an absolute monarchy'. Popular fears that George III had such aspirations at the beginning of his reign, unfounded though we now know them to have been, were not just the invention of Burke. The king still chose his own ministers, and his favour was essential in normal times; but he had to accept his ministers' policy. George I stopped attending the Cabinet not because of any lack of linguistic ability but because he had so little authority there. The Commons could also in effect veto the king's choice of ministers and in time of crisis a minister like Pitt might be imposed on a reluctant monarch. In 1729 Townshend insisted that the king must never allow himself to lose credit and influence with Parliament: 'The confusions and misfortunes that attended the reigns of King Charles I and II and King James, in differing with their Parliaments, are too notorious to be forgot.' In the King's Speech of 1734 Walpole made George II associate the monarchy with 'religion, liberty and property', the old Parliamentarian trinity. George exaggerated when he spoke of himself as 'a King in the toils', and complained that 'ministers are the Kings in this country' (1745); but he had to accept ministers who could ensure him a majority in the Commons. 'The next great policy of the constitution,' Charles Yorke explained to his brother in 1746, 'is this, that whatsoever the King does should seem to come *ex mero motu*; the result of his own wisdom and deliberate choice. This gives a grace to government in the eyes of the people, ánd here is the dignity of the monarchy.'

2

Yet what had replaced the monarchy? In 1703 Defoe wrote "'Tis in the power of the gentry of England to reform the whole kingdom, without either laws, proclamations or informers; and without their concurrence, all the laws, proclamations and declarations in the world will have no effect; the vigour of the laws consists in their executive power.' On paper the alterations to the old constitution were minimal. After 1688 any change seemed dangerous to the ruling oligarchy. The Tory Parliament in 1710 passed an act which established a landed qualification of £600 a year for a knight of the shire, £300 a year for a burgess. Swift thought this act 'the greatest security that ever was contrived for preserving the constitution, which otherwise might in a little time lie wholly at the mercy of the monied interest'. But in fact the main effect of the act was to reinforce existing social pressures on the monied men to set themselves up as landed families. Soon the Tory Bolingbroke was assuring 'the Bank, the East India Company and in general the monied interest' that anything which damaged them would also adversely affect 'multitudes of our own party'.

The arts of Parliamentary management were made necessary by the triumph of the monied interest. 'The House of Commons,' observed Dr Johnson, 'is no longer under the power of the crown, and therefore must be bribed.' Prosperity and the concentration of wealth in the early eighteenth century, together with the *relative* economic decline of the lesser gentry, made politics too expensive for some of those whose exclusive preserve it had hitherto been. The South Sea Company was said to have paid out £1,500,000 in bribes to public figures in 1720. The monied men were quite happy to leave the details of administration to those whose traditional function it was, secure in their ultimate control through the Bank of England and the great companies which advanced money to the government. But the 'natural rulers' had to group themselves in packs, united by kinship or geography, in order to hunt down the spoils of office; and they had to accept the leadership of one of the big families. The independent country gentleman was an ineffective political figure: not till the rise of new wealth, new classes, could the power of the great Whig dynasties be challenged; and this is after our period ends.

The effect of the Septennial Act, extending the life of Parliaments from three to seven years, and of an act of 1729, ostensibly directed against bribery, was to raise the price of a seat in the Commons, to the advantage of those with big money. So the constitution, devised to protect the landed interest, was gradually but inexorably twisted to the purposes of monied men. The price of a borough seat advanced in the eighteenth century from £1,500 to about £5,000: Clive was said to have paid £30,000 for his. There were regular borough brokers, who from the sixties advertised their wares in the newspapers. Around 1780, wrote Sir Lewis Namier, 'various nabobs returning from "India's plundered land" tried to insure against inquiries into the origin of their fortunes by providing themselves with seats in Parliament'. In 1754 the Tories spent more on the Oxfordshire contest than the government spent on the whole general election.

Gradually, as the Tory backwoods gentry slipped into the background, the distinction between landed and monied interests, so vital to Swift, lost its sharpness. Part of Walpole's achievement, Dr Plumb suggests, was to complete the reconciliation of these interests, the final rout of Toryism. For all practical purposes England was a one-party state. Significant political disputes were conducted within the ruling Whig party – usually over questions of foreign policy. Speaker Onslow deplored divisions in the House because the object of debate should be not to emphasize differences but to produce an agreed decision on the right policy for ministers to pursue. As this oligarchy closed in, most members even of the nominal narrow electorate were effectively disfranchised. Country gentlemen decided county elections among themselves: 'probably not more than one in every twenty voters at county elections could freely exercise his statutory rights', Sir Lewis Namier thought. If he were a gentleman of landed property, said Dr Johnson in 1775, 'he would turn out all his tenants who did not vote for the candidate whom he supported'. In all except the largest boroughs disputed elections were rare after 1720. In 1761 23 out of 44 towns with over 500 voters went to the polls; of 201 towns with less than 500 voters, only 18 polled.

A House of Commons so elected consisted of members more interested in the spoils of office than in political principles. Thus the system first evolved by Danby in the sixteen-seventies was gradually extended and perfected. Walpole matured and monopolized this system of government patronage. Appointments of neither subordinate local revenue officers nor cathedral canons were too trivial for him to be concerned with.* A hard core of 'King's Friends' was formed in the House, consisting mostly of placemen. Over and above this the ministry of the day relied on the votes of the various 'connexions' who held office. Government was a continual process of barter and manoeuvre. In the last resort a connexion could withdraw from a government, which might then find itself so weakened that it would

*Plumb, 1956–60, II, pp. 92–3, 97.

have to be reconstructed. The secret of political success in normal times was assiduous application to the day-to-day questions of patronage and place, such as the Duke of Newcastle showed. A man like the elder Pitt, the hero of the City of London, could force himself into power in time of grave emergency, but he never exercised the sort of arts which could have given him a permanently stable following. The system was suited to an age when no strong passions divided the political nation, but it made for inertia, lack of political drive: great issues were faced by governments only when they could no longer be avoided.

The system bred its own opposition to reform. At the beginning of George III's reign roughly half the M.P.s owed their seats to patrons. Those who had purchased a borough would gain no return on their investment so long as they remained in opposition. Obsolete places, which had become, in Burke's words, 'only a genteel excuse for salary', had to be preserved in order to satisfy the rapacious demands of politicians, of whom there were always too many chasing too few jobs. Yet without distributing enough places to managers of the groups comprising the House of Commons, government could not have been carried on. The settlement of 1688 had been designed to prevent royal government acting independently of the will of the landed families represented in Parliament; it perpetuated a spoils system for which the descendants of those families scrambled, a system which prevented strong government action except in times of acute crisis. Everybody in politics wanted to become the King's Friend, for though the King had no independent power, the major spoils of office were distributed in his name and often with his direct participation. The 'outs' inevitably looked to the Prince of Wales. The fact that George III's eldest son was not born until 1762 may have helped to persuade the 'outs' that the whole system must be reformed, and that they must appeal to public opinion for support. It may have made more acceptable Burke's new political myth, which justified the growth of party to the point of organizing opposition to the executive and offering an alternative government. Previously groups out of office had merely made nuisances of themselves until they were taken in. So principles were beginning to re-enter politics as our period ends: external public opinion was beginning to express the moral repugnance which the system of corruption and family graft roused in those outside the charmed circle.

Walpole came to power thanks in large part to his skill in clearing up the mess after the bursting of the South Sea Bubble, with a minimum of scapegoats. George I had been Governor of the Company, so the revelation of too many scandals might have shaken the Hanoverian settlement itself. This covering-up operation ensured Walpole the support of the royal family, as well as popularity in Parliament. His policy when in power was one of peace abroad in order to keep taxes low at home, to please the gentry. Yet his fiscal policy favoured manufacturers; he removed nearly all export duties on English manufactured goods, as well as import duties on some raw materials needed for industry. Bounties were given to stimulate sugar refining and the manufacture of sailcloth and silk; export duties remained only on industrial raw materials like coal and lead, and on unfinished cloth. In order to keep wages low an act was passed in 1726 prohibiting combinations of workers. Walpole's support in the City came from the ruling oligarchy. In 1724 his government disfranchised 3,000 freemen and confirmed the veto claimed by aldermen, a reversion to practices which had been disputed ever since the democratic sixteen-forties. (This act was repealed in 1746.) No longer were the Whigs the party which always favoured a wide franchise against oligarchy. Walpole was hated by ordinary citizens of London, it was said, 'because he never did anything for the trading part of it, nor aimed at any interest of theirs but a corrupt influence over the directors and governors of the great monied companies'. In 1742 the City of London petitioned officially for bills against places and pensions, and for repeal of the Septennial Act, as guarantees against the corruption of Parliament.

3

Slowly public opinion began to become a force, especially from the establishment of annual sessions of Parliament after 1689. Dissenters were perhaps the first to organize themselves as pressure groups, operating in what was to become the typical British middle-class way of working on ministers and civil servants behind the scenes rather than by public demonstration or petition. These latter techniques had been used by Levellers and Shaftesbury's Whigs, but fell into disfavour from the eighties, and were not revived until the new social force of Wilkesite radicalism arose in the seventeen-sixties. The press helped to give expression to this new middle-class opinion. Notwithstanding attempts by governments to restrict the circulation of newspapers by means of stamp duties, the English press from 1695 onwards enjoyed a freedom from censorship before publication which was unique in Europe. In 1700 no newspaper was published outside London; by 1760 there were more than 130, most of them opposition in tone. By 1782 there were eighteen London newspapers. Since provincial newspapers depended on London for their news, the effect of their circulation was to create a *nation.al* public opinion, led by London. Walpole abandoned his excise scheme in 1733 and changed his foreign policy in 1742, Pitt came to power in 1757, not in response to royal wishes or those of a majority in the House of Commons, but because of pressure from a powerful merchant interest with popular support. Wilkes's election in 1774 was a triumph for public opinion against king and House of Commons. It was the Wilkesite movement which finally brought to an end the Commons' obstinate opposition to the publication of their debates.

4

English fiscal policy from the sixteen-forties onwards can be seen as a battle between land tax and excise: a battle which is linked with disagreements over foreign policy. The wars of Cromwell, William and Anne were financed by increasing the land tax; the intervening periods saw it reduced. In the sixties, Pepys tells us, 'the country gentlemen are for a land tax and against a general excise, . . . because they are fearful that if the latter be granted they shall never get it down again'. The court party wanted a general excise for exactly this reason. By the eighteenth century the landed interest associated the land tax with the national debt.

Walpole's peace policy, his salt tax of 1732 and his Excise Bill of 1733 all resulted from a determination to keep the land tax low. Excise aroused the fury of the lesser citizens of London, who thought that the beer of the poor was being taxed to pay interest to fundholders. In the thirties malt and beer taxes brought in a quarter of Walpole's revenue from taxation. Land tax rose again with war in 1740 and 1756. But by 1780 the land tax brought in, on an average, only twenty-two per cent more than in William III's reign; the excise brought in more than five times the figure in William's time.

Excise was unpopular because of the brutality with which it was collected. Men feared, or pretended to fear, that excise-men would form the nucleus of the sort of bureaucracy which the Stuarts had been prevented from building up. Their very existence seemed to violate the principles of 1688. The great households brewing their own beer escaped the tax because they would never allow inspection by excise officers: as usual the smaller men paid. (Another effect of excise was to favour concentration of the brewing industry in fewer and larger firms.) The salaried bureaucracy of excise-collectors was also unpopular because of its efficiency. The cost of collecting taxes was lower in England than anywhere else in Europe.

5

The power of J.P.s, those 'freedom-loving tyrants', increased steadily after 1688. Quarter sessions no longer transacted business in public, and became less responsive to outside opinion as presentments by juries were replaced by presentments by individual J.P.s. Much business was delegated from all the magistrates in quarter sessions to one or more J.P.s acting with a minimum of control or supervision. Dismissal from the bench was virtually unknown. J.P.s regulated wages, at least down to the mid-eighteenth century, and controlled poor relief. They thus combined administrative with judicial functions, a combination which in the Star Chamber had been vigorously opposed by the gentry themselves. After 1732 all J.P.s had to have an estate of £100 a year. They inevitably shared the outlook of the employing class in industrial disputes: when, towards the end of our period, employers in the clothing industry began to set up committees to prosecute workers charged with embezzlement or bad work, it seemed quite natural that the inspectors whom the employers' committees appointed should be licensed by J.P.s.

In the corporate towns 1688 confirmed the authority of self-perpetuating oligarchies, who also in effect chose M.P.s. No government took action to limit their powers and privileges, or to call them to account. But after about 1760, in some of the economically advancing areas, a new spirit was abroad. A number of towns secured private acts of Parliament empowering them to set up paving commissioners, lighting commissioners, improvement commissioners, to make towns more comfortable places to live in. Many urban parishes employed regular doctors. Increasingly urban administration was being professionalized, while that of the counties remained incorrigibly amateur. This created a unity of interest in efficiency between the administrative class and the new industrial magnates, so badly organized nationally: it looks forward to Benthamism.

'Laws grind the poor, and rich men rule the law', sang Goldsmith. The law did not protect the weak, ignorant and simple. False pretences was not a legal offence until 1757, to the advantage of fraudulent company promoters. Between 1688 and the end of our period the number of offences which carried the death penalty rose from about fifty to nearly five times that number. The vast majority of these were offences against property, and most offenders, in London at least, were under twenty-one years of age. A man was hanged for stealing one shilling, a boy of sixteen for stealing 3s. 6d. and a penknife, a girl for a handkerchief. A boy of eleven was hanged for setting his master's house on fire. Many more were sentenced to transportation. The law, in Mr Thompson's words, 'was both dispassionate in its adjudication of substantial property rights and passionately vengeful against those who transgressed against them'. 'The laws of the land,' said Fielding's Lawyer Scout to Lady Booby, 'are not so vulgar as to permit a mean fellow to contend with one of your ladyship's fortune.' In *Amelia* the magistrate 'had too great an honour for truth to suppose that she ever appeared in sordid apparel'. Prisons, which were run on private enterprise principles, financed by fees payable by prisoners, were horribly insanitary.

6

The Union of England and Scotland in 1707 greatly increased what was already the largest free trade area in the world. Adam Smith thought this was one of the main reasons for England outstripping France. The old Scottish coins were called in and replaced by English currency. The payment of £400,000 compensation to Scotland was a great stimulus to her economy. The Union hit the Scottish clothing industry hard; but access to colonial trade made Glasgow by the end of our period the chief tobacco port in the United Kingdom. Glasgow's growth in its turn stimulated industrial development in the hinterland. The long-term effects of the Union were 'entirely beneficial to the Scots economy', Professor Hamilton thought. The Scottish corn and cattle trade to England prospered. English capital was invested in Scotland, and encouragement was given to the Scottish linen industry. Revenue from duties collected by the Scottish commissioners of excise rose six times from 1707 to 1780.

The defeat of the '45 brought an extension of London influence over the Highlands of Scotland similar to that which the outcome of the civil war had brought to the dark corners of northern and western England a century earlier. The clans were disarmed, hereditary jurisdictions and military service were abolished. Estates were confiscated and sold to monied Lowlanders. New roads and bridges were built, judges went on circuit, Highlanders were forcibly educated in English. Dr Johnson noted the social consequences. 'When the power of birth and station ceases, no hope remains but from the prevalence of money. Power and wealth supply the place of each other. . . . The chiefs, divested of their prerogatives, turned their thoughts to the improvement of their revenues, and expect more rent as they have less homage.' The evictions and depopulation which followed were the work of the chiefs themselves, 'degenerated from patriarchical rulers to rapacious landlords'. Jacobitism survived as a consolatory legend; but the cultural golden age of Scotland followed the defeat of the '45, the age of Adam Smith, David Hume, William Robertson, Adam Ferguson, Robert Wallace, Lord Kames, John Millar, William Ogilvie, James Boswell, Robert Burns and James Watt.

2

TRADE, EMPIRE AND
FOREIGN POLICY

Wealth, howsoever got, in England makes
Lords of mechanics, gentlemen of rakes:
Antiquity and birth are needless here;
'Tis impudence and money makes a peer. . . .
Fate has but very small distinction set
Betwixt the counter and the coronet.

– D. DEFOE, The True-Born Englishman (*1701*)

I

BETWEEN 1700 and 1780 English foreign trade nearly doubled;
it trebled during the next twenty years. Shipping doubled too.
The same years 1700–80 saw a shift from an economic map in
which Europe was still England's largest market to one in which
it had been replaced by the colonies. This expansion was aided
by deliberate government policy – e.g. the removal of all export
duties on British manufactures and corn, though important
industrial raw materials still had to pay duty. It was also aided by
British control of the seas, which lasted for exactly a couple of
centuries after the conclusion of the War of Spanish Succession.
James Thomson wrote *Rule Britannia* in 1740.

'Trade in England,' wrote Defoe in 1726, 'neither is or ought
to be levelled with what it is in other countries; or the tradesmen
depreciated as they are abroad. . . . To say a gentleman-trades-
man is not . . . nonsense.' The transition from trade to landed
family was now common. Consequently, though landlords still
dominated governments, they were well aware of the importance of 'our trade, which is so much the vital breath of this
country that the one cannot subsist whenever the other is
stopped'. That was Lord Hervey in 1734; the Duke of Newcastle
was 'bred up to think that the trade of this nation is the sole
support of it', and endeavoured always 'to contribute all that was

in my power to the encouragement and extension of the trade and commerce of these kingdoms'.

Professor Weimann has pointed out how many of Defoe's characters combine the careful calculating qualities attributed to the protestant ethic with an adventurousness, a buccaneering spirit which at first sight goes oddly with an emphasis on thrift and prudence. He relates the combination to the role of English merchants in the eighteenth century, when fortunes were made in India and the West Indies by methods little removed from piracy or plunder. Yet the nabobs, East India merchants and West India planters returned to England and became respected members of society, with who knows what degradation of its standards. At the same time, in trade, the navy and the civil service, younger sons of the aristocracy were beginning to learn the self-discipline and responsibility which made their successors in the nineteenth century such a formidable social group. There were advantages in having a navy as the country's main defensive force, and paying foreigners to do land fighting. Technical skill is needed to sail a ship, and, for all the flogging, some minimum of cooperation and understanding with the crew. Even if press-ganged, freer men are needed to sail a ship than to master Prussian parade-ground drill. Any one with the habit of command could be an army officer; a modicum of self-discipline and social responsibility was necessary for a successful naval officer.

2

'All this great increase in our treasure proceeds chiefly from the labour of negroes in the plantations,' said Joshua Gee in 1729, with a frankness that few historians have emulated. The slave trade was essential to the triangular imperial trade which grew up under the Navigation Acts. It seemed to economists an ideal trade, since slaves were bought with British exports, and transported in British ships. Moreover slave labour prevented the plantations draining England's population, a matter that was beginning to worry publicists after a century of complaint that the country was over-populated. This consideration accounts too for the high esteem in which tropical colonies were held.

The main base for the English slave trade was Jamaica, captured in 1655. The Royal African Company was founded soon after the restoration, under the patronage of the Duke of York, to oust the Dutch from the monopoly position in slaving which their seizure of Portuguese ports on the West African coast had given them. The first Dutch war opened India and the Far Eastern trade to English merchants; the second Dutch war West Africa and the slave trade. The ending of the Royal African Company's monopoly in 1698, coupled with the increasing demands of the sugar plantations in the West Indies, led to a rapid extension of the British slave trade. The great prosperity of Liverpool and Bristol in the eighteenth century was based very largely on this trade.

The War of Spanish Succession won for England the coveted *Asiento*, the monopoly of supplying slaves to the Spanish American empire, which France had proposed to secure for her merchants by annexing Spain. England replaced the Netherlands as the greatest slave-trading nation in the world. The South Sea Company was started by the Tory government in 1711, to trade with the Spanish empire after the conclusion of peace, especially in slaves. During its boom period the company was able to rival the Bank of England and the East India Company, to bribe ministers and the king. It was not so pleasant for the slaves as for those who profited by them. Owing to 'commercial inefficiency bred from meretricious politics', the historian of the South Sea Bubble tells us, 'mortality on the South Sea Company's slavers was heavier than on those of the more experienced Royal African Company' – where it had never been light.* After 1730 Parliament granted £10,000 a year for forts on the Gold Coast to protect the interests of the slavers. Pitt's famous words in 1739, 'where trade is at stake it is your last retrenchment; you must defend it or perish', lose something of their glamour when we recall that the trade in question was mostly in human beings. Pitt's own strategy in the Seven Years War took account of slaving interests: Senegal and Goree were captured in 1758.

The slave trade was believed to be the most profitable of all branches of English commerce. Slaves sold in the West Indies

* Carswell, pp. 53–8, 65–7.

for five times what it cost to buy them on the African coast, so losses (up to twenty per cent) in the horrible conditions of transit need not trouble the slavers unduly. There was little vocal opposition to the trade between the sixteen-fifties and the loss of America, except from a few Quakers: an honourable exception is John Dunton, in his *Athenian Oracle*, published in the sixteen-nineties. West India planters opposed the conversion of slaves to Christianity, and their education. The Society for Propagating the Gospel allowed no Christian instruction to be given to its slaves in Barbados. Pitt destroyed a scheme to teach negroes in the American colonies to spin and weave cotton. Colonial legislative assemblies were not allowed to prohibit or restrict the activities of slavers.

The consequences of the slave trade in brutalizing English opinion, and in fostering the Puritan tendency to hypocrisy, should not be underestimated. Even during the American revolution only one English commander suggested freeing slaves and using them against the rebels: rather lose an empire than keep it by such means! Although Moors occur in Elizabethan and Jacobean masques as evil figures, this seems to have been because of the Mohammedanism attributed to them as well as because their skins were of the devil's colour. Many other early references to Moors or negroes – Pocahontas, *Othello*, Ben Jonson's *Masque of Blackness*, Middleton's *The Triumphs of Truth*, Massinger's *The City Madam*, early seventeenth-century poems about flirtations between black and white boys and girls, Mrs Aphra Behn's *Oroonoko* – suggest that an attitude of racial discrimination was the result, not the cause, of the profitable slave trade: in the seventeenth century far greater generalized contempt seems to have been shown for the Irish than for negroes. Indeed in 1693 Thomas Rymer thought it necessary to criticize Shakespeare for showing so little colour prejudice in *Othello*. Something had happened in the generations which intervened.*

Inevitably, those who looked upon black labourers in the West Indies as chattels would extend this attitude to white labour in England. The slave trade also had deep and lasting effects on

*E. Jones, *Othello's Countrymen* (1965), *passim*.

relations between England and the extra-European world, whose memory was not obliterated by later English vigilance in suppressing the slave trade once this country had ceased to profit by it.

When I think of the colossal banquets of the Barbados planters [wrote Richard Pares], of the money which the West Indians at home poured out upon the Yorkshire electorate and Harriette Wilson, of the younger William Beckford's private orchestra and escapades in Lisbon, of Fonthill Abbey or even of the Codrington Library, and remember that the money was got by working African slaves twelve hours a day on such a [starvation] diet, I can only feel anger and shame.

The modern historian who adopts the most optimistic attitude to the position of workers in the Industrial Revolution has only one reference to the slave trade in his *Economic History of England in the 18th Century*, and that to 'an attempt . . . to mitigate' its 'worst horrors'.

3

The most approved trade in the eighteenth century was that with Portugal, because it appeared to be an alternative to trade with France. The only interest to favour the latter was the East India Company, which needed French bullion. French wines, by contrast, had to be purchased with English bullion. In the early eighteenth century demand for English manufactures (notably light textiles) was increasing from Portugal and Brazil. It helped a great revival of Exeter as a port. Especially after the Methuen Treaty of 1703 Portuguese trade, and particularly the gold of Brazil, contributed to the establishment of London as the bullion market of the world. This facilitated London's trade with the Far East and helped to purchase naval stores from the Baltic. Anti-French economic policies date back to the Commonwealth. Between 1649 and 1657 there was an embargo on French wines and wool and silk manufactures. Parliament again in 1678 forbade the import of French wines, brandy, textiles, salt and paper. Repealed under James II, the prohibition was renewed in 1689: the English paper industry grew up under this protection. The Whig war of Spanish succession was brought to an end in 1713 by a Tory peace; but Harley's commercial treaty with France was repudiated by Parliament.

The Hanover Tories ('Whimsicals') arose in opposition to the French commercial treaty. They were those who supported the woollen and silk manufactures, the port wine trade and the established protective system as a whole. By giving 'trade and the protestant succession' a majority in the House of Commons they showed how far the Tory party had ceased to be a mere party of the landed interest. A commercial treaty was signed with France in 1786 only after the decline of the Portuguese trade.

4

There were for eighteenth-century England two alternative foreign policies, expressing different economic interests. One group (Stanhope, Carteret, Chatham) held that war and colonial conquest were the way to national wealth and power. (Stanhope also wanted greater freedom for dissenters.) Pitt had the strong support of London and other citizens, concerting his policies with City merchants. Another succession of ministers (Harley, Walpole, Bute) wanted peace in the interests of the landed class, whose taxes financed war: they disliked commercial adventures. Walpole in a sense succeeded to the Tory 'little England' policy, just as Pitt took up the aggressive policy of Oliver Cromwell and William III. But Walpole's era of peace also allowed the development of some of England's greatest assets – the technical skill of her craftsmen and the methods of mass production supplying the home market. 'If England had enjoyed unbroken peace,' wrote Professor Ashton, 'the Industrial Revolution might have come earlier.' This conclusion is debatable, since government contracts and military expenditure also stimulated many branches of industry – iron and steel, brass and copper, coal, clothing. But at least it points the contrast between the two policies. There is a nice irony in the thought that the monied interest, the aggressive group, may have delayed the coming of the Industrial Revolution; and the enemies of the monied interest may have contributed to the triumph of a wholly capitalist civilization.

The conclusion is also debatable since England's wars led to the acquisition of new territories and new markets. Contemporaries had few doubts that, in the words of Lord Holderness, 'our trade depends upon a proper exertion of our maritime strength'. 'The rise of the British economy,' writes Professor Wilson, 'was based, historically, on the conscious and successful application of strength; just as the decline of the Dutch economy was based on the inability of a small and politically weak state to maintain its position against stronger states.' It would be nice if it had been otherwise; but even the most liberal historians cannot have their cake without breaking eggs.

The elder Pitt's foreign policy had one great difference from that of Stanhope and Carteret: he virtually abandoned any English share in continental fighting. This was left to foreigners subsidized by England. So Pitt escaped the stigma of sacrificing English lives to the interest of Hanover, and was left free to concentrate on the world-wide struggle for trade with France. (Carteret, by contrast, called commerce-destroying 'vexing your neighbours for a little muck'.) In the Seven Years War, Wolfe's recovery of Canada (surrendered by Charles I 130 years earlier) opened the fish and fur trades to England, and a new supply of naval stores. (Wolfe was well aware of what he was doing: 'French fishing in the Gulf of St Lawrence,' he wrote to Pitt in November 1758, 'is, in a great measure, ruined'.) The capture of Guadeloupe brought a new supply of sugar. The conquest of Senegal and Goree opened up the gum and slave trade of West Africa. Clive meanwhile was establishing a territorial power in India which would guarantee monopoly control of its trade. An attack on Manila gave control of trade in China tea. But many of these gains were surrendered at the Peace of Paris, made by a recrudescent landed interest. (Bute was compelled to accept the French terms, among other reasons, because the City said it could not raise money so long as he was in office.) Guadeloupe and Goree were restored, the advantages of Canada were lost by restoring French fishing rights. From this treaty, flouting Pitt and the City, Professor Plumb dates the dawn of bourgeois radicalism, in which at last industrial interests began to speak for themselves, in alliance with the left wing of the Whigs.

One consequence of the existence of two rival foreign policies was the reputation of *perfide Albion*. War-party governments made the promises necessary to gain alliances and win wars; peace-party governments disavowed these commitments in order to make peace. There was little continuity of foreign policy in the eighteenth century. The Catalans and the Dutch were let down in 1713, the Emperor in 1733, Frederick the Great in 1763. Periods of war were periods of national unity (at least within the ruling class); periods of peace those in which internal divisions were most obvious. A series of bad harvests between 1708 and 1713 contributed to popular clamour for peace; but perhaps the rise of internal differences forced Walpole into war in 1739. Were faction squabbles the cause or the effect of struggles for peace in 1710–13 and 1760–63? Pitt's foreign policy ended Jacobitism, just as Cromwell had hoped by his anti-Spanish policy to reconcile the Cavaliers to his government.

And of course there were divisions within the commercial interest, as there had been in the seventeenth century. The West and East India interests, and slave traders, seem to have been those most anxious for war. Exeter's trade prospered in the War of Spanish Succession, possibly because of illegal exports through Portugal to Spain; it was badly hit by the later wars of the century.

The landed interest allied with the clothing interest to carry the peace of Paris, retaining Canada rather than the sugar island of Guadeloupe. Clothiers no doubt saw the advantages of the North American colonies *as markets*, at a time when Europe was trying to shut out English cloth. Exports to North America nearly tripled between 1744 and 1758. The Peace of Paris was a turning point in English colonial policy; henceforth greater stress was laid on colonies as markets than as sources of supply. For the rapid growth of population in North America (from 200,000 to 2,000,000 between 1700 and 1770) meant that its imports of English commodities – like guns, axes, buttons, leather goods, household goods, etc. – increased, also about ten- or twelve-fold. In the eighteenth century English armies stationed there added to the demand for goods. The prosperity of English iron manufactures, so important a feature of the eighteenth-century economy, depended largely on the American market. Production for this market led to new divisions of labour in the metal industries. And then followed West African and Indian demand for cotton manufactures. In 1700–1701 America and the East and West Indies had taken thirteen per cent of English exports; in 1772–73 they took forty-six per cent; imports from these areas were thirty-three per cent in 1700–1701, sixty per cent in 1772–73.

There were many contradictions within the old imperial system. The clothing interest succeeded in excluding Indian calicoes from the English market; but the East India Company had to sell them, and so they competed in the European market with English textiles. The East India trade offered no market for English exports, and there was general disapproval of the export of bullion. These contradictions were resolved only with the rise of the English cotton industry. The system as a whole, which had been built up as a rival imperial monopoly of colonial trade and shipping to that of the Dutch, was losing its *raison d'être* with the defeat of England's Dutch and French commercial rivals. The mercantile system became a clog rather than a protection; but many vested interests had to be broken down before it could be changed. The rude shock of the American revolution and Irish revolt were needed first.

An essential prerequisite for industrial revolution was large and stable colonial monopoly markets. The conquest of India was in due course to open up such a market for the English cotton industry. The West Indies declined in importance from the mid-century because their slaves and absentee planters offered no significant market for English manufactures. The traditional West Indian colonies supplied raw materials, non-competitive with products of the home country, to be processed for re-export; the new empire was seen as an indefinitely expanding market for English manufactured goods. By the time the old imperial monopoly broke down, in the seventeen-seventies, the English cotton and metal industries had developed to a stage at which their products could re-enter and capture the European markets. So we can trace five periods of English export trade: (1) down to *c.* 1600, the old draperies, exported mainly to the North European market; (2) *c.* 1600–50, the New Draperies, catering especially for the southern European market; (3) *c.* 1650–1700, colonial monopoly, entrepôt and re-export; (4) *c.* 1700–80, manufactured exports especially to the colonies; (5) after 1780, England as the workshop of the world.

5

The navigation laws worked increasingly to the disadvantage of North America as population there increased. The New England colonies fitted into the navigation system only with difficulty. They had no tropical products to export, and they resented being dependent on Britain for all manufactured goods, instead of being allowed to develop their own industries. An act of 1699 forbade the export of cloth manufactures from the colonies, even to another American colony, and the American cloth industry was suppressed in 1719. American iron was allowed into England duty-free, but in 1750 the erection in America of any new slitting or rolling mills, forges or steel furnaces was prohibited. Even a friend of America like Pitt stated that he would not allow a nail to be made in the colonies without permission of the British Parliament. The development of coal-mining in Cape Breton was prohibited lest it should encourage iron manufacturing in America, though the prohibition meant that England continued to export coal to America which she could ill spare. In 1732 Parliament forbade the export of hats made in America.

The American colonies were thus in theory as oppressed as Ireland. But, because of the distances involved, these laws could not be enforced. There was a thriving trade in smuggled beaver hats between the colonies, and the act of 1750 about ironworks was disregarded. And there were compensating advantages from the imperial connexion. American shipbuilding, cheaper than English, was encouraged. By 1730 about one in six of English ships was American-built; by 1774 perhaps one in three. But the principles underlying English policy were deeply resented. By an act of 1729 American timber and naval stores were virtually commandeered for England, in disregard of the rights of private property which it had cost so much to establish in seventeenth-century England. 'That grand principle in nature, "that what a man hath honestly acquired is absolutely and uncontrollably his own",' Massachusetts explained to Chatham in 1768, 'this principle is established as a fundamental rule in the British Constitution.' The Americans asked only for the rights of pro-pertied Englishmen as established in 1641 and 1688. 'What we did,' said Jefferson, 'was with the help of Rushworth, whom we rummaged over for revolutionary precedents of those days.'

The fact that regulations were not enforced created a habit of lawlessness and contempt for English authority. Hence the un-expectedly fierce opposition in America when the British government tried to impose import duties in order to help to pay for British troops in America. The effect on American opinion of the act of 1765 which asserted the sovereignty of the English Parliament over the colonies was rather like that of James I's constitutional theory on early seventeenth-century Englishmen: they could not refute it as law, but they found it intolerable in practice.

6

As the East India Company's business expanded, it began to want to establish a territorial power in India in order to pay for fortifications by taxing those whom the forts held down. The Charter of 1661 recognized the company's right to tax, and gave it power to wage war against non-Christian peoples. By 1684 Sir Josiah Child was advocating 'absolute sovereign power in India for the Company'. In the mid-eighteenth century Clive began to execute this policy, to his own and the company's great financial advantage. Over £2 million a year was added to the company's revenue. (The directors of the company, it was said, had the disposal of 'several governments of much greater value than any in his Majesty's gift'.) This revolution in the company's power and status caused more active government interest in the company's affairs from 1766 onwards, 'not to give good government to the Indian possessions', Dr Sutherland emphasizes, 'but with the intention of providing for the state a share in the revenues which were coming to the Company' now.* In 1767 the company agreed to pay £400,000 a year to the Exchequer.

The great wealth won by the plunder of India enabled the plunderers to buy their way into English politics. Clive himself acquired first a Parliamentary seat, then a peerage. It was alleged that between 1757 and 1766 the company and its employees received £6 million from India as gifts. Warren Hastings prided himself on never defrauding the company: before accepting money he asked himself only 'this, whether it would go into a black man's pocket or my own'. In thirteen years he remitted to England over £218,000 which he had saved from black men.† There had been nothing like it in history since the Spanish *conquistadores* looted the Aztec and Inca civilizations of America in the early sixteenth century. The Wilkesites, with some support from the independent country gentry, led an attack on the company's monopoly, attributing to Clive's activities 'the late famine in Bengal and the loss of 3 million of inhabitants'. Finally, after Warren Hastings's deliberate policy of expansion had made British rule paramount in India, the English government took over a larger share of responsibility for governing India (Lord North's Regulating Act of 1773, Pitt's India Act of 1784). Hastings was impeached and a host of scandals revealed: but his policy was continued. Meanwhile tea imports rose from 54,600 lb. in 1706 to 2,325,000 lb. in 1750; the price fell from £1 to 5s. a lb.

It is difficult to establish any direct connexion between wealth amassed in the plunder of India and other colonies and the capital which financed England's Industrial Revolution. It is even more difficult to believe that there is no link between the two. But there were other connexions. A pamphleteer of 1696 foresaw that 'the East India trade by procuring things with less and consequently cheaper labour is a very likely way of forming men upon the invention of arts and engines, by which other

*Sutherland, pp. 33–4, 56 and *passim*.

†P. J. Marshall, 'The Personal Fortune of Warren Hastings', *Economic History Review*, 2nd Series, XVII, p. 291.

things may also be done with less and cheaper labour, and therefore may abate the price of manufactures'.

7

In the eighteenth century smuggling was almost a national sport, with popular sympathies on the side of smugglers against customs officers. The severe laws against wool export were ineffective: in 1696 penalties had to be reduced in order to encourage prosecution of smugglers. Before and after the Union of 1707, smuggling and Jacobites throve together in Scotland. In England Sir Robert Walpole himself engaged in smuggling even when he was Secretary at War. In 1733 illicit trade with France and Holland was estimated at one-third of the legitimate trade. Liverpool's slave trade could not have existed without the beads smuggled in from Holland, and much illegal sugar came from the French West Indies. At the end of our period scarcely one-third of the tea consumed in England seems to have been imported legally; and a great deal of English wool was smuggled to France. In America smuggling was almost a patriotic duty. Adam Smith thought that the chief French and English merchants were engaged in smuggling, and himself sympathized with the smuggler, who 'would have been, in every respect, an excellent citizen had not the laws of his country made that a crime which nature never meant to be so'. In the seventeen-fifties and sixties Wesley had the greatest difficulty in persuading Methodists in Cornwall, Sussex, Cumberland and Dover to give up smuggling.

Professor Ashton describes Smith as 'tolerant and cynical', but this is to miss his point. Smith was first and foremost a moralist, and he meant what he said about the immorality of the customs laws. They were class legislation, which artificially kept up prices to the detriment especially of poorer consumers. The cost of collecting the customs was believed to be many times what was collected. Whenever we are tempted to think of the eighteenth century as lawless, we should recall the class nature of the laws and justice against which rebellion was directed. Men might be transported for infraction of the game laws. Some of

England's most admirable and enterprising citizens transgressed these laws, with wide public approval. It was hardly 'cynical' to be tolerant of those who risked their lives to get cheaper tea than the nabobs of the East India Company thought was good for Englishmen. In any case, as many contemporaries pointed out, the criminal was only carrying to their logical conclusion the doctrines of individualism which were preached in so many pulpits.

3

TOWARDS INDUSTRIAL
REVOLUTION

To hold the lower orders to industry and guard the morals of
the poor is the truest patriotism. – DEAN TUCKER, Reflec-
tions on Various Subjects (*1752*)

They starve and freeze and rot among themselves; but they
beg and steal and rob among their betters. – HENRY FIELD-
ING, A Proposal for Making an effectual Provision for the
Poor (*1753*)

I

THE price paid for social stability in 1660 – the survival of the
power of the gentry and the restoration of monarchy, peerage
and Church of England – was a slowing-down of certain aspects
of economic development. There was no seventeenth-century
industrial revolution parallel to those in agriculture, trade and
finance. Iron was the chief bottleneck holding back the advance of
industry, so long as pig-iron could be obtained only in small
quantities (through lack of fuel), and bar-iron had to be labori-
ously hammered. Machinery could be produced on a large
scale only when obstacles to the use of coal for mass production
of iron had been overcome. In the late seventeenth and early
eighteenth centuries iron production was actually declining.
Labour costs were higher than in Sweden or Russia. Yet the
industry was heavily protected from 1690 onwards, which made
foreign imports very expensive, and so kept home production
profitable. The high cost of farm tools was a bottleneck in
agriculture too.

Professor Nef thought it puzzling that so little should have
been done in England in the later seventeenth century to develop
new processes for making iron. Coke was not substituted for
charcoal in the iron industry for more than a century after it was
used for drying malt. The steam engine, which the Marquis of

Worcester claimed to have invented in the fifties, and with which experiments had been conducted since the early seventeenth century, came very slowly into industrial use only a century later. In part this was due to the ending of the all-European price revolution in the mid-seventeenth century; but there were special factors diverting capital away from the basic English industries.

Two of the bottlenecks – coal and iron – were industries in which, necessarily, landowners were prominent. And though they had never been averse to exploiting their mineral resources, they were under continuing social pressure to maintain a high standard of ostentatious expenditure. There was an inevitable tendency for them to take short-run views, to be interested in quick returns, to be reluctant or unable to invest large capital sums in the hope of long-term returns. As John Webster observed in 1671, the property rights of kings and great land-lords held up the development of English mining by smaller capitalists. The strict settlement in particular* held back capital investment in mining as well as in agricultural improvements. One of the main objects of Defoe's *Compleat English Gentleman* (1729) was to persuade gentlemen to invest in productive activity, not merely to consume. Nor were merchants interested in financing speculative projects on other people's land. Advance in these sectors had to wait for slower accumulation by humbler freeholders and lessees.

The new epoch in iron opened when the Darbys started smelting with coke at Coalbrookdale from 1709 onwards, though it was forty or fifty years before the new processes were widely adopted. The peaceful age of Walpole was one of relative stagnation for the iron industry; but war stimulated its development. From about 1750 a break-through occurred: cast iron began to be produced sufficiently cheaply and on a huge enough scale to replace wood in machines. From this side too England was ready for the Industrial Revolution. The completely iron mould-boards and all-iron ploughs which were invented in the seventies also helped to transform agriculture. From the nature of the case the later iron industry required heavy capital investment, and

*See pp. 146–8, above.

was run on fully capitalist lines. The Carron works in Scotland, which specialized in armaments manufacture, started with a capital of £12,000 in 1760, raised to £150,000 by 1774.

But in the seventeenth and early eighteenth centuries the purchase of a landed estate continued to be the ultimate aim of every ambitious trader or entrepreneur. In the Netherlands, by contrast, little land was available, and it was severely taxed. So in Holland son succeeded father in merchant dynasties, whereas in England capital was continually being withdrawn from industry and trade to investment in land. By the time the strict settlement slowed down land sales, there were plenty of openings for investors in the sector of trade and finance.

Landlords, increasingly perhaps as the eighteenth century advanced, sought prestige through conspicuous investment rather than conspicuous consumption – buildings, parks, paintings. But such investment, though it created some employment, stimulated the economy far less than a planned programme of investment in the capital goods sector and in improving communications would have done. Landlords in many cases initially opposed the improvement of water communications. The Royal Society did not fulfil the role of Bacon's House of Solomon, controlling and directing the economy. Royal patronage and the need to stress its political safeness led to an influx of dilettante gentlemen. When the Society turned its attention to agriculture, industry or navigation, its inquiries were narrowly utilitarian; and the greatest scientists, under Newton's influence, withdrew to the Olympian heights of abstract mathematics. Scientific advance in the eighteenth century came from the societies established in the Midlands and North of England by craftsmen and industrialists – the Lunar Society of Birmingham, the Manchester Literary and Philosophical Society.

Government policy before 1688 had contributed to this slowing down of industrial advance. Dissenters, the most industrious group in the population, were in many cases ruined by persecution. The Clarendon Code made life especially difficult for urban nonconformists. Birmingham flourished because it was not a chartered borough and its dissenters were not purged; but in this respect it was lucky. Defoe thought Bristol's prosperity was held back by 'the tenacious folly of its inhabitants' in clinging on to 'that corporation-tyranny'. A Parliamentary report of 1751 laid it down that 'the most useful and beneficial manufactures are principally carried on, and trade most flourishing, in such towns and places as are ... not liable to corporation bye-laws. ... A great part' of 'the laws relating to trade and manufactures ... ought to be entirely repealed', having 'become prejudicial to trade in its present state'.

The Navigation Acts diverted capital to colonial trade and shipbuilding, in the long run to the advantage of the economy as a whole: but in the short run to the disadvantage of industry. 'The development of the English entrepôt in these decades [1660–1760],' writes Professor Davis, 'involved large investments in commerce not accompanied by industrial investment', except in industries concerned with processing colonial goods. 'Foreign trade ... was in this period making exceptionally small demands for new industrial investment in relation to its requirements for its own financing.'

The Commercial Revolution, with its over-emphasis on the financial sector of the economy – banking, insurance – to the detriment of technology, ended in the fiasco of the South Sea Bubble. The South Sea Company drew investments from all corners of the three kingdoms, and from all but the poorest classes. But when the Bubble burst, the reaction was the more widespread. The premature sophistication of the economy was succeeded by a generation of timidity and lack of enterprise. Its historian suggests that the Bubble lengthened the gap between Commercial and Industrial Revolutions. The Bubble Act of 1720 forbade the formation of joint-stock companies without royal charter, and so increased the difficulty of raising capital for industrial enterprise. Yet heavy capital outlay was necessary for the development of industries like mining and iron and steel production. The new industries of the eighteenth century were built up slowly and painfully by their founders, with little help from the few provincial banks. The survival of guild regulations till 1688, and of the great trading companies' monopolies, also restricted economic activity.

Meanwhile most real wages rose slowly, despite the prevailing assumption that low wages were essential if English merchants were to compete with the Dutch. If wage regulation had been effective it would have restricted the home market to the advantage of exports. The object of the Act of Settlement of 1662, in Professor Ashton's words, was 'to keep people and resources apart'. Though it does not seem to have checked migration to larger towns, it may well have slowed down the development of rural industry. The corn laws and the bounty helped to keep food prices high and rents higher. The 'disappearance of the small landowner' ultimately cleared the decks for a fully capitalist agriculture; but during the transitional period it had the reverse effect, since the medium-sized freeholder, clinging desperately on to his holding, could not afford to be as experimental as his Dutch counterpart. Big landowners, unless exceptionally enterprising, did not need to adopt technical improvements so long as prices were artificially bolstered. Smaller landowners, especially after 1688, were hard hit by the land tax. It was only with the lower food prices of the 'agricultural depression' of the seventeen-thirties and forties that industrial costs were reduced and the purchasing power of the lower classes increased.

The usury laws, forbidding private entrepreneurs to offer more than six per cent interest on loans from 1651 to 1714, five per cent after 1714, diverted resources from industry and agriculture to the state, since the government could offer what rate it pleased. Moreover, since membership of the House of Commons was a great asset in the quest for government contracts, 'no small part of the resources of the larger London merchants went to the purchase of seats and to maintaining connexions with the sources of patronage' (Ashton). This was less of a drain on economic activity than when early Stuart courtiers had to be bribed: but a drain it was. The banking system evolved only after 1694, and then was closely tied to government loans. The National Debt was the first *safe* long-term investment other than land. The credit system was for long based entirely on London. The largest stockholders in the Bank of England were the South Sea and East India Companies, and other Londoners. The slow development of provincial banking meant that local industries were starved of capital to the advantage of big foreign-trading capital.

The aggressive foreign policy waged after 1688 was largely economic in motivation, and contributed both in the short run (protective tariffs, government contracts) to industrial advance, and in the long run (conquest of India, West Indies, Canada) to the dominant position in the world economy which England attained. Nevertheless, it too diverted assets from investment in peaceful construction. In 1715 a Board of Trade inquiry reported that 'the funds and stocks settled in the late wars render a more certain and greater gain than any foreign trade whatsoever', with the result that English capital was diverted from the carrying trade. 'To found a great empire for the sole purpose of raising up a people of customers,' wrote Adam Smith, 'may at first sight appear a project fit only for a nation of shop-keepers', and to the detriment of home consumption. The interest on the National Debt was greater than the whole value of colonial trade.

2

Where did the capital for the Industrial Revolution come from? Spectacularly large sums flowed into England from overseas – from the slave trade, and, especially from the seventeen-sixties, from organized looting of India. 'The early iron industry of South Wales,' Professor Ashton noted, 'was largely the creation of tea-dealers and other traders of London and Bristol, and the Clyde Valley owed much of its industrial equipment to the tobacco merchants of Glasgow.' But it is not always easy to trace connexions so directly. There is not much evidence that the plunder of India flowed directly into industry: much of it was spent on conspicuous consumption, and on buying political immunity for the plunderers. A certain amount of capital came from abroad, especially from the Netherlands, seeking safer and more profitable investment in the country of its now victorious rivals. Landowners, especially those owning coal-bearing land, also contributed. But in the early stages of England's industrial development we should probably attach even more significance to family and group savings of small producers who ploughed their profits back into industry or agriculture. Gregory King thought that in 1688 the largest total contribution to savings came from freeholders and farmers who would often themselves be industrialists. The 'prevalence of small yeoman capital', 'small independent men of energy', was thought by Miss Mann to have had something to do with the success of the Lancashire cotton industry in its early stages. Matthew Boulton began the expansion of his Soho works on the savings of his father's lifetime in the hardware industry. Certainly the brewing industry seems to have pulled itself up by its own bootstraps. Its historian emphasizes especially the Quaker contribution.

Members of sects evolved a group loyalty in the dark days of persecution in the later seventeenth century. They were likely to deposit their savings within a family or sectarian group. Capital thus remained in industry, not flowing out into land or the funds. The sects inherited a dislike of conspicuous expenditure: their exclusion from the universities and the great world of politics lessened the temptation for sons to dissipate the wealth of their fathers. As communications improved, economies of time could release resources for further investment: and nonconformists on religious grounds thought time should not be wasted. Moreover, the Quakers especially had far-flung connexions, extending in the case of the Barclays from London to Norwich, to the Midlands, to Philadelphia. This did not make marketing any more difficult. In times of crisis family and sectarian loyalties might save a firm from the failure of confidence which was the main hazard of a growing business. Here was perhaps one of the main contributions of nonconformity to the Industrial Revolution.

3

The Commercial Revolution not only created an expanding colonial market for English manufactures: it also helped to cheapen, diversify and expand the production of manufactured goods, to stimulate new industries. This dialectic between home and imperial markets is of the greatest importance in accounting for the Industrial Revolution. So is the dialectic of war and peace, war stimulating some industries, peace stimulating trade and other industries. Government contracts encouraged large-scale production – of ships, guns, uniforms, boots, sailcloth beer. But in the last resort we come back to the home market. The rise in population which took place simultaneously in England, Ireland and China stimulated industrial development in England only, because only in England did a larger population mean larger effective demand. By inland trade, said Defoe, 'innumerable families are employed, and the increase of the people maintained, . . . by which increase of trade and people the present growing prosperity of this nation is produced'. The destruction of domestic workshops in town and country, and the commercialization of farming, created the demand which was to absorb the products of factory industry. Unlike France, where the most important industries, and those encouraged by governments, were luxury industries, in England the expanding industries were textiles, stockings, hardware, catering for a mass market. French visitors to southern England noted that peasants did not wear wooden shoes or eat black bread (though they still did in the North). As the market was nationalized by slowly improving communications, so the annual fairs (so disruptive of the regular rhythms of an industrial economy) sank into insignificance. Middlemen came to the consumer and to weekly fairs in market towns. There were more village shops. In the later seventeenth century Quakers were thought odd because their yea was yea and their nay was nay: they refused to haggle at the market, insisting on a single price for all customers. By 1780 fixed prices were becoming generally accepted.

The process, once begun, was self-perpetuating. The extension of retail trading offered greater choice to more people, and so stimulated demand. Inventions in one sphere created new tastes, new demands, in another: when pewter gave way to glass it helped the sparkling Burton ales to compete with the cloudy London porter. When skilled labour was dear, and costs were rising, as they began to do in the newly developing industrial districts of the North, it paid to introduce labour-saving machinery. In the long run this lowered prices of most consumers' goods to a level at which at least some wage-earners could afford to buy them. Standardized products like Boulton's Birmingham brass buttons, or Wedgwood's pottery, began to supply an ever-widening home market before they went into the export business. 'We think it of far more consequence to supply the people than the nobility only', Boulton said. This was wise, as well as no doubt inspired by democratic sentiments.

Gregory King thought the average income of Englishmen in 1688 was £8–9 a head: labourers, cottagers and paupers averaged less than £3 3s. 0d. a head. This made him think England richer than any country in the world except the Netherlands. A century later the national average income had probably doubled. Apart from such guesses we know nothing of the extent of the home market. Davenant calculated that domestic demand for textiles was three times that of the foreign market. A guess of 1721 put the total home market at six times the foreign market. Eighty years later Macpherson assessed it at thirty-two times. In Scotland at the end of our period the home market took four times as much as the export market. Of the significance, and the rising significance, of domestic demand there can be no doubt. It may well be that the apparent pause in England's economic advance between 1720 and 1740 is in part an optical illusion caused by looking only at exports, and that the development of home industries was in fact creating a greater self-sufficiency. In explaining the prosperity of the West Riding, Defoe put first 'the travelling merchants', who 'go all over England with droves of pack horses', selling goods 'for the clothing the ordinary people'. From about 1750 there seems to be some evidence that wage-labourers were acquiring the habit of working harder and spending more, on things like boots and clothing, rather than taking more leisure when their minimum demands were satisfied. All roads thus led to expansion of the home market. Commercialization of farming, enclosure and eviction, and the undermining of small, self-sufficient craftsmen's households, created a market for products of large-scale manufacture. Those at the bottom of the ladder had to buy more, the more fortunate both bought and consumed more.

Finally, lest our emphasis on the growing industrial sector should get our perspectives wrong, let us recall that right down to the end of our period we can hardly speak of a *class* of manufacturers acting together: more often one section opposes another, as the wool trade fought against the cotton industry. Gregory King in 1696 had no category for manufacturers; in 1803 Colquhoun put their number at 25,000. Arthur Young estimated in 1770 that sixty-four per cent of England's national income derived from the soil, and only thirty-six per cent from trade and industry. Nearly half the population was still engaged in agriculture. Only at the very end of our period do industrial crises begin. Earlier crises originated in the agricultural sector.

4

One essential prerequisite for industrial and agricultural advance was an improvement in transport and communications. It requires an intellectual and imaginative effort to conceive of all the consequences of their backwardness. Transport by road was at least four times as expensive per ton-mile as by canal: twenty times as expensive for coal, some said. One horse could draw eighty times as much in a canal barge as by cart on a soft road, and four hundred times as much as a pack-horse could carry. So the fact that between 1600 and 1760 England's seven hundred miles of navigable rivers had been nearly doubled was of crucial importance. Before the canal era of the seventeen-sixties, ordinary strong beer had an economic marketing area of about four to six miles. This effectively limited expansion of the industry outside London, and preserved home brewing. Canals made possible the sale of ale brewed from the uniquely suitable water of Burton-on-Trent, not only to Liverpool but also to the Baltic countries and to India.*

Unlike road and sea transport, canals were unlikely to be affected by bad weather. Their significance was very great for the transportation of coal, so heavy and bulky and yet so vital for many industries. Before the canal era inland coal prices used to rise sharply after heavy rainfall. Canals halved the price of coal in Manchester. Turnpike roads and canals were the essential basis

* Mathias, *The Brewing Industry in England, 1700–1830*, pp. xxii–iii, 16, 175.

of the prosperity of the Staffordshire potteries. Birmingham no longer exported through London, but direct. Cheaper coal meant cheaper bricks for building the new industrial towns.

Coal was important for agriculture as well as for industry. Eighteenth-century open-field farmers were still burning manure as fuel: cheap transport for coal was essential if the ground was to be fertilized. Lime burned with coal was indeed widely used as a fertilizer. Improved communications also made marketing easier, not only of grain. Canals brought the long-staple wool of Lincolnshire and Leicestershire to the West Riding. Better roads made it possible to bring livestock to the London market in winter, so ironing out seasonal variations in prices. In 1767 the improvement in the quality of English roads was emphasized as the characteristic of the age most likely to impress posterity.

Turnpike roads helped London: canals, usually started on local initiative, helped especially the outlying industrial areas. Bad communications had kept England divided into self-contained economic regions. In 1700 wages in the North were barely half those of London, two-thirds of those paid in the West. By 1790 they had nearly caught up with those paid in the capital, and had far outstripped the West. Rents were steady in Durham from 1660 to the end of our period, but they rose in the Midlands between 1640 and 1690, in Norfolk between 1718 and 1745. The navvies who dug canals may, like the New Model Army a century earlier, have helped to spread new ideas to the outlying areas.

5

Among many streams contributing to the English Industrial Revolution, not least important was the tradition of skilled craftsmanship, especially in clock- and instrument-making, built up during the two centuries before 1780. The original impetus seems to have come from the demand for nautical instruments and chronometers for navigational purposes: but the skills soon extended into other fields. The English school of clock-making which grew up in the early seventeenth century became famous throughout Europe. Most of the leading clockmakers were Quakers. The industry's high degree of specialization taught

Petty the importance of division of labour. In the early eighteenth century clock-making became a mass-production industry which captured the European market. John Harrison, who at last solved the problem of determining longitude at sea, was a clock-maker; so was John Kay, who helped Richard Arkwright with his spinning frame (1768). (The John Kay who invented the flying shuttle in 1733 described himself as an engineer.) Arkwright himself falsely claimed to be a clockmaker, to enhance his standing and prestige. Benjamin Huntsman, another clockmaker, invented the process for making crucible steel in the quest for a stronger steel for clock springs. Newcomen, whose steam engine was invented in 1708, was a locksmith, James Watt a maker of scientific instruments.

There was consequently a solid basis of technical skill and ingenuity for the advances of the Industrial Revolution. France, whose economic level in so many respects compares with that of England until the mid-eighteenth century, lacked just this basis of widespread skilled and educated free craftsmanship – carpenters, locksmiths, millwrights, clock- and instrument-makers. Kay's flying shuttle (and other inventions) were successful in England, where they were taken up by weavers; they failed in France, where they were taken up by the government. English labourers had to be introduced into France to develop the cotton industry, hampered by corporations and regulations. On the other hand eighteenth-century French inventions in clock-making and textiles came to fruition in England. English craftsmen were gadget-minded. Most of the famous mechanical inventions of the eighteenth century were the result of many previous experiments, the 'inventor' being the lucky man who broke through. With all its defects, the Royal Society helped to diffuse interest in scientific matters: so still more did the dissenting academies. It was a great piece of good fortune for England that after 1660 the nonconformist middle class was excluded from Oxford and Cambridge, where they would have learnt to despise science. The connexion between dissent and scientific invention was as close in the eighteenth century as relations between Baconianism and the Parliamentary cause in the early seventeenth century. Joseph Black, educated at

Presbyterian Glasgow, and the political radical Joseph Priestley, teacher at a dissenting academy, picked up the science of chemistry where it had got bogged down at the restoration. The actuarial calculations which the Unitarian Richard Price placed at the disposal of the Equitable Insurance Company were an application to business life of principles which he had found valuable in religious thinking.*

The metal trades of Birmingham, Staffordshire and Sheffield trained many of the great eighteenth-century inventors. Matthew Boulton's success in perfecting the steam engine was due to the fact that 'his factory was one huge laboratory of applied mechanics' (Mantoux). So we reach the stage at which machines make machines: the superlative skill of the handicraftsman begins to be superseded. Only in the later stages of the Industrial Revolution did the industrial organizer come to the fore, himself devoid of technical skill, but gifted with ability to make use of the talents of others. Arkwright is the personification of this type, which was to make the profits out of the Industrial Revolution. Few of the great inventors died rich.

6

The Lancashire cotton industry dates from the seventeenth century. It was from the start organized upon a capitalist basis. It developed especially after the revolution, when legal decisions exempted unincorporated towns and villages from the operation of the Statute of Artificers. Lancashire adopted the Dutch ribbon loom, a complicated piece of machinery which was kept out of many continental countries by guild hostility. It probably established itself in Manchester during the interregnum, and its use extended after the restoration when the organized London weavers were rioting against it. Lancashire wages were low, and its cheap cotton goods were soon very popular in the home market, bought by 'all the mean people, the maid servants and indifferently poor persons'. Being washable, cottons must have been good for the health of their wearers, though at the expense of more work for housewives.

*I owe this point to my friend and former pupil Mr Peter Brown.

The cotton industry benefited from protective measures against Indian calicoes. It was doubly linked to the slave trade; West African slaves were paid for either by Indian cotton goods or – whenever supply from India was interrupted – by Lancashire cotton exports; slave labour in the West Indies and America produced raw cotton for the Lancashire industry. In return, the planters bought Manchester cottons to clothe their slaves. Liverpool, which became the cotton port, was the great centre of the slave trade. Its population increased ten times between 1680 and 1760. By the latter date it had replaced Bristol as second port to London. Between 1700 and 1780 British imports of raw cotton increased from one to five million pounds, by 1789 to thirty-two and a half million. Between 1750 and 1769 the export of British cotton goods increased ten times; and from about 1770 they began to capture the European market.

In the early eighteenth century the brewing industry interestingly anticipates some of the developments characteristic of the later Industrial Revolution. The basis for its capitalist expansion was the concentration in London of a large population which no longer brewed its own beer, because it was composed of wage-labourers who had lost their agricultural holdings. This expansion was based on mass production from single units employing great fixed capitals. The size of the London market permitted mass distribution and undercutting the prices of small producers. Production was on such a scale that price fluctuations arising from variations in the harvest could be overridden; from 1722 to 1760 the price of beer in London was constant at 3*d*. a quart pot. 'Before the mid-eighteenth century a large porter brewery was as different from the inn brewhouse as the later cotton mill was from a cottage workshop.' A revolution in managerial techniques and finance naturally followed, as well as the development of subsidiary trades in by-products hitherto wasted, and subsidiary industries like the manufacture of barrels.*

*Mathias, op. cit., pp. 11, 13, 25, 28, 41, 53, 63, 73, 112 and *passim*.

Climatologists note that after the cold epoch extending from 1550 to 1700, the weather was much better in the first half of the eighteenth century: there were indeed fewer bad seasons than in the second half of the century. With so many people living near the borderline of starvation, the difference made by good harvests and warm winters was incalculable. Burials in London continued to be more numerous in the early months of each year, and varied considerably with the severity of the winter. As late as January 1767 a Lancashire J.P. thought that 'numbers of poor people must inevitably have starved' if the bad weather which cut south Lancashire off from Yorkshire and Cheshire had continued. A bad harvest might *lower* industrial wages, since shortage of money decreased the demand for labour. The whole economy was still geared to the weather, and consequently the ending of 'the little ice age' round about 1700 must have had a considerable effect.

We still know too little about rates of population change in the eighteenth century, except in Scotland, but the picture becomes a little clearer than in previous centuries. The first three-quarters of the seventeenth century had seen a relative stagnation in population growth in England. Plague was frequent, with especially severe outbreaks in 1625 and 1665. But by the end of the century it was extinct and did not recur even in the famine years 1693–99. Victory over plague gave stimulus to and confidence in further medical advance, and also created the possibility of a *stable* industrial society in urban conglomerations. There was a sharp decrease, in the century after 1650, in deaths from deficiency diseases, rickets and scurvy. In the first half of the eighteenth century, with plague over and the lowest classes able to buy more food, population began to expand significantly again – slowly till about 1750, faster from 1750 to 1780.

The rate of expansion varied from region to region in this period (as no doubt it had done earlier, but this cannot be documented). Towns continued to be killers, and especially London, in which typhus, typhoid and smallpox raged. In eighteenth-century Nottingham one child was buried for every two baptized. In Lancashire in the fifties the death-rate in towns was more than twice what it was in villages. There seems to have been a sharp increase of population in the first half of the century in the north-west of England – areas of *rural* industry recently incorporated within the London market, and so enjoying rising prosperity. Men married early, and the birth-rate was high where child labour helped to balance the family budget. This upsurge of population to meet the increasing demand for labour may have been an essential pre-condition for the Industrial Revolution in which Lancashire played so prominent a part. Wages rose while labour remained scarce, and so purchasing power was increased to form the market for increased output of consumer goods.

To the effects of the rising birth-rate throughout the eighteenth century must be added a fall in the death-rate (in London at least) from about 1750, after it had reached a peak between 1720 and 1740. The fall seems to have been due to greater resistance to disease, thanks to a rising standard of living. The seventeenth-century Agricultural Revolution, new crop rotations and improved communications led to increased production, and reduced the violent fluctuations in food prices from year to year that had so frequently brought famine in the past (and which the ten-yearly averages of the textbooks so often conceal). More fresh meat was now available in winter, cheaper potatoes all the year round, and more butter and cheese were being eaten. There were no great improvements in medical knowledge, but there were some changes for the better. Military and naval experience started new ideas about hygiene; the value of fresh air and ventilation was beginning to be recognized, and the desirability of isolating infectious cases. Smallpox inoculation began to have significant results from about 1760. Dispensaries for the poor, a London doctor said in 1775, had caused a total revolution in the attitude of the common people towards disease and its cure. Hospitals may or may not have been beneficial. In the early nineteenth century they probably killed more than they cured. But we need not read the later evidence back into our period, when country hospitals were just beginning in a small way. We do know that one child out of every fifteen born at the

British Lying-in Hospital died between 1749 and 1759; one out of every 118 fifty years later. In 1767 it was made compulsory for London parishes to send pauper children into the country to be nursed.

Cheaper cotton underwear and cheaper soap, new ideas on clothing and feeding infants, on relating diet to specific diseases, on the use of antiseptics, all helped. Towns, led by Manchester, were being made more healthy as the eighteenth century progressed, especially after the sixties: streets were widened and paved, drains covered in, water supplies improved, houses rebuilt in brick to replace vermin-infested mud or timber, roofed with slate rather than vermin-infested thatch. The Great Fire of 1666 had destroyed London's wooden houses; thanks to the shortage of timber they were replaced by healthier brick buildings. Cheap iron pots, pans and beds, as well as cheaper pottery, also made for greater cleanliness.

Diet improved too. Sugar imports to Great Britain increased from 10,000 tons in 1700 to 150,000 tons a century later. This encouraged consumption of fruit, jam and puddings, which helped to vary diet, especially in winter. Rice began to be imported from the mid-century. The potato was establishing itself as a field crop, especially in Lancashire: some historians think that it contributed to the population explosion by making earlier marriages economically possible. On the other side, between 1615 and 1700 consumption of tobacco rose from one-fiftieth of an ounce per head of the population to forty ounces. But this was mostly smoked in pipes, or taken as snuff, so it may not have contributed substantially to mortality rates. As tea grew cheaper (thanks to smuggling, among other things) it helped to replace alcohol. Gregory King thought the average household spent more per week on beer and ale than on any other single commodity – more than on meat, butter, milk and cheese together. From the reign of William III Parliament encouraged distilling, from home-grown wheat and barley, and so the drinking of gin and whisky as substitutes for French brandy. Consumption of spirits per head, notably of gin, trebled between 1710 and the seventeen-forties till it was checked by increased duties in 1751.

There seems to have been a steady migration of skilled craftsmen from London to the provinces, again in consequence of the extension of London civilization. These migrants included schoolmasters and surgeons, which helps to explain the rise in literacy and may help to explain the fall in the death-rate.* Even the rise of factories was beneficial in one respect, in that many unhealthy manufacturing processes were removed from the home. Though enormous numbers were still executed for offences against property, juries were increasingly reluctant to convict; the proportion of those condemned who were actually hanged had declined since the early seventeenth century and was still falling. In 1750–52 the first motions for reducing the number of offences liable to the death penalty passed the House of Commons, only to be defeated in the Lords. But transportation and emigration continued, as did the practice of releasing criminals and debtors from gaol on condition of joining the armed forces.

We should not exaggerate the effects of any of these changes taken singly: overcrowding in factory towns was soon to work against many of them. But the impact of a falling death-rate after 1740 on a rising birth-rate meant that the population as a whole rose sharply in the last decades of our period. And this upsurge, unlike anything that had happened before, was not checked after a few years but continued into the 'population explosion' of the later decades of the century.

Population trends and their effects are still fairly mysterious: we must be very tentative in any conclusions we draw. For instance it may be less true to say that the high death-rate in early eighteenth-century London was due to gin-drinking than that gin-drinking was due to the high death-rate. Mr Edward Thompson has recently cogently argued that 'a substantial decline in infant mortality and increase in life expectation among several millions in the middle classes and aristocracy of labour would mask, in national averages, a worsening position in the working-class generally'. Ironically, expanding population – and the expansion seems to have been most rapid·in the north-west – meant a surplus of child labour for the factories. To illustrate Mr Thompson's point, between 1750 and 1769 sixty-three per cent of children died in London under five years of age; but of

*Cranfield, p. 212.

257

children born in London workhouses, or received there at less than twelve months old between 1763 and 1765, only seven per cent survived.

The seventeenth-century emphasis on export convinced most economists that labour costs must be kept as low as possible: only those with an eye on production for the home market could agree with Child's view that high wages offered 'infallible evidence of the riches of that country', and were 'the test of a nation's wealth'.* An industrial revolution depends on an expansion of the home market no less than on exports; mass production must bring the price of consumer goods down to a level at which mass demand becomes effective. Hence the importance of rising wages in the North, hitherto of relatively little significance as a market. Higher and steadier wages made the factory system just tolerable by creating the market for its products. Wages in and near great towns, Adam Smith observed, were often twenty to twenty-five per cent higher than a few miles away.

Though real wages rose in the late seventeenth and early eighteenth centuries, they never allowed for luxury. The unskilled worker ate little meat; and in the North potatoes and black bread were eaten instead of cheese, meat and white bread. From the sixties the position of the workers seems to have worsened in the South and West, though it continued to improve in the North. Because of the chronic shortage of currency in the eighteenth century, wages tended to be paid at irregular intervals, often in coins of large denomination, which had to be changed at the local inn; or in credit notes or goods – a form of truck.

8

At the beginning of the eighteenth century more than one in five of the population was receiving poor relief, though real wages had risen for all but the poorest. It was still assumed that a man's wages could not support a large family. Of children of the poor Locke said in 1697: 'What they can have at home from their parents is seldom more than bread and water, and that very

*But see Richard C. Wiles, 'The Theory of Wages in Later English Mercantilism', *Economic History Review*, Second Series, XXI, pp. 113–26.

scantily too.' Locke himself, and Defoe after him, used this to argue in favour of female and child labour. The pauper wore distinctive dress, and was forbidden to beg.

At the end of Charles II's reign the cost of the poor rate was estimated at some £650,000 to £700,000; by the end of our period it had risen to nearly £2 million. There was probably a growth of pauperism in the early eighteenth century. After 1722 paupers who refused the workhouse test could be denied relief. The increasingly savage penalties for offences against property in the thirties and forties (and the game laws) perhaps testify to growing pauperization. By 1740 it was a capital offence to steal property worth 1s. As the cost of poor relief rose, so did the determination of parishes to keep it down. The poor laws had power not only over those actually chargeable but also over those likely to become so. Many parishes were humane to their own settled poor; but the law encouraged them to be brutal to strangers. Every wage-labourer was a potential charge on the rates in old age or sickness. Immigrants must therefore be prevented from acquiring a 'settlement', a claim on the parish to relief as a right. Pauper children were apprenticed outside their own parishes, for the same reason. 'All who ... become noisy and are not content with some small allowance, as 1s. per week at furthest, are sent to the workhouse.' With this threat before them, many of the poor 'have made shift with one shilling where four before would not have contented them'. The inefficiency of the methods of relieving the poor was paralleled only by the corruption of its administrators.

Poor relief, as Lord Townshend observed in 1730, was a subsidy to wages. It helped to keep England's manufactures cheap. 'Were it not for what they receive out of the tax ... they would not knit or spin for so small wages as they receive for that work, because they would starve by it.' It depressed wages generally. The years 1763–73, which saw a great expansion of trade and national prosperity, also saw an unusually large increase of pauperism and outdoor relief. This vast subsidy to the employing class, at the expense of all taxpayers, compares with the corn bounty paid to landowners, again at the expense of the community at large.

4
FACTORIES AND THE
WORKING CLASS

Manufactures . . . prosper most where the mind is least con-
sulted, and where the workshop may, without any great effort
of imagination, be considered as an engine, the parts of which
are men. . . . We make a nation of helots, and have no free
citizens. – ADAM FERGUSON, An Essay on the History of
Civil Society (*1765*)

I

IT has become fashionable of late to argue that the miseries of
the workers during the Industrial Revolution are the *ex post facto*
invention of sentimental historians, especially of those pioneers,
J. L. and Barbara Hammond. It can be shown statistically that
both the national income and average wage rates went up after
1780. Therefore, it is argued, factory workers must have been
better off. Statistics and imagination are for the historian what
oil and petrol are to the internal combustion engine: an excess
of the one will not compensate for the lack of the other. The
Hammonds opened up a new field of study – ordinary people.
History will never look the same again after their work. There is
room for detailed criticism of their conclusions in the light of
more recent statistical evidence; but the Hammonds were more
gifted with historical imagination than their critics, and we should
be foolish to dismiss them too cavalierly.

It is, for instance, not enough to demonstrate simply that in
the same number of hours a man could earn more in a factory
than as a domestic worker. At home, however long his hours, he
was his own master. If he chose to take an hour or a day off, and
be that much the poorer, he was free to do so: and this freedom
could not be measured in cash. In the factory his nominal earn-
ings might be higher. But this was offset by a strict discipline,
of a sort to which he was entirely unaccustomed, enforced by

severe fines for trivial misdemeanours, so that even the net financial outcome might be less: in working long hours not of his own choosing his sense of personal freedom and dignity was impaired. We may suppose, looking back after two centuries, that the imposition of labour discipline was easily accepted because its necessity is obvious to us: men have to start at a given time in the morning, work regular hours, continuously, at such speeds and in such temperatures as are required for the industrial process. But all these must have seemed enormous hardships, and intrusions on his liberty, to the former domestic worker, with no clock in his house, living perhaps some miles from the factory, and with no means of transport other than his legs. Above all, he abandoned the right to choose when he worked, for how long and at what intensity: and what is freedom, as Milton asked, but choice? Arguments based on nominal wage rates, and on assumptions about purchasing power, may be misleading, for we do not know what proportion of factory workers at any given date retained a plot of land on which they could grow their own food. Factories paid wages more regularly; but they increased the differential between skilled and unskilled. The rising prices of the later eighteenth century were tolerable for the skilled, whose wages were rising as fast or faster; not for domestic and unskilled workers. But even if all that the optimists claim about working-class standards of living could be proved, men still do not live by bread alone.

We look back with twentieth-century preconceptions. After two hundred years of trade union struggle, wage labour has won a respected and self-respecting position in the community. But if we approach wage-labour from the seventeenth century, as men in fact did, we recall that the Levellers thought wage-labourers had forfeited their birthright as freeborn Englishmen, and should not be allowed the vote; that Winstanley thought wage-labourers had no share in their own country, and that wage labour should be abolished. This traditional attitude, together with the fact that many factories looked like workhouses, and were often consciously modelled on them (paupers too had been thought unworthy of the franchise by the Levellers) may help us to understand why independent craftsmen clung so hard to economically untenable positions; why the early Lancashire spinning factories were staffed so largely by women and pauper children, the latter of whom had no choice in the matter, and by Welsh and Irish labourers (Highlanders in Scotland), who lacked the English craftsman's tradition of self-help and self-respect. In the parish *cahiers* of grievances in France in 1789, Sir John Clapham suggests, the position of day-labourer 'is seldom referred to except as a kind of hell into which peasants may fall if things are not bettered'.

Freeborn men still felt that to go voluntarily into a factory was to surrender their birthright, which a Leveller had defined as property in one's own person and labour. We should not allow hindsight to prevent us from entering imaginatively into such feelings. If we grasp the aura of unfreedom which still clung around wage-labour in the eighteenth century we shall not be so impressed by statistics which suggest that wage-labourers might be better off than free craftsmen or squatters on commons; and we shall understand why the freer craftsmen formed the vanguard of early trade unionism.

Before the Industrial Revolution there was in England, as in any backward economy, seasonal unemployment and permanent underemployment. So long as the labourer had a holding he was cushioned against all but very long periods of unemployment; and this enabled his employer under the putting-out system to have more workers on his books than he normally needed, so as to be able to mobilize them all to meet a sudden increase in demand. When bad times came they were thrown on to the parish. Irregularity of labour was built into the system. This brought its own attitude towards labour. Malachi Postlethwayt attributed the high quality of English manufactures to the frequent 'relaxation of the people in their own way', their freedom to work (within limits) when they felt like it. This freedom was more highly prized than continuity of labour. Hence men observed St Monday as a day of leisure, and sometimes even Tuesday, making up by intensive labour at the end of the week; hence the total break in labour in many industries at harvest time, at the annual fair or wake; or in London on hanging days. Hence the tendency, so deplored by economists, to work less when food was cheap.

It was said in 1747 that a man 'who can subsist on three days a week will be idle and drunken the remainder of the week'. Men were better clothed and fed when prices were high. In London there was a standing pool of unemployed labour. Elsewhere the pool was less obvious, and consisted of labour which was not fully employed, including squatters and paupers as well as domestic workers. This meant, among other things, that recruits for the armed forces could be obtained in time of war without much strain on the economy: fully employed craftsmen were rarely conscripted. A regular factory system necessitated a regular army.

We should not idealize the domestic system. Time was wasted; labour was under-employed most of the time; accident might reduce men to dependence on poor relief or on the moneylender. Industrial relations were, as Professor Ashton has pointed out, 'depersonalized' in the textile trades long before the coming of the factories: for the instruments of production belonged to the capitalist and thousands of domestic workers never set eyes on their employer. Domestic workers embezzled their employers' raw materials; employers paid in kind at inflated prices. A worker in domestic industry, obtaining his raw materials on credit or otherwise receiving advances from his employer, invariably got into debt, and so was bound to his boss. It was considered bad form to take a man on without the consent of his previous employer. A workman in such a position had virtually no bargaining power; the system precluded the possibility of collective bargaining. Long hours, truck and irregular payment of wages were all to be found under the domestic system. It meant hard labour at low remuneration for men, women and children. It is absurd to attack the factories as though they introduced child labour: it had long existed in the home. The factories shocked philanthropists by bringing it into the public view, and making brutally clear the dependence of the capitalist's profit on such labour.

Nevertheless, when all is said, there is a difference between child labour at home (except where parents were exceptionally brutalized, or in the case of pauper apprentices, who were often savagely treated) and child labour in factories. Even a pauper apprentice had the chance of learning some skill which might enable him ultimately to set up as a free craftsman: factory children learnt nothing that would help them to escape. It was long considered a disgrace for a self-respecting man to let his children enter a factory. Pauper children shipped north from London workhouses in order to save ratepayers the cost of their maintenance were particularly unprotected. From the age of seven children in factories had to work twelve to fifteen hours a day (or night), six days a week, 'at best in monotonous toil, at worst in a hell of human cruelty'. 'The tale never ended of fingers cut off and limbs crushed in the wheels.' Foremen's wages depended on the work they could get out of their charges. The story of these children is, as Professor Ashton mildly remarks, 'a depressing one'. One of the worst counts against early Methodists is their condonation of child labour because they were convinced of the dangers of idleness to the originally sinful. It is part of a general hostility to diversion which contributed so much to the bleakness and barrenness of the age of industrial revolution.

From the economists' point of view there was everything to be said for switching from domestic to factory system. It was so much neater and tidier. The domestic worker often had to make fantastically long journeys to obtain his raw materials and market his wares. In the East Midlands hosiery trade two and a half days each week might be so spent. The advantages of concentration leading to specialized division of labour are obvious. Discipline was hard to learn, but – as in any backward economy – was essential to rising productivity. Wages were paid more regularly by factories – though still not always punctually. Crises of over-production were thought to be less likely. Economies of large-scale production were as obvious in industry as in agriculture. What was lost by factories and enclosure was the independence, variety and freedom which small producers had enjoyed: an enforced asceticism, the Webbs called it. To resentment at loss of freedom we must add hatred for the new absolute and uncontrolled power which the capitalist employer obtained over his employees – especially where wages were paid, wholly or in part, in IOUs which had to be redeemed at a truck shop owned by the employer. Some of them exploited their monopoly to charge exorbitant prices. The relations of employer and wage-labourer, wrote Dean Tucker in George II's reign, 'approach much nearer to that of a planter and slave in our American colonies than might be expected of such a country as England'. The words 'master' and 'servant' of the acts dealing with labour relations sum up the reasons for hostility. A servant was unfree, had forfeited his birthright as a freeborn Englishman. Behind this attitude there were centuries of history.

The new industrial masters soon became as rich as bankers, merchants or great landlords. But they had none of the traditional sense of responsibility, however inadequate, which characterized some landlords and heads of households. The relationship between master and servant was defined by the cash nexus. Labour was one of the factors of production, whose cost must be kept as low as possible. 'Raising the wages of day labourers is wrong,' thought Dr Johnson; 'for it does not make them live better, but only makes them idler.' Such comfortable maxims were now applied to men who had no agricultural holdings to save them from starvation in unemployment, and to give them liberty to stop work when it became intolerable – say owing to illness. For the overwhelming majority of the population the words of William Hutton in 1780 – 'every man has his fortune in his own hands' – must have seemed the bitterest irony. What most men felt was not that new doors had been thrown open but that old rights had been taken away. Arnold Toynbee's verdict of 1884 still stands: 'The more we examine the actual course of affairs, the more we are amazed at the unnecessary suffering that had been inflicted upon the people.'

Machine-breaking was the logical reaction of free men who even under the domestic system had rarely owned their own implements, and who saw the concentration of machinery in factories as the instrument of their enslavement. In the late seventeenth century London weavers had rioted to smash Dutch looms when introduced by French ribbon-loom weavers; mechanical saw-mills were broken in London in 1763 and 1767. In 1727 smashing stocking frames was made a capital offence. In 1753 John Kay's house was wrecked because of his labour-saving inventions and he fled the country. In 1768 Blackburn spinners destroyed Hargreaves's jennies; a decade later there were systematic attacks on Arkwright's machines. It was not only illiterate workers who reacted in this way. In 1755 Lawrence Earnshaw invented a cotton-spinning machine, but at once destroyed it rather than take bread out of the mouths of the poor. But this soon changed. Arkwright in the sixties had none of the qualms about the social consequences of his invention that Lewis Paul had felt about a less complex machine thirty years earlier.

Selective machine-breaking against particularly resented employers was a primitive form of industrial protest. Early working-class action first tried to get Parliament to stop the flow into the factories by appealing to Elizabethan apprentice regulations; when that failed they turned to organized machine-breaking. ('Whenever the legislature attempts to regulate the differences between masters and their workmen,' Adam Smith observed, 'its counsellers are always the masters.') Other early forms of industrial action were what Dr Hobsbawm has called 'collective bargaining by riot', and price-fixing by riot, of which twenty-four incidents have been traced in 1766 alone.

2

As workers ceased to market their own products, and came to depend on the employer for this, so they became interested in high wages rather than high prices for their products. They ceased to have common interests with employers in restricting output and maintaining standards of quality. So guilds gradually gave way to organizations which could fight better for the wages and living conditions of those with only their labour to sell.

The great power of the state and the employing class was brought to bear against any attempt by working men to organize to protect their position. In 1719 workmen (but not inventors) were forbidden to take their skills into another country. By an act of 1726 combinations of workers were severely repressed: fourteen years' transportation for using violence in labour disputes, death for wilful machine-breaking. But employers had the right to combine, 'with the utmost silence and secrecy,' says

Adam Smith, to 'sink the wages of labour'. Neither trade unions nor their individual members were likely in normal times to take legal action against employers who paid in truck, for fear of victimization. In 1719, when the keelmen of Newcastle struck for higher wages, a regiment of soldiers and a man-of-war were sent to answer them. Next year, after a strike of some 7,000 journeymen tailors in London, combination was forbidden in that industry by Act of Parliament, in 1726 in the weaving and wool-combining industries, following riots and loom-breaking in the West country, in 1749 in the silk, linen, cotton, fustian, iron, leather and other industries, in 1777 among hatters. In 1757, after a strike, the system of wage assessment by J.P.s was finally discarded in the clothing industry: wages were left to free negotiations between the unequal parties. Ironically, it was now labourers and consumers who sought protection from a maintenance of the Elizabethan system of regulation – of wages, prices, standards, conditions of apprenticeship, etc. *Laissez faire* suited manufacturers and middlemen better than control by country justices who might have some sense of local solidarity and considerable dislike of rich upstarts.*

Employers could bring actions for conspiracy against members of trade unions, and could prosecute individuals for stopping work. Nevertheless, among skilled or semi-skilled workers there were already some fairly strong trade unions, often disguised as clubs or friendly societies, providing sick and funeral benefits. A good example is the keelmen's fund at Newcastle-on-Tyne, established in 1699, with which a hospital was built. But in 1712 the fund was alleged (by employers) to be 'spent in encouraging mutinies and disorders among the keelers'.† There are many other examples of clubs in the early eighteenth century acting as organizations for putting wage demands. In 1773 the Spitalfields weavers got an act of Parliament to regulate their wages and working conditions, thanks to their own organization and the help of a Wilkesite Lord Mayor of London.

*This is the social basis for the 'Tory radicalism' referred to on p. 214, above.

†There had been a keelmen's strike for higher wages as early as 1654 (Howell, *Newcastle upon Tyne and the Puritan Revolution*, p. 292).

5

AGRICULTURE AND
AGRARIAN RELATIONS

In the commercial state there is no natural check which may
establish the security of the cultivator; and his lord has hardly
any obvious interest but to squeeze his industry as much as he
can. . . . The rights of the higher orders are rendered perfectly
secure, while those of the cultivators are laid open to their
oppressors. – WILLIAM OGILVIE, Essays on the Right of
Property in Land (*1781*)

IN the favourable climate of the eighteenth century the capitalist development of agriculture was extended. 'The eighteenth century gentry,' in the words of Mr Thompson, 'made
up a superbly successful and self-confident capitalist class. They
combined, in their style of living, features of an agrarian and
urban culture.' He refers to 'the profoundly capitalist style of
thought of the class – zestfully acquisitive and meticulous in
attention to accountancy. . . . *Laissez faire* emerged, not as the
ideology of some manufacturing lobby, not as the intellectual
yarn turned out by the cotton mills, but in the great agricultural
corn-belt. Smith's argument [in *The Wealth of Nations*] is
derived, very largely, from agriculture.'

Enclosure facilitated draining of wet lands. Drainage schemes,
cultivation of waste and moorland, new crop rotations, more
intensive cultivation, regional specialization – all this had led
to an increase in output. By the end of our period English wheat
land produced nearly forty per cent more per acre than French.
Despite the bounty on corn export, white bread was beginning
to become the staple diet even for the poor. From the mid-
century new land was coming into cultivation as agricultural
prices rose. Since the seventeenth-century Agricultural Revolution cattle could be kept alive through the winter. This, together
with improved communications, meant that fresh meat and more

corn were marketed all the year round: the consequent decline in consumption of salted meat must have had a good effect on health. Longer-lived cattle produced more manure, and so helped more intensive cultivation. The new grasses also improved the quality of sheep's wool. The number of sheep in England may have doubled during the last century of our period, and they grew fatter. But sheep were now bred for mutton as well as for wool, cattle for beef rather than as draught animals. Just as Boulton produced buttons for the people, not just for the nobility,* so Bakewell said he did not breed sheep for gentlemen's tables but for the masses. The Roast Mutton of Old England rather than beef was the cheap eighteenth-century meat. Enclosure reduced the incidence of infectious diseases among livestock, and facilitated selective breeding. The ending of seasonal slaughtering of animals, together with increased grain production and improved communications, led to greater stability of prices, fewer famines.

Increased food production did not necessarily mean an improved standard of living for those who grew it. The stimulus to agricultural revolution had come from the desire of landowners and capitalist farmers to make profits by producing for the market. The Norfolk system of intensive agriculture required substantial initial investment of capital: it was beyond the means of small men. But it brought great wealth to improving landlords: land values in Norfolk increased ten-fold between 1730 and 1760. The cheaper food of the agricultural depression of 1720–50 meant economic difficulties for smaller freeholders and tenants, and increased pressure to engross or enclose: all roads led to larger economic units, and depressed the independent small producer. The seventies was a period of 'open war against cottages': the phrase is Arthur Young's. The number of enclosure acts rises sharply after 1750, when expansion of population began to make itself felt; but resort to an act of Parliament, which cost about £2,000, may witness only to opposition to enclosure, that could not be overcome by less expensive means.

Enclosure of commons was praised by contemporaries because

*See p. 248, above.

it forced labourers to 'work every day in the year'; 'their children will be put out to labour early'. By depriving the lower orders of any chance of economic independence, the 'subordination of the lower ranks of society ... would be thereby considerably secured'. (These illuminating phrases come from official Board of Agriculture reports.)

It has become rather smart to sneer at old-fashioned historians who spoke of men being 'driven from the land' by enclosure, and to suggest that Parliamentary enclosures met with little opposition. Contemporaries thought otherwise. 'I had rather,' wrote Arthur Young, originally an advocate of enclosure, 'that all the commons of England were sunk in the sea, than that the poor should in future be treated on enclosing as they have generally been hitherto.' 'By nineteen out of twenty enclosure bills,' he added 'the poor are injured, and some grossly injured.'

There was no coercion, we are assured. True, when the big landowner or landowners to whom four-fifths of the land of a village belonged wanted to enclose, the wishes of the majority of small men who occupied the remaining twenty per cent could be disregarded. True, Parliament took no interest in the details of an enclosure bill, referring them to be worked out by its promoters, who distributed the land as they thought best. But the poorest cottager was always free to oppose a Parliamentary enclosure bill. All he had to do was to learn to read, hire an expensive lawyer, spend a few weeks in London and be prepared to face the wrath of the powerful men in his village. If he left his home after enclosure, this was entirely voluntary: though the loss of his rights to graze cattle on the common, to pick up fuel there, the cost of fencing his own little allotment if he got one, his lack of capital to buy the fertilizers necessary to profit by enclosure, the fact that rents, in the Midlands at least, doubled in consequence of enclosure – all these might assist him in making his free decision. But coercion – oh dear no! Nothing so unBritish as that. There was a job waiting for him, either as agricultural labourer in his village or in a factory somewhere, if he could find out where to go and if he and his family could trudge there. 'Only the really small owners,' say Professor

Chambers and Dr Mingay reassuringly, would be forced to sell out.

It is true too that in many villages population did not fall after enclosure. One explanation of this fact is that population was increasing anyway. Extension of the cultivated area and intensification of agriculture demanded more labour. But there is also more than one sense in which a family is 'driven from the land'. So long as it held its farm, however small, whether as freehold, copyhold or on a long lease, it had some security. Once the farm was lost, however 'voluntarily' it may have been surrendered, the fact that employment as wage-labourer was obtainable offered no equivalent security. 'As agriculture came to require more specialized workers,' Professor Ashton observes, 'less spinning and weaving was done in farmhouses and cottages, and indeed landlords sometimes prohibited the practice.' This transition from a mixed economy of domestic industry and part-time wage-labour to one of full-time wage-labour must have had catastrophic consequences for the total income of many families. From about 1765 the wages of agricultural labourers began to fall, and to need supplementation from poor relief. Marx may have over-simplified and foreshortened a complicated process when he spoke of the independent yeomanry being succeeded by a servile rabble of tenant farmers on short leases; but taking the long view that is precisely what happened. Enclosure was most easily effected in villages whose parochial organization was least democratic. Many small owners were bought out *before* enclosure, to facilitate it. Whether as cause or consequence of enclosure, such village self-government as existed in England disappeared. 'A rural democracy was practically non-existent,' wrote the unsentimental Sir Lewis Namier, since 'the yeomen farmers were declining in numbers and importance, the tenant-farmers at [Parliamentary] elections owed suit to their landlords, while village labourers had neither votes nor facilities for effective rioting' such as existed in the towns. Rural distress and protest were certainly on the increase when our period ends.

Looked at in retrospect, the whole process has an air of inevitability. The strict settlement and entail fortified the economic position of the great landowners, who had triumphed politically in 1660 and 1688. They could afford long-term planning and investment, and so regained some of the ground lost economically to the monied interest in the seventeenth century. The land tax made it impossible for the smaller gentry to accumulate the capital necessary for the new agriculture. Similarly smaller freeholders could not compete with leaseholders possessing greater capital resources. The fall of prices and rents in the depression after 1730 intensified their difficulties. Enclosure was a consequence as much as a cause of the disappearance of small freeholders. Yet the bounty helped bigger farmers by keeping up the price of corn and so artificially occasioning what Adam Smith called 'a constant dearth in the home market', which forced labourers to work harder and for longer hours.

The bitterness which marked relations between classes in the two generations after our period derived as much from a feeling that the poor had been swindled out of their land as from resentment at being forced into the factories. Hence the appeal to the working class of 'back-to-the-land' schemes far into the nineteenth century. In December 1634 the inhabitants of Boston, New England, in choosing men to make division of the town lands, left out magistrates resident in Boston, 'fearing that the richer men would give the poorer sort no great proportion of land'. In eighteenth-century England the allotment of land was made exclusively by 'the richer men', many of whom thought 'the poor ... had no legal title to the common land', and so rarely gave them any compensation. By all means let us be careful not to exaggerate, not to accept at face value propagandist statements by eighteenth-century agitators. But when we have made every possible allowance, given the enclosers the benefit of every conceivable doubt, there is still evidence for saying that enclosure brought untold suffering to countless numbers of English men, women and children – sufferings which can only be ignored or explained away by historians who have as little imagination as the often honourable men who inflicted them.

It is impossible to draw up a balance sheet on which pluses and minuses neatly cancel out – for eighteenth-century England or for any backward economy which rapidly industrializes itself. Collectivization in the U.S.S.R. in the nineteen-thirties can be condemned because it led to thousands of deaths from starvation; it can be defended because it made possible the production of sufficient grain for the Soviet Union to become an industrial power strong enough to withstand the Nazi onslaught in 1941. But it is too facile to say, in the case either of eighteenth-century England or twentieth-century Russia, that the statistical results *justify* the individual suffering. We can only record both. No calculus tells us that a fifty per cent increase in cotton exports is worth purchasing at the cost of one thousand women who died prematurely and two thousand stunted children.

The whole story of enclosure and industrial revolution reveals the dual standard of rationality which the eighteenth century had inherited from John Locke. The luxury expenditure of the rich, it was generally agreed, was good because it created work; the luxury expenditure of the poor was bad because it showed they were earning too much. Most of the propertied class had no doubts at all that the lower classes should not take independent economic decisions, should be forced to work harder in unfree circumstances, without sharing significantly in the product of their labour, provided total national wealth was increased. 'The poor have nothing to stir them to labour but their wants,' said Mandeville, 'which it is wisdom to relieve but folly to cure.' The only way to make the lower orders temperate and industrious, said a pamphlet of 1739, was 'to lay them under the necessity of labouring all the time they can spare from rest and sleep, in order to procure the common necessities of life'. The bounty on corn export and the enclosure of commons were both praised for this reason. Walpole in 1732 preferred a salt tax to a tax on candles because the former would fall mainly on the poor and force them to work. The very poor tended to make their own tallow candles, not to buy them.

Such attitudes are explicable, if not very attractive, in the eighteenth century: less explicable is their perpetuation by twentieth-century historians, who dismiss as mere sentimentality any concern for those who carried the burden of industrialization and the rationalization of food supplies; and who call for impossibly rigorous standards of proof before they will abandon their assumption that all must have been for the best because total national wealth was increasing. Historians have still found no answer to the question which Arthur Young put into the mouth of a victim of enclosure: 'If I am diligent, shall I have leave to build a cottage? If I am sober, shall I have land for a cow? If I am frugal, shall I have half an acre of potatoes?'

6

RELIGION AND
INTELLECTUAL LIFE

The genius of [dramatic] poetry consists in the lively representation of the disorders and misery of the great; to the end that
the people and those of a lower condition may be taught the
better to content themselves with privacy, enjoy their safer
state, and prize the equality and justice of their guardian laws.
– LORD SHAFTESBURY, Advice to an Author, *1710*

The true Christian will never be a leveller. . . . He who wor-
ships God in spirit and in truth will love the government and
laws which protect him without asking by whom they are
administered. – ARTHUR YOUNG, An Enquiry into the State
of the Public Mind among the Lower Classes (*1798*)

Are not religion and politics the same thing? – WILLIAM
BLAKE, Jerusalem

I

THE rising agricultural prosperity of the late seventeenth and
eighteenth centuries made the Church of England an institution
fit for aristocrats to serve in; deaneries and canonries, in Ireland
as well as in England, took their place beside army commissions
for hungry younger sons. Bishops had always been safe government voters in the House of Lords, who could be relied upon to
throw out any bill to reduce the number of placemen in the
Commons. Their votes twice saved Walpole from defeat in the
excise crisis of 1733. Nor was there too much damned merit
about the Hanoverian church: in 1729 George II declared his
intention of giving preferment to all clerics who were gentlemen
of quality. Walpole used the church for patronage purposes, and
the Duke of Newcastle perfected the system. So the church, like
the state, became impervious to reforming movements. Con-
vocation, in which Tory rank-and-file attacked Whig bishops,
ceased to meet after 1717: the Church of England lapsed into a

lethargy from which the efforts of some recent historians have only partially rescued her.

The Toleration Act of 1689 recognized the fact that radical Puritanism could not capture the Church of England, but that it had come to stay; and the fact that protestants of all kinds would combine against any resurgence of popery. The attempt to turn England by political means into a holy community was defeated, and dissenters accepted a subordinate position as a series of disunited sects. Dissent inevitably became 'sectarian' in the pejorative sense of that word. The cosmic battles which Milton and Bunyan depicted were succeeded by sterile controversies over deism and unitarianism. Tolerated dissent lost its missionary zeal, grew respectable and prosperous. Eighteenth-century dissenters organized themselves to put pressure on governments to obtain alleviations of their unprivileged position. But always the knowledge that an overthrow of the Whig régime would be far worse for them than its maintenance prevented them going very far – just as the Puritans had accepted Elizabeth as the lesser evil. The very poor, at least in towns, probably did not go either to church or to chapel. Dissenters had as little to say to the lowest classes as had the established church. But from the middle of the eighteenth century a quite new interest was shown in foreign missions, a reflection of England's new status as a great extra-European power.

Wesley was the first even to preach seriously to those who had lost their birthright and whose only earthly consolation was gin: though the consolations he offered were not in this life. As Sir Charles Grandison put it, the Methodists 'have really . . . given a face of religion to subterranean colliers, tinners and the most profligate of men, who hardly ever before heard the word or thing'. But Wesley was an unbending high Tory. 'The greater the share the people have in government,' he said, 'the less liberty, civil or religious, does a nation enjoy.' We need not argue that Methodism saved England from revolution to agree that its influence on the outcasts of society was in a profoundly non-revolutionary direction. Wesley, on the other hand, was no enemy of the bourgeois virtues, or of technical innovation. 'Gain all you can,' he told his adherents, 'by using in your business all the understanding which God has given you. . . . It is a shame for a Christian not to improve upon [his forefathers] in whatever he takes in hand.'

Yet even Methodism seemed subversive to some of the upper classes. The 'haughty' Duchess of Buckingham found its teaching 'tinctured with impertinence and disrespect towards their superiors. It is monstrous to be told that you have a heart as sinful as the common wretches that crawl the earth' – a remark that tells us less about Methodism than about the ruling class. But it was the old dissent rather than the new that produced political radicals in the later eighteenth century: Wilkes was the unexpected end-product of a tradition of which Richard Price and Joseph Priestley were more orthodox representatives.

One subject that, so far as I am aware, has never been properly investigated, is the political effect of surviving anti-papist sentiments on eighteenth-century Englishmen. In 1702 the House of Lords declared that the war against France was being waged for religion, liberty and property – a continuation of the Good Old Cause of the sixteen-forties! In the seventeen-twenties, Dr Plumb tells us, 'every reprisal taken by the Spanish against English piracy [in the New World] was magnified into an act of fiendish Catholic cruelty'. During the Seven Years War Samuel Richardson thought he saw 'the whole protestant interest at stake': there was strong clerical support for Wolfe's campaign against the Scarlet Woman in Canada, and Frederick the Great enjoyed surprising popularity as a Protestant Hero. In the Gordon Riots a new social element seems to have entered in, since rioters turned their attentions largely against *rich* Roman Catholics.

2

Although higher education languished in the eighteenth century, industry called for a greater degree of literacy and proficiency in arithmetic; similar demands came from the lower ranks of the civil service. At the lowest level this education was provided by the charity schools, of which there were a great many. The charity school movement began as an activity in which Anglicans and nonconformists co-operated, but by the Schism Act of 1714 dissenters were driven out and the movement was captured by high church elements suspected of Jacobitism. This perpetuated a confessional split in elementary education such as already existed at higher levels. The charity schools taught 'the duties of humility and submission to superiors' as well as the three Rs; for, as Mrs Sarah Trimmer put it, 'children fed by charity ought in a more special manner to be clothed in humility'. In consequence the schools were not universally popular with the lower orders, who anyway could often not afford to lose the earning capacity of their children. Charity schools were more effective in towns, where semi-skilled labour was needed, than in the countryside: farmers disliked any form of education for the poor who formed their pool of casual labour. 'The principle of any plan to employ the poor should be to inure them to the lowest and most early labour,' said a critic of the charity schools in 1767.*

The old post-1660 hostility to education as politically dangerous was still widespread: 'Nineteen in twenty of the species were designed by nature for trade and manufacture,' said a letter in *The Grub-Street Journal*; 'to take them off to read books was the way to do them harm, to make them not wiser or better, but impertinent, troublesome and factious.'† The new literacy, however, had much to do with the extension of newspaper-reading, especially in the provinces, and so with the formation of a wide public opinion outside 'the political nation'. It was both cause and effect of the rapid eighteenth-century expansion of the paper industry. By 1781 Dr Johnson spoke of England as a 'nation of readers'. A year later the existence of names rather than signs over shops struck a foreign visitor to London as unusual. Although there had been public libraries from the seventeenth century, the circulating library dates from the early years of the eighteenth century, and testifies to the spread of the habit of reading to a lower class in society: again to the accompaniment

---

*Jones, pp. 74, 78, 95, 112, 130. For a searching criticism of Miss Jones's thesis, see Joan Simon, 'Was there a Charity School Movement? The Leicestershire Evidence', in *Education in Leicestershire, 1640–1940* (ed. Brian Simon, Leicester University Press, 1968, pp. 55–100).

†Cranfield, p. 53.

of cries of alarm from their betters at this debauching of the minds
of ploughboys and servants.

3

The eighteenth century saw an extension of professionalism into
the arts, as rich patrons succeeded the court. They employed not
only sculptors, painters and architects but also musicians and
landscape gardeners. Reynolds, Gainsborough and Romney
catered for an aristocratic clientele: Hogarth's cheap engravings
raised a popular art form to new levels, and their commercial
success revealed the existence of hitherto unsuspected new classes
of consumers for works of art, parallel to the new bourgeois
audience which was making it possible for some novelists and
essayists to live by their pens. National pride entered into it. The
Royal Academy was established in 1768, and Wilkes proposed
the establishment of a National Gallery.

An interesting literary fashion was the cult of crime and
roguery. *Moll Flanders*, *The Beggar's Opera* and *Jonathan Wild*
are 'literary' examples of the genre, just as the vogue of books
about pirates and highwaymen, and *The Newgate Calendar*,
testify to a similar interest at a lower level. This lower-class
literature reflects a genuine social reaction: sympathy for smugglers and highwaymen, moral support for condemned criminals
at Tyburn, all bear witness to a popular hatred of the state and
its law. It illustrates that hostility towards regular and disciplined
labour which made free craftsmen resent the factories so much.*
But in the hands of Defoe, Swift, Gay and Fielding the literary
form serves a more complex purpose. *The Beggar's Opera* and
Jonathan Wild deliberately compare the ethics of criminals with
those of accepted economic individualism or political competition, with the same ironic intention as Swift in *Gulliver's Travels*,
or Richardson when he made Lovelace defend his sexual promiscuity as far less harmful than the warlike exploits of universally applauded 'royal butchers'. The years of Walpole's rule, so
peaceful, so prosperous, seem also to have been years of spiritual
desolation as men contemplated the barren mechanical universe

*See pp. 260–65, above.

of Newton, and the new dismal science of economics which
Mandeville took to its logical conclusion. *Robinson Crusoe* – a
younger son like Lemuel Gulliver – personifies the prudence,
the careful calculation, of economic man; his resourcefulness,
adaptability and application are admirable. But he sells into
slavery the Moorish boy who helped him to escape from cap-
tivity. Profit conquers gratitude and humanity. Warmth and
social solidarity were what was lacking in this atomized and
individualized society;

> 'That independence Britons prize too high
> Keeps man from man, and breaks the social tie,'

Goldsmith was to say. The utter filth in which Gulliver's Yahoos
lived gains in point if we accept the Freudian equation of human
excrement with money; for the monied interest was Swift's
greatest bugbear.*

We may reflect incidentally on the fact that Ireland produced
many of the most serious social critics writing in English after
1688 – Congreve, Swift, Berkeley, Goldsmith, Sheridan. For the
exploitation of Ireland was naked and unashamed, and its basis
in religious inequality ensured that some intellectuals were its
victims. Social issues were not smothered to the same extent as
they were in England, a society in which Puritanism had gone
sour, had turned into humbug. The high ideals of Bacon, Vane,
Milton, Bunyan, George Fox, had led to the South Sea Bubble
and the workhouse test, to charity schools which applied the
joint-stock principle to charity, once the holiest of the three; to
a society in which the vices of the rich were not prosecuted with
anything like the same vigour as the vices of the poor. The real
horror of Swift's *Modest Proposal for preventing the Children of
Poor People from being a Burden to their Parents or Country,
and for making them beneficial to the Publick* (1729) is that his
suggestion that the Irish should serve up their children as food
perfectly catches the smug note of detached benevolence in
the literature of the voluntary societies: with the further horror
that perhaps it really was no less benevolent than to keep Irish
children alive in a country so plundered by Englishmen.

*Cf. the interesting pages on Swift in N. O. Brown's *Life against Death*
(1959), Part v.

Hypocrisy and humbug, great wealth based on starvation wages and the slave trade, an established church whose Archbishop (Tillotson) said religion was identical with self-interest. The word 'respectable' began to acquire overtones of moral excellence ('a most respectable man') shortly after the words 'prude' and 'indelicate' established themselves in the language. It was difficult to find ways out of the moral wilderness of Yahoo society. The third Earl of Shaftesbury advocated a thin depersonalized religion of benevolence, Bishop Berkeley suggested that matter, time and space were illusions, Fielding thought we could all have a jolly time if we meant well, and at least had no use for formal hypocrisies; Richardson, whom Fielding thought so old-maidish and prim, contrasted the institutions of Clarissa Harlowe's society – property-marriage, greed, individualism, the values of the market – with the protestant principles to which that society still paid lip-service but which could not be realized on earth. A nostalgic romanticism was one way out; or the emotional self-indulgence of Methodism; or Blake's rejection of the whole Newtonian universe, the whole humbug to which he thought institutionalized Christianity had been reduced.

Many mid-eighteenth century novelists have a real and personal sense of the suffering and degradation which poverty brought with it. In this still relatively fluid society, they knew that even well-born persons might 'be exposed by indigence to a relapse in point of morals', and that 'without money there was no respect, honour or convenience to be acquired in life'. The words are Smollett's in *Ferdinand, Count Fathom*, but many similar passages could be found in Fielding. The latter's friend, William Hogarth, the first English-born painter of genius, castigated upper-class profligacy, idleness and debauchery in paintings whose close and faithful observation of ordinary people mark the final triumph of Dutch bourgeois standards in England: Hogarth was named after William III. His portraits too introduce a spontaneous and direct realism, a conscious reaction from the grand manner, that was as new as Fielding's teeming novels. With Hogarth, as with the great novelists, English middle-class art came of age in the eighteenth century.

7

RETROSPECT

In every commercial state, notwithstanding any pretension to
equal rights, the exaltation of a few must depress the many. –
ADAM FERGUSON, An Essay on the History of Civil Society
(*1765*)

BY 1780 the Industrial Revolution is upon us. 'After 1782 almost
every statistical series of production shows a sharp upward turn,'
wrote Professor Ashton. We may conclude by drawing together
a few symbolic examples of the ending of one age and the coming
of another around 1780. The Derby, for instance, was first run
in that year. The last Cornish speaker had died two years earlier.

By 1780 James Watt had entered into partnership with
Matthew Boulton, symbolically linking the captain of industry
with the scientist-inventor; and they had begun supplying
steam-engines for the market. In 1779 a cast-iron bridge had
been built across the Severn. Self-sharpening hardened cast-iron
plough-shares came in the eighties. At about the same time
Henry Cort perfected the puddling process, after which wrought
iron could be produced cheaply with coal, and the industry leapt
ahead. For over 15,000 years there had been practically no improvement in lighting-systems; in 1782 the invention of the
Argand lamp in France gave a ten-fold increase in light from a
single wick. By 1780, though enclosure was in full swing, England
had ceased to be a corn-exporting and was becoming on balance
a corn-importing country – so great was the consumption in
towns by the new working class whose formation dates from
these years. In 1782 Gilbert's act legalized the system whereby
industrial wages were explicitly subsidized from parochial rates.
In 1780, for the first time, a government thought it worth taxing
retailers' shops. It is from the eighties that the growth of country
banking becomes really pronounced. The consolidation of
industrial capitalism is marked by a great increase in patents and
bankruptcies in the years after 1782.

The American Declaration of Independence (1776) caused a polarization in politics. It strengthened the movement for reform in England. Wilkes received enthusiastic support from the American colonists. In 1776 he moved in the House of Commons a bill for redistributing the franchise. Burke, with the support of Bristol, the second city in the kingdom, appealed from the Old to the New Whigs, demanding economic reform and a reduction of placemen. From 1779 Wyvill's Yorkshire movement took the lead in organizing petitions for Parliamentary reform. Next year the Society for Promoting Constitutional Information was formed: it welcomed Paine's *Rights of Man* no less than it did the American and French revolutions. In 1780 too the Commons passed the famous resolution declaring that 'the power of the crown has increased, is increasing and ought to be diminished'. Two years later George III was forced to accept a government which he detested. A revival of party rivalries based on principle had begun, ending the Namier age. The rule of the oligarchy seemed moribund. It was to survive in fact for another fifty years; but this is no part of our story.

The War of American Independence saw England in a dangerous position of political isolation: even the docile Dutch joined the armed neutrality of 1780. The American revolution shattered the old colonial system. Ireland took advantage of England's extremity to extort (by threat of armed revolt) freedom of trade with the American and West Indian colonies. By 1782 she had won home rule and religious equality for Roman Catholics. Adam Smith's *Wealth of Nations* (1776) inaugurated a new epoch of economic thinking, both about internal economic policy, a more complete *laissez faire*, and about empire. The first convict settlement in Australia was made in 1788, five years after England accepted the loss of the Thirteen Colonies.

But 1780 was also the year of the Gordon Riots, the last large-scale appearance of no-popery as a political force, the first confused harbinger of working-class revolt. The Gordon Riots came at England's nadir in the War of American Independence, and Gordon himself was a supporter of the American cause. But the riots marked the end of such unity among the radicals as the Wilkesite movement had produced. Wilkes himself defended the

Bank of England against the rioters, and disappeared from politics. Richer London merchants ceased to oppose the crown; the political regrouping which led to the emergence of the younger Pitt and the new Toryism began. We should be very wary of accepting the old clichés which depict Pitt as an ardent reformer whose benevolent schemes were frustrated by the French revolution and the obstinacy of George III. By 1789 Pitt had been in office for five years, and had done little to follow up the political reforms of 1780–82. Between 1787 and 1789 he actively opposed nonconformist attempts to secure repeal of the Test and Corporation Acts. His own reforming efforts were always half-hearted and never pressed home; it is reasonable to suppose that they were never very seriously intended, were sops to public opinion. What Pitt did take seriously, and carry out very skilfully, was the manipulation of this public opinion by management and bribery of the press.

In the intellectual sphere the new spirit is even more marked. The year 1776 saw the publication of *The Wealth of Nations*, *Common Sense*, Bentham's *Fragment on Government* and the first volume of Gibbon's *Decline and Fall of the Roman Empire*, coinciding with the beginning of the fall of the first British Empire. The eighties saw the foundation of literary and philosophical societies at Manchester and many other towns. The political radical Priestley inaugurated a scientific revival parallel to Wesley's religious revival. And we can date the beginnings of romanticism * also from about 1780. Macpherson's *Ossian* had taken the public by storm twenty years earlier. Percy's *Reliques of Ancient Poetry* was first published in 1765, and ran to three editions in ten years. Chatterton's Rowley poems appeared in 1777, Blake's *Poetical Sketches* in 1783. 'Verses which a few years past,' wrote Vicesimus Knox in 1778, 'were thought worthy the attention of children only, or of the lowest and rudest orders, are now admired for that artless simplicity which once

---

*Adjectives approximating to the word 'romantic', Mr Bateson pointed out, were invented between 1650 and 1659 by no less than seven writers (F. W. Bateson, *English Poetry: A Critical Introduction*, 1950, p. 95). In yet another sphere the age of radicalism and industrial revolution was returning to the neglected heritage of the seventeenth-century revolution.

obtained the name of coarseness and vulgarity.' The lyric, derived from the popular ballad, had forced its way up and was soon to be considered the truest form of poetry. Gothic architecture, the Lake District and water colours of wild mountain scenery were already fashionable. Industrialism had made its lasting mark on literature and art.

Part Five

CONCLUSION

The historical method is supposed to prove that economic changes have been the inevitable outcome of natural laws. It just as often proves them to have been brought about by the self-seeking action of dominant classes. . . . The more we accept the method of historical inquiry, the more revolutionary shall we tend to become in practice. – ARNOLD TOYNBEE, The Industrial Revolution (*1884*)

So we have moved from a backward economy to one on the threshold of industrial revolution, from an agricultural to an industrial society; from a society in which, as Dr Johnson put it, influence was gained by 'promiscuous hospitality' to one in which 'the way to make sure of power and influence is by lending money confidentially to your neighbours . . . and having their bonds in your possession'. We have moved from a society in which it was taken for granted that a fully human existence was possible only for the narrow landed ruling class to a society in which an ideology of self-help had permeated into the middle ranks. The economists were newly conscious of scarcity because of the new prospects of abundance. In these 250 years we pass from universal belief in original sin to the romanticism of Man is good. We have moved, too, from an England which had virtually no overseas possessions except Ireland to the break-up of the first British Empire and the first stirrings of Irish nationalism.

By 1780 England had increased vastly in wealth, in the externals of civilization; but it was still a very undemocratic society. Despite the seventeenth-century revolution, the House of Lords, the monarchy, the Church of England still occupied privileged positions. Adam Smith, the high priest of capitalism and *laissez faire*, said in 1776 that 'civil government, so far as it is instituted for the security of property, is in reality instituted for the defence of the rich against the poor, or of those who have some property against those who have none at all'. This had seemed true both to Gerrard Winstanley and to John Locke, though Winstanley disapproved and Locke approved. And Smith's words almost echo Sir Thomas More's description of government just before our period begins:

. . . a certain conspiracy of rich men procuring their own commodities under the name and title of the commonwealth. They invent . . . all means and crafts, first how to keep safely, without fear of losing, that [which] they have unjustly gathered together, and next how to hire and abuse the work and labour of the poor for as little money as may be. These devices, when the rich men have decreed to be kept and observed under colour of the commonalty, that is to say, also of the poor people, then they be made laws.

More's Utopia was a communist society which rejected private property. From the seventeen-seventies and eighties reformers like Spence, Ogilvie and Paine began to attack the monopoly ownership of great landlords. The Industrial Revolution was to give birth to a working–class movement which would challenge private property in a rather more serious manner than More, would pick up ideas which Winstanley had thrown on to apparently stony ground during the English revolution and would conceive of a society in which wage labour would be abolished and common freedom established.

BOOKS FOR
FURTHER READING

There is a bibliography at the end of my *Century of Revolution*, to which the reader is referred for works of seventeenth-century England published before 1960. In the list which follows I have reproduced no titles recommended there.

ANDREWS, K. R. (1964), *Elizabethan Privateering*, Cambridge.

ASHTON, R. (1960), *The Crown and the Money Market*, Oxford.

ASHTON, T. S. (1948), *The Industrial Revolution*, Home University Library.

(1955), *An Economic History of England: the 18th century*, Methuen.

(1959), *Economic Fluctuations in England, 1700–1800*, Oxford.

AYLMER, G. E. (1961), *The King's Servants: the Civil Service of Charles I*, Routledge and Kegan Paul.

BERESFORD, M. W. (1954), *The Lost Villages of England*, Lutterworth Press.

BINDOFF, S. T. (1950), *Tudor England*, Pelican History of England, Vol. V.

BOWDEN, P. J. (1962), *The Wool Trade in Tudor and Stuart England*, Macmillan.

CAMPBELL, M. (1942), *The English Yeoman under Elizabeth and the early Stuarts*, Yale.

CARSWELL, J. (1960), *The South Sea Bubble*, Cresset Press.

CLAPHAM, SIR J. H. (1951), *A Concise Economic History of Britain from the earliest times to 1750*, Cambridge.

COLE, G. D. H. and POSTGATE, R. W. (1938), *The Common People, 1746–1938*, Methuen.

COLLINSON, P. (1967), *The Elizabethan Puritan Movement*, Cape.

CRANFIELD, G. A. (1962), *The Development of the Provincial Newspaper, 1700–1760*, Oxford.

DAVIS, D. (1966), *A History of Shopping*, Routledge and Kegan Paul.

DAVIS, R. (1962), *The Rise of the English Shipping Industry*, Macmillan.

DEANE, P. and COLE, W. A. (1962), *British Economic Growth, 1688–1959*, Cambridge.

DICKENS, A. G. (1964), *The English Reformation*, Batsford.

Books for Further Reading

DICKSON, P. G. M. (1967), *The Financial Revolution in England*, Macmillan.

ELTON, G. R. (1955), *England under the Tudors*, Methuen History of England, Vol. IV.

EVERITT, A. M. (1966), *The Community of Kent and the Great Rebellion*, Leicester.

FERGUSON, A. B. (1965), *The Articulate Citizen and the English Renaissance*, Duke.

GEORGE, D. (1953), *England in Transition*, Penguin Books.

HALLER, W. (1963), *Foxe's Book of Martyrs and the Elect Nation*, Cape.

HAMMOND, J. L. and B. (1948), *The Village Labourer*, Guild Books.
(1949), *The Town Labourer*, Guild Books.

HARDING, A. (1966), *A Social History of English Law*, Penguin Books.

HILL, C. (1964), *Society and Puritanism in Pre-Revolutionary England*, Secker & Warburg.
(1965), *Intellectual Origins of the English Revolution*, Oxford.

HOSKINS, W. G. (1950), *Essays in Leicestershire History*, Liverpool.

JONES, M. G. (1938), *The Charity School Movement*, Cambridge.

KERRIDGE, E. (1967), *The Agricultural Revolution*, Allen & Unwin.

MARSHALL, D. (1956), *English People in the 18th century*, Longmans Green.
(1962), *18th century England*, Longmans History of England, Vol. VII.

NAMIER, SIR LEWIS (1957), *The Structure of Politics at the Accession of George III*, Macmillan, 2nd ed.
(1961), *England in the Age of the American Revolution*, Macmillan, 2nd ed.

PEARL, V. (1961), *London and the Outbreak of the Puritan Revolution*, Oxford.

PLUMB, J. H. (1950), *England in the 18th century*, Pelican History of England, Vol. VII.
(1956–60), *Sir Robert Walpole*, Vols I and II, Cresset Press.
(1967), *The Growth of Political Stability in England, 1675–1725*, Macmillan; Peregrine Books 1969.

RAMSEY, P. (1963), *Tudor Economic Problems*, Gollancz.

ROOTS, I. (1966), *The Great Rebellion*, Batsford.

ROWSE, A. L. (1941), *Tudor Cornwall*, Cape.
(1950), *The England of Elizabeth*, Macmillan.

RUDÉ, G. (1962), *Wilkes and Liberty*, Oxford.

SIMON, J. (1966), *Education and Society in Tudor England*, Cambridge.

STONE, L. (1965), *The Crisis of the Aristocracy, 1558–1641*, Oxford.

Books for Further Reading

SUTHERLAND, L. S. (1952), *The East India Company in 18th century Politics*, Oxford.

TAWNEY, R. H. (1912), *The Agrarian Problem in the 16th century*, Longmans Green.

TAWNEY, R. H. and POWER, E. (ed.) (1953), *Tudor Economic Documents*, 3 vols. Longmans Green.

THIRSK, J. (1957), *English Peasant Farming: the Agrarian History of Lincolnshire from Tudor to Recent Times*, Routledge and Kegan Paul.

(ed.) (1967), *The Agrarian History of England, 1500–1640*, IV, Cambridge.

THOMPSON, E. (1963), *The Making of the English Working Class*, Gollancz; Penguin Books 1968.

TREVOR-ROPER, H. R. (1967), *Religion, the Reformation and Social Change*, Macmillan.

WADSWORTH, A. P. and MANN, J. DE L. (1931), *The Cotton Trade and Industrial Lancashire*, Manchester.

WALKER, D. P. (1964), *The Decline of Hell*, Routledge and Kegan Paul.

WALZER, M. (1966), *The Revolution of the Saints*, Weidenfeld and Nicolson.

WATT, I. (1963), *The Rise of the Novel*, Penguin Books.

WERNHAM, R. B. (1966), *Before the Armada: the Growth of British Foreign Policy*, Cape.

WHITE, H. C. (1944), *Social Criticism in Popular Religious Literature of the 16th century*, Macmillan, New York.

WILLIAMS, E. (1945), *Capitalism and Slavery*, Oxford University Press.

WILSON, C. (1965), *England's Apprenticeship, 1603–1763*, Longmans Green.

WRIGHT, L. B. (1935), *Middle-Class Culture in Elizabethan England*, Chapel Hill.

INDEX

Abacus, the, 209

Africa, 59, 72, 158, 160, 162, 229, 232, 234, 253

Africa Company, the Royal, 173, 228

Agricultural Revolution, the, 14, 150, 153, 154, 240, 255, 268–9

Agriculture, Board of, 270

America, 22, 25, 45, 71, 72–3, 80, 81, 93–4, 99, 157–9, 165, 178, 233–6, 253

American Independence, Declaration of, 283

War of, 283

American Revolution, 229, 234, 283

Amsterdam, 155

Anabaptists, 111, 118, 143, 205

Andrews, Prof. C. M., 161

Anne, Queen of England, 41, 161, 215, 221

Antwerp, 53, 74

Apothecaries, Society of, 108

Apprentices, apprenticeship, 27, 84, 92–6, 174, 263, 266–7

Arkhangelsky, Prof. S. I., 134

Arkwright, Richard, 251–2, 266

Armada, the Spanish, 42

Armaments industry, 94, 170, 233, 247

Arminians, 114

Articles, the, 55, 111

the 58, 111, 205

Artificers, Statute of, 1563, 32, 57, 82, 92–6, 174, 252

Ashton, Prof. R., 54, 106

Ashton, Prof. T. S., 148, 184, 230–32, 238, 244–5, 263–4, 271, 282

Asiento, the, 228

Astronomy, 15, 72

Atheism, atheists, 117, 205, 214

Atlantic Ocean, 71, 164

Aubrey, John, 33, 63, 111, 116, 147, 207

Australia, 283

Avon, river, 167

Bacon, Sir Francis, 32, 48, 68, 73, 95, 97, 99, 112, 157, 201–4, 208, 242, 251, 280

Baillie, Robert, 50

Bakewell, Robert, 269

Bale, John, Bishop of Ossory, 21

Baltic Sea, 81, 150, 158–60, 230, 249

Bancroft, Richard, Archbishop of Canterbury, 112, 113

Bank of England, the, 19, 184–6, 139, 214, 217, 228, 244, 284

Bankruptcy, 49, 282

Banks, provincial, 244–5, 282

Banks, Sir John, 183

Baptists, 130, 190

Barbados, 75, 229–30

Barbon, Dr Nicholas, 184

Barclay family, 246

Barley, 71

Barley, Mr M. W., 55

Barnes, Ambrose, 144

Barnstaple, 185

Barrowe, Henry, 43

Bate's Case, 104

Bateson, Mr F. W., 284n.

Baxter, Richard, 117, 147, 178

Baynes, Captain Adam, 180

Beaumont, Joseph, 201

Beckford, William, 230

Becon, Thomas, 36

Beef, 55, 269

Beer, brewing industry, 17, 85, 88, 105, 170, 180, 222, 247, 249, 253, 256

Beggars, 45–6, 58, 94, 98–100

Behn, Mrs Aphra, 229

Belgium, 88

Bengal, 237

Bentham, Jeremy, Benthamism, 223, 287

Berkeley, George, Bishop of Cloyne, 280–81

Berkshire, 70

Bible, the, 39, 55, 199–200

Bills of exchange, bill-brokers, 186

Index

Birch, Col. John, 187
Birley, Dr Robert, 197
Birmingham, 90, 139, 167, 169, 172, 242, 248, 250, 252
Birthright, 261
Bishops, 47, 64, 114-15, 122, 135, 140, 190-92, 197, 200, 275
Black, Joseph, 251-2
Blackburn, 169, 266
Blackstone, Sir William, 32
Blake, Robert, 157
Blake, William, 275, 281, 284
Blood, circulation of the, 209
Blyth, Walter, 150
Bolingbroke, Henry St John, Viscount, 160, 214-17
Bombay, 162
Boroughs, rotten, 218-19
Boston, New England, 272
Boswell, James, 225
Boulton, Matthew, 246, 248, 252, 269, 282
Bowden, Professor P. J., 62, 65, 84
Boyle, the Hon. Robert, 165
Bradford, 175
Braithwaite, Richard, 61
Bramston, Sir John, 108
Brandy, 230
Brass, 88, 95, 231
Bray, Vicar of, 215
Brazil, 162, 230
Bremen, 159
Brewing, see Beer
Brill, Bucks., 143
Bristol, 133, 138-9, 167, 175, 178, 228, 242-3, 245, 253, 283
Brooke, Sir Basil, 88
Brown, Mr Peter, 252
Browne, Robert, 111
Brownists, 111
Buckingham, Edward Stafford, Duke of, 34
Buckingham, Katherine Sheffield, Duchess of, 277
Buckingham, Sir George Villiers, Duke of, 38, 73, 75, 77, 78, 80, 104, 120, 197
Building industry, 85, 88, 138, 171, 250
Bunyan, John, 117, 172, 195, 276, 280
Burbage, James, 89

Burford, 21
Burghley, Sir William Cecil, Lord, 66, 74, 79, 106
Burke, Edmund, 215
Burlamachi, Philip, 122
Burns, Robert, 225
Burton, Robert, 115, 121
Burton-on-Trent, 247, 249
Bury, Lancashire, 22
Bute, John Stuart, Earl of, 231-2
Butler, Samuel, 149

Cabinet, the, 216
Calais, 25, 42, 78
Calico, 163, 234
Calvinism, Calvinists, 41, 195-6, 200, 204
Cambridge, 133
  University of, 40, 51, 65, 89, 133, 194, 251
Cambridgeshire, 167
Canada, 73, 232-3, 245, 277
Canals, 21, 187, 249
Candles, 180, 273
Canterbury, Archbishop of, 35, 112
Cape Breton, 235
Capital, accumulation of, 15, 61, 67, 72, 76-8, 146, 160-61, 181-2, 237, 240, 246
Cardiganshire, 22
Carlisle, 133
Carlisle, James Hay, Earl of, 75
Carron Works, 242
Carteret, John, Lord, 231-2
Castile, 93
Castles, 21, 34, 85
Catalans, the, 233
Catherine of Braganza, Queen of England, 162
Catholics, Roman, 20, 112, 114-15, 128, 154, 165, 214, 277, 283
Cause, the Good Old, 15, 143, 215, 277
Cecil, Sir Robert, Earl of Salisbury, 103-4, 120, 146
Cecil, Sir William, see Burghley, Lord
Censorship, 109, 190-91, 205, 221
Chamber, the royal, 28
Chamberlain, John, 105
Chamberlen, Dr Hugh, 184
Chambers, Prof. J. D., 270-71

Index

Index

Index

Index

Index

Plymouth, 138
Pocahontas, 229
Poland, 87
Poor, the, 45–6, 56, 60, 87–8, 94, 98, 106, 110, 145, 153, 178, 182, 248, 258–9, 273, 277–8, 281, 290
Poor Law, 45, 56, 58, 84, 119, 145, 151, 259
Poor Relief, 28, 54, 58–9, 64, 258–9
Pope, the, 34, 37–8, 41–2
Popish Plot, the, 42
Population, 13, 44–7, 57, 62, 82–4, 227, 247, 254–8, 271
Port, 158, 231
Portland, Richard Weston, Earl of, 104
Portugal, 158, 162, 164, 173, 228, 230, 233
Post Office, the, 168
Postlethwayt, Malachi, 262
Potatoes, 153, 165, 255–6, 258, 274
Potteries, the, pottery, 248, 250, 256
Poulett, John, Lord, 133
Povey, Thomas, 158
Preaching, 27, 64, 111–12, 191, 198
Presbyterianism, Presbyterians, 129–30, 134, 143, 190, 193, 205, 252
Press, the, printing, 38, 197–8, 221
Pretender, the Young (Prince Charles Edward), 213
Price, Richard, 252, 277
Price Revolution, the, 13, 61, 65–8, 82–4, 87, 102, 241
Prices, 46, 57, 62, 82–4, 109–10, 153, 244, 247, 253, 255, 261, 272
Priestley, Joseph, 252, 277, 284
Prisons, 47, 224
Privateering, privateers, 66, 77–8
Privy Council, the, 50, 120, 135, 140, 197, 209
Privy Seal, the, 28
Proletariat, 15, 59, 63, 170, 174
Protections, 49
Providence Island Company, 79, 156
Prynne, William, 128, 200
Puckle, John, 174
Purgatory, 40
Puritanism, Puritans, 25, 41, 43, 55, 64, 67, 79, 89, 98–9, 111–13, 117–18, 137, 140, 191, 193, 195–6, 229, 276, 280

Purveyance, 105, 107
Putney Debates, the, 127
Pym, John, 79, 96, 128–9, 180, 213

Quakers, 86, 117–8, 140–41, 195, 200, 229, 246–7, 251
Quarles, Francis, 60

Radicalism, 214, 221, 232–3, 284
Ralegh, Sir Walter, 13, 30, 41, 52, 79, 81
Ramsay, Dr G. D., 92
Reformation, the English, 17, 25, 28, 34–8, 40–41, 47–8, 64, 78, 109–10, 116, 138, 199, 201–2
Rents, 65–8, 101–2, 115, 164–5, 244, 250, 269, 272
Republicanism, 214; see also Commonwealth, the
Reresby, Sir John, 67, 177, 197
Restoration, the, 136, 140–41, 176, 180, 192, 196, 205, 240, 251–2
Retail trade, 85; see also Shops
Retainers, 29, 35
Reynolds, Sir Joshua, 279
Ribbon loom, the, 173, 252, 265
Rice, 256
Richardson, Samuel, 196, 277, 279, 281
Ridley, Nicholas, Bishop of London, 37
Roads, 22, 167, 187, 249–50
Roberts, Mr R. S., 209
Robertson, William, 225
Rochester, Bishop of, see Sprat, Thomas
Rogers, J. E. Thorold, 58, 184
Roll, Dr Eric, 161
Rolling mills, 172, 235
Romanticism, 281, 284, 289
Rome, 31, 34, 78–9, 202
Romney, George, 279
Root and Branch Petition, 1640, 122
Roses, Wars of the, 25, 29–30
Royal Academy, 279
Royal Exchange, 53
Royalists, 131, 133, 149, 233
Royal Society, 140, 145, 153, 207, 242, 251
Ruhr, the, 88
Rushworth, John, 236
Russia, 72, 99, 160, 240

302